Inclusive Education

Inclusive Education

Examining Equity on Five Continents

Edited by

Alfredo J. Artiles, Elizabeth B. Kozleski, and Federico R. Waitoller

HARVARD EDUCATION PRESS

Cambridge, Massachusetts

Library of Congress Control Number 2011937680

Paperback ISBN 978-1-61250-115-4
Library Edition ISBN 978-1-61250-116-1

Published by Harvard Education Press,
an imprint of the Harvard Education Publishing Group

Harvard Education Press
8 Story Street
Cambridge, MA 02138

Cover Design: Sarah Henderson
Cover Photo: Jaime Monfort/Getty Images
The typefaces used in this book are ITC Stone Serif for text and ITC Stone Sans for display.

CONTENTS

INTRODUCTION

Equity in Inclusive Education
Historical Trajectories and Theoretical Commitments

Elizabeth B. Kozleski, Alfredo J. Artiles, and Federico R. Waitoller

I keep coming back—simplistically and idealistically—to the notion of opposing and alleviating coercive domination, transforming the present by trying rationally and analytically to lift some of its burdens, situating the works of various literatures with reference to one another and to their historical modes of being. What I am saying is that in the configurations and by virtue of the transfigurations taking place around us, readers and writers are now in fact secular intellectuals with the archival, expressive, and elaborative, and moral responsibilities of that role.

—*Edward Said,* Culture and Imperialism[1]

We present in this chapter a historical sketch of inclusive education and current conceptualizations of this movement. Our review owes much to the notion that ideas like inclusive education exist in contrapuntal relationships to political, social, and economic trajectories within and outside of national borders. Appropriated by conservatives, liberals, and radicals alike, the construct *inclusive education* is simultaneously used to promote globalization; erase cultural, ethnic, linguistic, and indigenous identities in search of a common core within all humans; and to identify and give voice to the experiences and lives of peoples who live at the margins of social institutions and, in doing so, make visible power-laden polycultural discourses that construct differences. It is in pursuit of the latter—to make visible the discourses of difference that are being engaged in inclusive education projects—that we commit our collective efforts to understanding how inclusive education is being constructed in multiple scales: local, national, and global.

The purpose of this edited volume is to take a critical look at the global movement called *inclusive education* through an equity prism. Despite the impressive growth in interest and enthusiasm around inclusive education throughout the world, how it is defined and implemented, and for whose benefit, remains at best incompletely understood.[2] Further, questions and considerations of equity have been neglected in gauging the impact of inclusive education on students, families, and communities.[3] For these reasons, this volume addresses equity concerns that emerge in the implementation of inclusive education models in nine nations from five continents.

A central focus of our analyses is how disparate approaches to inclusive education in various countries are mediated by (1) the official and implicit purposes and goals of public education, (2) access to an array of intellectual, human, and material resources, and (3) collective understandings and educational responses to sociocultural differences. This analytic perspective allows the authors of the chapters herein to situate inclusive education in their nation's larger projects of collective identity formation and social engineering that are pursued in part through inclusive social and educational policies and practices.

GENESIS

This volume builds on work that we have been doing at Arizona State University's Equity Alliance. The Alliance aims to generate research knowledge on important contemporary issues surrounding educational equity through various projects. Contributors met three times over the course of two years at Stanford University, Leibniz University (Hannover, Germany), and Arizona State University to challenge one another's assumptions about inclusive education, its implementation in each of our countries, and the ways in which projects of inclusive education affected students with a variety of difference markers, including citizenship and immigration status, language usage, ability, race, ethnicity, gender, and religion. Berhanu makes the observation that, increasingly, research on difference and diversity points to the important role that social construction plays in determining what indices are included within the parameters of normalcy and what is relegated to the margins and beyond.[4] By investing inclusive education with the agenda of moving the boundaries for children who are identified with a number of those markers, it becomes imperative to understand how those boundaries come to exist and are maintained, and how they intersect with and/or amplify one another.[5]

Historical Trajectories

Scandinavian countries, along with the United States, Canada, and England, were among the pioneers in inclusive education.[6] The attraction of inclusive education is reflected in the number of countries that officially align with this movement and the preeminence of international agreements endorsing inclusive education signed in the last twenty years. Although a distinctive feature of inclusive education theory is the attention to multiple forms of difference, the bulk of this research focuses on ability differences (i.e., students with disabilities).[7] Multiple professional discourses about inclusive education can be grouped into two strands.[8] The first is concerned with *justification* of the need for inclusive education. The second focuses on the *implementation* of inclusion.

Inclusive education has meant anything from physical integration of students with disabilities in general education classrooms to the transformation of curricula, classrooms, and pedagogies, and even the transformation of entire educational systems.[9] Yet, despite efforts to expand and extend its meaning and practice, in most cases the inclusive education movement has focused on students with disabilities' access to and participation in normative contexts (i.e., nondisabled cultures).

A variety of political and social pressures for deinstitutionalization and normalization began a period of intensive efforts on the part of grassroots organizers, families, and scholars in several economically vibrant countries such as Denmark, France, the United States, and England beginning in the 1960s. Legislation soon followed that established a set of principles to guide increasing inclusion in mainstream settings in mental health, adult disability services, and education systems.[10] These trends bypassed other countries that were also riding the economic growth waves of the latter part of the twentieth century. The Netherlands, the former Soviet Union, Brazil, Hong Kong, Taiwan, and Japan can be included in this group.[11] Poverty and economic challenges, as well as politically repressive governments, impacted the participation of countries such as China, India, Mexico, Nigeria, Pakistan, Spain, South Africa, and the Palestinian territories.[12]

A second generation of inclusive education efforts followed the signing of the Salamanca Statement in 1994.[13] Ninety-two nations committed to the ideal of inclusive education and went on to promote inclusive education in country-specific visions and principles. For instance, South Africa embraced inclusive education, but policy and practice laid out a continuum of services much like those that emerged in the aftermath of the 1975 federal legislation in the United States.[14] It is these uneven and locally interpreted versions of inclusive education that occupy much of the analysis in this book and point to the complex cultural practices that are deeply embedded in the way that human rights are conceptualized and implemented for some but not all in both first- and second-generation versions of inclusive education.

Contemporary Contexts

There are groups of students in every educational system that struggle to learn, lag behind, and/or experience a disproportionate failure rate. Many other children have yet to access educational opportunities; UNESCO estimates this number to be more than 900 million children.[15] Inequitable historical legacies and systemic conditions, among many other factors, shape this state of affairs. A first-order challenge for educational leaders, therefore, is to address these educational inequities. The international inclusive education movement promises to assist education leaders to ensure that children everywhere have access to education. There is increasing recognition in many countries that a policy of inclusion—whereby students with special needs and learners who are marginalized or excluded from school because of their ethnicity, ability level, language background, social class, or gender are taught in ordinary schools with various forms of special supports—is preferable to segregation in special programs, tracks, or schools.[16] More than a set of strategies to merely place students in ordinary classrooms and schools, inclusive education is based on a comprehensive educational philosophy and is guided by a set of principles to transform all spheres of activity in educational systems.[17]

Notwithstanding the excitement around and contemporary spread of inclusive education, several key difficulties have emerged. For example, inclusive education has largely ignored the complex histories and sociocultural conditions of developed and developing nations that shape how inclusive agendas are defined and implemented. In the United States and Western Europe, the trend is toward comprehensive inclusive educational systems. However, approaches to mandating inclusive education have created country-specific unintended consequences that constrain progress toward inclusive schools and systems. Further, disconnects between the intent and practice of inclusive education create conundrums for reformers. In contrast, in Latin America and most parts of Asia and sub-Saharan Africa, financial constraints limit the coverage and extent of such policies. Globalization has also created paradoxical situations that have at times deepened educational and social inequities.[18] Many developing nations are still struggling to achieve universal school *access* and *completion*, whereas developed nations are concerned with equity in *participation* and *outcomes* across diverse groups.

Even in postindustrial nations, there remain children and youth who are excluded from public education, and critical opportunity disparities have been documented. For instance, researchers in the United States have documented that although inclusive education has gained considerable strength, not all students are benefiting from it. More specifically, some racial minority students tend to be disproportionately identified with disability labels and placed in more segregated programs than their White counterparts, although the students are identified *with the same disability*. Furthermore, the bulk of inclusive education research in the United States rarely acknowledges and addresses the sociocultural backgrounds and experiences of racial minority students, who happen to comprise the majority of students in these programs.[19]

It is interesting that a global movement that emerged out of equity concerns might (unintentionally) create inequitable educational experiences for some groups. Unfortunately, only a few researchers have begun to question these results and document some of the potential unanticipated consequences of inclusive education within and across national contexts.

But the greatest challenge to inclusive education is arguably found in the failure to address power issues at the individual, family, organization, and system levels in explicit and systematic ways.[20] Perhaps one of the insidious forces that blocks attaining the ideal of inclusive education is the failure of proponents to acknowledge and address the historical sediments of oppression that are layered within institutions. And because of the cultural perspectives and understandings of how ethnicity, race, gender, language, citizenship, and other markers of difference are conflated with ability, examining these power questions is laced with the blindness and unconsciousness of familiarity.

CULTURAL HISTORICAL FRAMEWORK TO GROUND INCLUSIVE EDUCATION

The work of the international team that contributed to this volume is grounded in a *cultural historical perspective* to examine equity in inclusive education. We use this term in a broad sense to identify theoretical commitments to historical analyses that take into account the mediating force of culture when examining change processes, though we should note that contributors were influenced by a host of theorists across disciplines.[21] Thus, we assume the goals and purposes of public education and the ways in which it defines and addresses *differences* interact to shape local versions of inclusive education within each nation. Based on the interplay of these themes, educational systems create structures, designate roles, allocate resources in various domains (e.g., curricular planning, funding, personnel preparation), and design monitoring systems to track inequities to advance—or give the illusion of advancing—inclusive agendas. Our comparative framework enables us to understand the complex local equity conditions of inclusive education within a nation while it also allows us to discern regularities and discontinuities across national contexts.

Consistent with the perspective used in this volume, chapters are focused on multiple levels. For instance, broader analyses can trace changes at the cultural historical level (e.g., national or institutional levels). In turn, *life history analyses* focus on the level of individuals to chart change trajectories over time. The examination of microgenetic change (i.e., moment-to-moment history of events) is also possible, though it is not represented in this volume. Analyses at each of these levels are concerned with the role of cultural practices and the regulative, interpretive, and instrumental dimensions that help interpret the cultural work of an inclusive education system.[22] Perhaps in examining inclusive education from one or more of these dimensions, researchers might discover silences about certain inclusive education issues, groups, or practices. Further, by filtering activity through these dimensions, intended outcomes of inclusive education might become more sharply focused and more available for assessment, review, and critique. In this spirit, contributors examined national habits, the organization of schools, the experiences of teachers, and the viewpoints of families in connection to projects of inclusive education.

Waves of Inclusive Education

The participating countries were selected based on two key considerations in the study of equity in inclusive education. First, a country's historical commitment to inclusive education and its attendant historical legacies about *difference* shape a number of conditions that mediate the nature and qualities of inclusive education. We are targeting first-generation (United States, England, Austria, Germany, and Sweden) and second-generation (Argentina, South Africa, Kenya, and India) inclusive education nations. Inclusive education models in countries with different historical commitments to this approach are affected differently by economic opportunities, systems of stratification, policy climates, levels of investment in social policies, educational expectations for the citizenry, cultural forces, social movements, and so forth. We are also interested in tracing differences *within* the first- and second-generation groups, since local educational systems create distinct norms and regulations and disparate opportunities for groups to benefit from inclusive programs.

Second, we theorize that globalization and the tensions observed in a given nation between cultural continuity and change also shape how equity is addressed in inclusive education. The United States, for example, has experienced long-standing pressure to cope with rapidly shifting demographics and has produced distinctively paradoxical responses throughout its history to address differences (e.g., assimilation of immigrants, exclusionary and inclusive responses for people with disabilities, and racial and linguistic minorities). These responses have changed over time, depending on multiple factors and conditions. The United States continues to grapple with how to respond to differences in equitable ways; and because it is a major hub of economic and cultural activity, globalization forces also affect how equity is addressed in education policy and practice. Other developed nations in Western Europe were characterized by significant intranational homogeneity and were somewhat insulated from the massive immigration waves observed in the United States. This does not mean, however, that Western European nations were free of tensions related to various forms of difference. More recently, globalization has been transforming rather rapidly the socioeconomic and cultural conditions of these nations; notions such as national identity, citizenship, and inclusion are now heatedly contested. Thus, the institutional resources and historical conditions that permeate these debates and developments are played out in very different ways across nations.

The second group of nations in this project varies from the preceding examples of how globalization and social change might mediate the nature and development of inclusive education. South Africa, for instance, is engaged in a process of defining its emerging democratic identity after a brutal period of racial oppression. We also observe in this nation the tensions between western and indigenous identities. Greater diversity in a given society could forge a more complex social change climate, since resistance movements and mechanisms and networks for building and maintaining pressure on state bureaucracies to alter the status quo might have deeper roots and greater leverage. Unfortunately, we do not know yet how these forces and developments are molding the processes and outcomes of inclusive education and their consequences for educational equity.

We are therefore targeting countries that embody variations along key dimensions that include the interaction between a historical commitment to inclusion and the sociocultural conditions of a nation's development level, the influence of globalization, and the intensity of social changes to examine equity issues that affect inclusive education. Comparative analyses that account for these complex dimensions and nuances of local contexts will enable us to trace regularities across and within national contexts.

SIGNIFICANT GAPS IN THE INCLUSIVE EDUCATION LITERATURE: AN EQUITY AGENDA?

As explained above, this book addresses significant gaps in the inclusive education literature by using an equity prism. The design of the book challenges the long-standing assumption in this literature that a laudable idea—inclusive education—can travel seamlessly across cultures and contexts. Instead, the contents suggest that national leaders and local actors appropriate inclusive education in the midst of complex historical and cultural contingencies. Thus, the analyses in this volume deepen how inclusive education is defined, studied, and implemented across nations and cultural communities. This is indeed a significant contribution to the literature in light of the advent of globalization and the increasing cultural diversity of communities around the globe.

The chapters in this book refine our cultural historical lens and generate cutting-edge research questions and policy refinements that need to be addressed in order to support, extend, and critique the United Nations agenda on inclusive education. If inclusive education has such far-reaching equity implications for marginalized groups across the globe, we ought to refine the theoretical formulation of this movement through a culturally and historically situated research program. The chapters in the second section of the book offer urgently needed insights for future policy and research on inclusive education that is mindful of equity.

All the chapters are concerned with inclusive education as an issue of educational access and equity. We conceptualize inclusive education as a means to provide students with educational access and opportunities to participate in society. By incorporating voices from different countries, this volume provides insights and descriptions of the different contexts where inclusive education is conceived and implemented. Importantly, we ground our collective scholarship in a view of inclusive education that entails access, participation, and outcomes for all students who are marginalized in educational systems because of gender, caste, ethnic identity, socioeconomic status, race, language, immigration status, and ability level. The chapters provide *emic* perspectives on inclusive education—that is, most lead authors are natives of the target countries and have extensive experience working in the educational systems of these countries or coauthor chapters with inclusive education professionals who are currently working in the target country. And they do so with multidimensional conceptualizations of equity and inclusion that require systematic attention to the role of culture, history, and context. Thus, inclusive education is situated in larger cultural historical contexts (e.g., purposes of schooling, definitions, and responses to *difference* in educational contexts). This perspective demands the examination of unexplored questions from an interdisciplinary perspective, such as: What are the intended and actual outcomes of inclusive education? What are the consequences of these outcomes regarding participation in society? How do constructions of *difference* draw stratifying lines that benefit some groups but not others? What are the historical legacies that mediate the development and outcomes of inclusive education? These critical questions redirect the reader's gaze from the technicalities of inclusive education (e.g., strategies for development of inclusive settings) to the ideologically charged forces and processes (e.g., historical legacies of marginalization, meaning of inclusive education, and so on) that enable and constrain the potential of educational equity in inclusive education.

OVERVIEW OF THE CHAPTERS

In this section, we offer a brief snapshot of each chapter so that readers have a conceptual map of the terrain explored in the book. In chapter 1, authors Luciak and Biewer explore the discourses and paradigms that frame inclusive education in Austria; in particular, the changes observed in the Austrian educational system as a result of increasing immigration that complicate the inclusive education project. The authors examine inequities experienced by immigrant students and students with special needs in the Austrian educational system in relation to five parameters: physical placement, inclusive curricula and pedagogy, educational attainment and achievement, transition to work, and social integration and participation. Using analyses at the cultural historical and life history levels, the authors compare differential outcomes for students identified as special needs and immigrant students. The authors trace the historical and cultural contexts that shape these differential outcomes and present two case studies to examine how students may experience different educational trajectories according to their background and starting position. Using these cases and the aforementioned inclusive education parameters, the authors examine the intersections between culture, language, race, and disability and their implications for equity in inclusive education in Austria.

In the chapter 2, Artiles, Kozleski, Waitoller, and Lukinbeal describe an interdisciplinary theoretical and methodological multilevel approach to studying racial inequity questions related to inclusive education. Theoretical insights from special education, educational anthropology, cultural geography, and cultural psychology are integrated as they examine equity issues in inclusive education in Chicago. Using evidence compiled from state, school district, and neighborhood data sets, the authors analyze the intersections and disconnects between localized practices, habits, routines, and perspectives, local school outcomes, and aggregated state data. The analysis shows the need to frame racial inequity questions beyond school walls through the examination of sociocultural processes that are distributed in time and spaces (e.g., neighborhoods, districts). The modeling approach offers an alternative way of using data to provide more robust analyses that will allow policy makers and researchers to use a paradigm that tracks inequitable practices as well as cultural resources and assets.

In chapter 3, Dyson, Jones, and Kerr suggest that England can be understood as a socially polarized country, marked by significant inequalities resulting from a strong association between social background and educational outcomes. Moreover, these inequalities are spatially patterned, with concentrations of poor social and educational outcomes in certain urban places. The authors report an analysis of placement patterns in inclusive education programs in urban school districts in England, examining how this concentration has been constructed and addressed by national education policy. Using a spatial perspective on inequalities, the authors analyze the efforts of *successive governments* to break the link between social disadvantage and low poor educational outcomes through area-based initiatives (ABIs), demonstrating that social disadvantage transcends individuals' traits. Drawing on a case study, the authors provide policy recommendations to address exclusion based on a richer understanding of area dynamics.

Chapter 4, on inclusive education in Germany, brings the perspectives of Löser and Werning to bear on inequities in the German educational system experienced by Turkish immigrant students who come from lower socioeconomic backgrounds and have learning disabilities. The German education system is grounded in a long tradition of organizing students into homogeneous learning groups in separate schools. This clustering by learning groups is particularly problematic for Turkish immigrant students. For instance, because of early exclusion and segregation, these students often do not have a chance to attend advanced secondary schools. The authors analyze the functions that segregation serves in maintaining disparate educational programs and educational achievement, the authors question child/family- and system-centered explanations that have been advanced to explain equity issues.

In chapter 5, Berhanu maps out the challenges and responses to inclusive education in Sweden from a cultural and historical perspective, discussing core educational and political concepts that bear on inclusive education practices in Sweden. His analysis is grounded in the assumption that policy and practice decisions involve dilemmas and tensions. From this vantage point, he examines the dramatic changes in the Swedish social welfare/educational policy, moving toward a neoliberal economic, cultural, and educational model. Berhanu examines the inequities that increased during this change and Swedish efforts in the past to promote equity through a variety of educational policies, arguing that those early educational policies, including the macro political agenda focused on the social welfare model, have helped to diminish the effects of social, cultural, and economic backgrounds on educational outcomes. He further argues for a varied social and educational measures combined with an effective monitoring system and a stronger partnership and transparent working relationship between central and local government systems.

In chapter 6, Ahram and Fergus focus on the racialization of disability in the United States. Using the findings from a project on special education disproportionality in suburban schools in New York, the authors examine the school conditions that contribute to barriers to equity in inclusive education. The authors examine the relationship between ability and racial differences and how school practices such as educational interventions and special education placement policies serve to reinforce this relationship. They discuss how teachers drew from deficit views of students and the "othering" of students and families to explain causes for disproportionality in their schools. Ahram and Fergus argue, however, that the special education placement process and the poor institutional safeguards that fail to support struggling learners have been the main contributors to disproportionality.

Chapter 7, Engelbrecht's examination of the South African journey, offers a fascinating glimpse of a nation in transition. In 1994, a newly elected democratic government in South Africa introduced a constitution that not only transformed the political system but also stressed the principle of education as a basic human right. This principle emphasizes equity, quality, and relevance of schooling and education and implies that all students have the right to equal access to the widest possible educational opportunities. Every education policy initiative since 1994, including policy on the implementation of inclusive education, has been founded on this principle. However, despite the fact that education has undergone fundamental transformation and indicators show that general access to basic education has improved, equity in relation to participation in inclusive education with specific reference to the acceptance of difference is questionable. In this chapter, Engelbrecht draws from a research project that aimed to pilot the index for inclusion in three schools to illustrate the ways in which relational dynamics influence the establishment of communities of practice that embrace diverse identities. She suggests that a shift toward the enhancement of equity of participation with an emphasis on dynamic interactive processes in school communities is needed in order to create more equitable inclusive school communities in South Africa.

Singal and Jeffery explore the implementation of inclusive education in India in chapter 8. India is a complex plural society, with a range of ethnic, linguistic, and religious diversity. As it stands on the threshold of economic change and social development, the focus on fulfilling the obligations of Education for All has become paramount. In this chapter, the authors examine efforts undertaken by the government to address issues of educational exclusion and the limitations in its approach. They begin by providing a brief overview of the Indian education system, paying particular attention to how the government has addressed the needs of certain groups who are disproportionately excluded from the system. The authors also highlight how the government's attempts at addressing unique educational needs inadvertently perpetuate inequalities. Using political and justice theory, Singal and Jeffery discuss policies' narrow conceptualization of educational equity in terms of access and resources rather than equality of participation. The chapter thus argues for an urgent need for the reconceptualization of notions of *difference* and *educational equity* in the Indian education system.

In chapter 9, Skliar and Dussel examine the status of inclusive education in Argentina. The authors begin by analyzing the legal framework, drawing from the national educational law and some city regulations, and then provide a snapshot on the educational situations of people with disabilities in Argentina drawing from the UN World Report *The Right to Education of People with Disabilities*. The authors argue that despite an increasing recognition of inclusion at the policy level, there have been limited resources to include students, and the percentage of those students included into general education settings is extremely low. In addition, Skliar and Dussel analyze the ways in which teachers in general education and special needs schools tend to talk about inclusive education, drawing from focus groups in which issues of diversity, difference, and living together were discussed. The authors leave the reader pondering a thought-provoking question that has implications beyond the Argentinian context: Is it possible to teach to live and to live together?

In chapter 10, Mutua and Swadener examine how the intersection of post-colonialism, culture, and disability have impacted equity issues in inclusive education in Kenya. The authors provide the historical and political context of inclusive education in Kenya and review and critique the traditional explanations for the lack of access and participation for students with disabilities. Drawing from narratives of Kenyan families, Mutua and Swadener use postcolonial and disability studies as lenses to understand how families address issues of access and participation for their children with disabilities. In doing so, they demonstrate how disability is a social relational condition inscribed onto people's bodies. Mutua and Swadener argue that pursuing equity and inclusion in Kenya requires understanding how local communities make meaning of and develop inclusive spaces for all children.

The volume concludes with a reflective commentary from McDermott, Edgar, and Scarloss on the cultural work of inclusive education. This analysis uncovers the underlying views of equity embedded in the inclusive education discourses. Tensions and contradictions among these discourses are identified. This chapter offers a lexicon about equity in inclusive education to interpret the national cases included in the volume.

SUMMARY

The challenge of the next generation of inclusive education research is to map the disparate and situated meanings of equity in inclusive education within and across national contexts, and trace their concomitant consequences for various groups of students. Future inclusion research should be ultimately concerned with building a theory of equity in diverse educational systems.

PART I

Equity Issues in First-Generation Inclusive Education

1

Equity and Inclusive Education in Austria
A Comparative Analysis

Mikael Luciak and Gottfried Biewer

This chapter, based on an analytical framework and paradigmatic case examples, provides a critical analysis on facilitators of and barriers to equity and inclusion in the Austrian education system, as seen in the case of immigrant students and students with disabilities. This comparative approach allows insight into the different strategies and measures meant to improve these student groups' educational situation, and discloses the ideological underpinnings on which the understanding of equity and inclusion are based.

Austria, a member state of the European Union, has a population of 8.3 million and is ranked twenty-fifth on the Human Development Index.[1] Since the late 1960s, low birth rates and an aging population have been offset by immigration. Today, about 15 percent of the population is foreign-born and 10 percent hold foreign citizenship. In Vienna, about one-third of the population has an immigrant background—that is, born either abroad or in Austria, but holding foreign citizenship.[2] If one includes descendants of immigrants with Austrian citizenship, the total population of people from families with an immigrant background is even greater. The majority of immigrants came from countries that are currently not EU member states (i.e., Serbia and Montenegro, Turkey, Bosnia and Herzegovina, and Croatia). The highest numbers of immigrants from EU countries come from Germany and Poland.[3] Austrian citizenship legislation is based on the principle of *ius sanguinis*—citizenship is passed on by parents and is not conferred by country of birth. Therefore, many second-generation immigrants who were born in Austria still hold foreign citizenship. About 40 percent of the student population in Vienna comprises non-native German speakers (German being the language of school instruction). Outside of Vienna, only about 10 percent of students are non-native German speakers.[4] Austria continues to be a primarily German-speaking and Roman-Catholic country; however, aside from immigrants, six officially recognized autochthonous minority groups (Slovenes, Croats, Hungarians, Roma, Czechs, and Slovaks) have lived in certain regions of the country for centuries and have retained a minority language in addition to German. According to estimates, their total number is less than 200,000; none of these groups exceeds 50,000 people.[5] The number of non-Christian religious denominations in Austria is rather small (less than 5 percent) but has increased, mostly due to Muslim immigrants from Turkey and Bosnia and Herzegovina.[6]

Existing studies on equity in the Austrian school system conclude that educational inequalities persist for students with lower economic backgrounds and for immigrant students, while gender and disability no longer constitute great barriers to equitable education.[7] However, these analyses are somewhat misleading. If the general categories *immigrants* and *students with disabilities* are differentiated, if intersections of diversity dimensions are accounted for (e.g., by disclosing how social class mediates ethnicity), and if equity and inclusion are defined and analyzed according to specific parameters, the above-mentioned conclusions come under question.

The current advancement of equity and inclusion in Austria is discussed in relation to historical developments and sociocultural conditions by underscoring the role of power relationships and structures of privilege in society. To this end, the following equity-related questions, originally proposed by the OECD and subsequently specified by Demeuse, Crahay, and Monseur, are asked in relation to the Austrian educational system: Does the system offer students with an immigrant background and/or with special educational needs (1) equity of access or equality of opportunity (i.e., is there an equal chance for progress in the educational system for all members of the school population?), (2) equity in relation to the environment for learning or equality of means (i.e., are there equitable conditions for learning for students from disadvantaged groups as compared with students from advantaged groups?), (3) equity in production or equality of achievement (i.e., do individuals from different backgrounds achieve equivalent educational outcomes?), and (4) equity in benefiting from the results of education (i.e., do all individuals, regardless of their background, have the same opportunities to apply their skills and knowledge in the job market and in society?). In addition to these four dimensions, the authors of this chapter add a fifth dimension: equity in relation to social integration (i.e., does the school environment foster interpersonal understanding, social contacts, and communal harmony?)[8]

Unless otherwise specified, the terms *students with an immigrant background* and *immigrant students* are used interchangeably, as are *students with special educational needs* (SEN) and *students with disabilities*.

THEORETICAL AND ANALYTICAL FRAMEWORK

Educational inclusion, as a theoretical concept, is "concerned with *all* students" and with finding appropriate ways of "responding to the diversity of needs of all learners."[9] However, efforts to transform school systems toward becoming more inclusive frequently focus on the educational situation of vulnerable, disadvantaged, and marginalized groups, as evidenced by the UNESCO Guidelines for Inclusion: "Inclusion invokes a particular emphasis on those groups of learners who may be at risk of marginalization, exclusion or underachievement."[10] From an ideological standpoint, the theory of inclusion relates to ethics, civil rights, and conceptions of social justice, but the parameters of inclusion can be conceptualized differently.[11]

Physical Placement and Access

There is broad consensus that inclusion refers to *placement* of all students in regular schools and classrooms regardless of individual differences or difficulties. The Salamanca Statement declared that "[a]ssignment of children to special schools—or special classes or sections within a school on a permanent basis—should be the exception, to be recommended only in those infrequent cases where it is clearly demonstrated that education in regular classrooms is incapable of meeting a child's educational or social needs or when it is required for the welfare of the child or that of other children."[12]

In most contexts, the terms *regular, general,* or *mainstream* schools or classes refer to comprehensive school systems during mandatory schooling, regardless of the different types of tracks or elective courses that can be chosen within that system. Segregated special schools are considered *nonregular* schools. In school systems in which comprehensive schooling applies only to primary schooling, different types of secondary schools are generally considered to be regular schools. However, it needs to be asked whether it is justified to speak of *inclusive* educational systems when socially disadvantaged and immigrant students are overrepresented in those types of secondary schools that are less academically challenging and lead to lower-level educational qualifications.

Inclusive Curricula and Pedagogy

Curricula and instruction ought to meet the needs of all learners. Individual, social, cultural, and linguistic differences must be considered within a common, diversified curriculum. Inclusive settings require student-centered educational practices by teachers who view their role as facilitators of learning rather than as transmitters of knowledge. As Thompkins and Deloney point out, "This means that teachers must discover where each of their students are academically, socially, and culturally to determine how best to facilitate learning."[13] Corbett and Norwich propose a conceptual framework that addresses the relationship between educational needs and pedagogies in the context of differentiation.[14] While the authors distinguish between common and specific or distinct, as well as individual, needs to be addressed by specific pedagogies, they regard these differences as complementary. The authors write that "pedagogy, therefore, also needs to be considered in terms of the relationships and balances between practices which are common to all, specific to some and not others and unique to individuals."[15] Making pedagogical adaptations in regard to forms of instruction, teacher-student interaction, learning styles, or level of learning objectives is not contradictory to inclusive pedagogy, particularly since it is assumed that all students benefit from differentiated teaching methodologies.

Educational Attainment and Achievement

Access to mainstream schools must be assessed beyond legal provisions. If students of particular groups show lower retention and higher dropout rates, repeat classes more often than others, and show comparatively lower educational attainment, the system's inclusiveness must be questioned.

It is generally agreed that inclusive educational settings must provide conditions for all students to achieve at their full potential. However, there are various ways to conceptualize and assess achievement. Black-Hawkins, Florian, and Rouse stress two relevant aspects.[16] First, in their view, "educational achievement is not limited to academic attainment" (i.e. literacy, numeracy etc.) but "students' social, emotional and creative development" counts as achievement as well.[17] Second, achievement must be understood in terms of progress made by learners over time. The authors point out that "it is possible for students to have achieved well, giving their starting point, but not to have reached the (arbitrary) standards as pre-specified by performance criteria."[18] Thus, results from standardized tests and student assessments, which do not account for progress, lack explanatory value.

Transition to Work

A useful assessment of inclusive educational practices must take into consideration students' participation in areas of life that extend beyond schooling. For example, school systems must prepare students for a successful transition from school to work and community life, taking into account each student's needs, abilities, interests, and preferences. Measurable discrepancies in outcomes related to this key transitional period would raise concern that certain needs, abilities, interests, and/or preferences are not receiving appropriate support.

Social Integration and Participation

There is widespread agreement that interpersonal contact in diverse settings fosters *social integration*. According to Gordon Allport's hypothesis, promoting interpersonal contact is an effective way to reduce stereotyping and prejudice, if "(1) there is equal status between groups, (2) there is a common goal shared by the groups, (3) the contact is sanctioned by institutional support, and (4) that it leads to a perception of common interests."[19] Thus, inclusive educational settings must foster the quality of social interaction, as well as mutual acceptance, feelings of belonging, and emotional well-being.

Another indicator of the educational systems' inclusiveness is the rate of participation, involvement, and activity of all learners. Limited active involvement of students during school lessons and in daily school activities points to a low level of inclusion.

CONCEPTUALIZING EQUITY

Overall, the concept of equity is based on the principle of fairness and social justice. By making reference to the equity framework developed by Berne and Stiefel, the UNESCO report *Educational Equity and Public Policy* distinguishes between three principles of equity: (1) horizontal equity (equality of treatment is fair on condition that members of a group are in the same starting position), (2) vertical equity (if people encounter different starting positions, special measures have to be taken to support members of disadvantaged groups in order to level the difference), and (3) equal educational opportunity (all students should have an equal chance to succeed, and educational success should depend on motivation and effort rather than, for example, on place of residence or availability of resources).[20]

Artiles, Harris-Murri, and Rostenberg, however, call for a transformative model based on a concept of social justice that presupposes acknowledgement of social contexts where "class, race, gender, and language background (among other markers) afford (or constrain) people's access to participate or secure resources in institutional contexts."[21] This view demands that the role of "power relationships and structures of privilege" be recognized in shaping "the goals of education, the curriculum, and the organizational structures and processes of schools."[22] Thus, a critical analysis of educational systems in regard to equity and inclusion needs to go beyond looking at accessibility, educational outcomes, or inclusiveness of curricula and pedagogies, and disclose the ideological underpinnings on which the understanding of equity and inclusion are based. Limited access to education, disproportionate educational attainment, or practices that do not recognize the needs of diverse student populations are clear indicators of inequity and lack of inclusion. However, in proposing measures and strategies to eliminate inequalities and injustices, not only standard practices but also the historically and culturally based values underlying these practices must be challenged. Furthermore, as argued by Ainscow, Booth, and Dyson, simply advocating for inclusion without fostering appreciation for its far-reaching practical consequences is not enough; people might agree on values, such as "those concerned with equity and participation until they start to look in detail at their implications for practice."[23]

In the rest of this chapter, facilitators of and barriers to equity and inclusion in the Austrian education system will be analyzed in light of the criteria stated above. First, we describe the study populations of this analysis and the availability of data.

STUDY POPULATIONS AND DATA AVAILABILITY

This chapter discusses educational inclusion in relation to two main groups of students: (1) students with an immigrant background and (2) SEN students. However, given that immigrant students are overrepresented in special education, the population of SEN students overlaps to some degree with the population of immigrant students. The term *students with an immigrant background* refers to students who themselves or whose parents were not born in Austria. However, this term is not an official category of education statistics. Rather, school statistics differentiate students by citizenship and language. In the school year 2007–08, 9.3 percent of all students had foreign citizenship and 16.2 percent had a first language other than German.[24] Neither data set reliably encompasses the entire group of students with an immigrant background. Naturalized immigrants are not included in data on foreign citizenship. Further, data on students' first language is imprecise because students with an immigrant background and their parents may declare either German or the national language of the parents' country of origin or a parent's minority language as the student's first language. Also, because ethnic group differences are not accounted for, it cannot be deduced whether a student of any given nationality might in fact belong to an ethnic minority group in the respective country.

Methods of statistical data collection on linguistic parameters frequently change. In the past, the terms *mother-tongue, first language, everyday speech,* and *colloquial language* have been used as study parameters— and these terms are not necessarily equivalent. At present, linguistic data collection records the colloquial language (i.e., the native language students actually speak in addition to German on a daily basis). This data is meant to inform the assessment of language support needs and the development of corresponding educational provisions. In practice, the lack of differentiation between first- and second-generation students, whose language competencies vary, results in inconsistent provision of German as a Second Language (GSL) teaching.

The second study population is SEN students. Until the early 1990s, all SEN students were categorized as having disabilities (i.e., learning or intellectual disabilities, motor or behavior disorders, and visual or hearing impairments) and were placed in different types of special schools accordingly. At present, official data categorize students only as having special educational needs rather than distinguishing them by disability, even though the diagnosis of a disability is still a prerequisite for receiving special needs education. According to Austrian school law (§ 8 SchPflG), special educational needs are declared as follows: "If a child cannot follow instruction at a primary or secondary school or at pre-vocational school . . . without receiving special support due to a physical or mental impairment, but is nevertheless capable of attending school . . . Unsatisfactory achievements at school without the qualifying characteristic of a disability do not justify a SEN."[25]

The fact that special-needs provision relies on a disability diagnosis constitutes a problem. Contrary to practice in other countries (e.g., Finland, United Kingdom), SEN students in Austria whose learning difficulties are not necessarily based on a disability, by law are not eligible to receive special-needs provision. However, overrepresentation of socially disadvantaged and immigrant students in special schools indicates that some students are falsely diagnosed with a disability. While their learning difficulties arise primarily from socioeconomic disadvantages and cultural and linguistic factors that surface in the interaction between the student and the educational environment, they are stigmatized as being organically impaired.[26]

Currently, the populations of SEN students in special schools can be distinguished by various forms of disability because each type of special school caters to the needs of students with particular disabilities. However, in integrative settings differentiated statistical data on SEN students' diagnosis are not made available, a fact that hinders educational planning and scientific research.

In the school year 2006–07, 3.4 percent of all students had special educational needs and two-thirds of all SEN students were males. More than half of the SEN student population was in integrated settings, but the ratio of integration varied regionally between 30 percent and 80 percent. Overall, only 1.6 percent of the entire school population is in segregated settings.[27]

HISTORICAL DEVELOPMENTS

Today's Austria must be understood within its historical context. Austria, formerly the central base of a multinational empire, has undergone a series of sociopolitical changes since 1774, when Empress Maria Theresa first introduced compulsory schooling. In 1869, a primary school law (*Reichsvolksschulgesetz*) established that the state rather than the church would control schools. Mandatory schooling was extended from six to eight years, though only a smaller group of students transferred to the academically more challenging bourgeois school (*Bürgerschule*) after five years of elementary schooling. Male and female pupils were taught in separate schools or classes, and women gained access to university education only after 1887.[28] During the Austrian-Hungarian monarchy (1867–1918), the Catholic Church and the Hapsburg dynasty were more willing to tolerate cultural and linguistic expressions of ethnic minority groups (*Volksgruppen*) in the Austrian region, while the liberal bourgeoisie—and many teachers—pushed for Germanization.

In the late eighteenth century, Enlightenment thinkers recognized the educability (*Bildsamkeit*) of children with sensory impairments, marking the beginning of Austria's strong tradition of providing education to children with disabilities.[29] Pioneers established educational institutions for sensory-impaired children; these schools obtained public financial support, whereas institutions for pupils with intellectual disabilities relied on private or clerical sponsors. Between 1857 and 1865, the educationist Jan Daniel Georgens and the liberal political activist Marianus Deinhardt established the educational institution *Levana*, one of the most notable pedagogical experiments in nineteenth-century Vienna, which aimed at the common education of mentally disabled and non-disabled children.[30] As this integrative pedagogical concept deviated radically from the ideas accepted at the time and thus was not state subsidized, Levana had no sustainable effect on the development of remedial institutions in the following decades.[31]

By 1900, about half of Vienna's two million inhabitants were immigrants, most from neighboring Bohemia and Moravia.[32] This influx stirred nationalistic sentiments in Austria's German-speaking population and propelled Vienna's mayor, Karl Lueger, to speak about the city's "endangered German character."[33] Fin-de-siècle Vienna was characterized not only by increasing nationalism but also by rising anti-Semitism.

After World War I, the tracking of eleven-year-olds into different types of secondary school remained a relic of the Austro-Hungarian monarchy. Children of peasants and workers mainly attended schools with lower educational demands, whereas children of the middle class and nobility tended to visit academically oriented secondary schools. The school reforms proposed by the social democrat Otto Glöckel in the 1920s marked the beginning of a discussion about a comprehensive secondary school system. Glöckel made a case for equal education of all children, regardless of gender, social origin, and religious denomination. A political compromise in 1927 led to harmonization of educational standards in the different types of secondary school for students aged ten to fourteen, although transfer to academically oriented tracks was still based on good grades and high teacher recommendations.[34] To this day, Christian conservative political parties defend this divided secondary school system, whereas social democrats advocate for comprehensive schooling.

In 1920, through the Treaty of St. Germain, Austria lost large parts of its territory and was obligated to protect minority groups. Ethnic minorities were in principle entitled to receive school instruction in their minority language, mostly at the elementary level.[35] At secondary levels, instruction was increasingly in German, due in part to a lack of financial resources for bilingual teachers and books in minority languages but also to political resistance against minority education.

Until the end of the First Republic, in 1934, Vienna was regarded as a center of remedial education that combined medical and pedagogical approaches for students with disabilities. In 1938, with the annexation of Austria by National Socialist Germany, the progressive tradition of remedial education began to come to an end. Political attitudes toward minorities in general became increasingly hostile. Ethnic diversity declined due to waves of emigration as well as the persecution, expulsion, and killing of minority group members. Instruction in minority languages ceased, and minority schools were closed. Before their persecution and murder in concentration camps, Jewish students, who generally had attended mainstream schools, were sent to segregated schools and eventually were prohibited from attending schools at all. Similarly, students identified as Roma, who also in part had been in segregated schools, were excluded from schooling. The ideology of creating a racially and genetically pure German nation also led to forced sterilization of people with disabilities and culminated in the so-called *euthanasia program*.[36]

After World War II, Austria again became an independent country. Constitutional rights secured in the Austrian State Treaty (1955) as well as bilateral agreements eventually led to the Minority Schools Acts, which granted autochthonous minorities specific language rights pertaining to elementary and secondary education. Between the 1970s and 1990s, Slovenes, Croats, Hungarians, Czechs, Slovaks, and Roma became officially recognized as minority groups. However, only members of the Slovene, Croat, and Hungarian minorities became entitled to instruction in their minority languages or to bilingual schooling. Only a small number of Roma survived the Holocaust and, for the most part, their children were sent to special schools.[37]

In the postwar period, Austria was still a country of emigration. This began to change in the 1960s, when labor was in short supply and foreign laborers were recruited from Yugoslavia and Turkey. In addition to labor migration, the demographic situation in the second half of the twentieth century was also characterized by the influx of refugees from various Communist countries. School policies concerning labor migrants were based on the initial assumption that eventually these groups would return to their home country. Migrant children were educated in mainstream schools but received native language instruction in order to facilitate reintegration into their country of origin. When it became clear that most labor migrants would stay in Austria permanently, school policies responded by promoting assimilation. However, in the 1980s and 1990s, the concept of intercultural education slowly began to emerge in the Austrian educational system. Students were offered GSL as well as first-language instruction. In the 1990s, intercultural learning was introduced as an *educational principle*, meant to underlie teaching in all subject areas and to target all students, rather than just minority students. Furthermore, in 1995, the integration of Austria into the European Union fostered awareness that students must be better prepared to live in a world characterized by increasing diversity and globalization.

In the second half of the twentieth century, Austria reestablished its special school system. At the time, the medical professions had considerable influence on the design of remedial education.[38] For several decades, *Heilpädagogik*, by the medical scientist Hans Asperger, strongly influenced special educators' views on children with disabilities and educational difficulties.[39] Disabilities were viewed as personal deficits requiring treatment. Special education was offered at segregated facilities. Until the early 1990s, the subdivided special education system included schools for children with learning disabilities, mental retardation, and physical as well as sensory impairments, and these schools were attended by 4 percent of all school-age children. Inclusive settings were not provided, although in some rural areas with limited delivery of special education, individual children with learning disabilities attended the local mainstream schools.

A systemic change in the special education system was implemented following discussions between parents and educators who argued that special education stigmatizes and marginalizes students and provides poor learning outcomes. In the early 1980s, this resulted in an integration movement, mostly led by parents of children with disabilities from the academically educated middle and upper class. Although initially met with resistance by government and school administrations, the campaign for integrative education became successful with the support of mass media, progressive teachers, and educational scientists.[40] The first integrated class was established in 1984. In 1993, Austria revised school legislation and established the right of parents of children with disabilities to choose between integrative and special school settings. The education act also included a change in terminology: children who previously had been labeled as students with various disabilities were now referred to as *students with special educational needs* (SEN). A nationwide system of integrated classes was gradually established, with permanent team teaching involving regular and special education teachers. Thus, integrated classes with four to six children with special educational needs now have better individualized resources than regular classes. Nonetheless, even though the Austrian educational system has become more inclusive over time, not all groups of students benefit from this development as will be shown in the subsequent case examples.

CASE EXAMPLES

The three paradigmatic cases described below illustrate how students may encounter significantly different educational experiences in the Austrian system depending on their backgrounds and starting positions. Case 1 describes a male student with an immigrant background from a working-class family; case 2 describes an Austrian female student with intellectual disability from a middle-class family; and case 3 describes a male immigrant ethnic minority student with learning difficulties from a lower-class family.

Case 1

Fifteen-year old Mehmet was born in Vienna and attends ninth grade at a prevocational school. He is finishing his final year of mandatory schooling after spending the last four years in a general secondary school. His parents migrated from the countryside of Eastern Turkey to Austria and now work long hours in low-paying jobs. Mehmet and his two siblings are Turkish citizens and have been raised primarily by their grandparents, who have low reading and writing skills. While Turkish is the children's first language, they often communicate in a German dialect with each other and their friends.

Mehmet did not attend kindergarten and went to primary school in a district of Vienna with a high immigrant population. Foreign citizens comprise about 35 percent of the district's population. In Mehmet's school, 80 percent of the students had a first language other than German.

Like several of his classmates, Mehmet received support in primary school from a Turkish native language teacher several hours a week during regular instruction. While Mehmet's parents had high aspirations for him, they were not able to help him much with his homework. His grades were low, and thus he attended a publicly financed after-school program twice a week. In his fourth year, Mehmet's grades had improved. Still, his main classroom teacher recommended that he transfer to general secondary school rather than the more challenging academic secondary school. In Vienna, about half of all ten-year-old students transfer to general secondary school, the other half to academic secondary school. However, the average representation of students with immigrant backgrounds in general secondary schools is over 57 percent, compared with only 26 percent in the academic secondary schools. In Mehmet's general secondary school, the representation of immigrant students was 90 percent, and several of his teachers felt overburdened with the cultural and linguistic diversity as well as with various social and disciplinary problems.

Mehmet, now in his last year of compulsory schooling, lacks the grades needed to advance to higher technical and vocational schools. Recently, Mehmet and his peers participated in the OECD Program for International Student Assessment (PISA), which for him and many other students with a first language other than German resulted in low outcomes in reading and math comprehension. He had difficulty understanding the work tasks, which were described in a rather sophisticated German. Mehmet always wanted to become an engineer, but given his low grades, he now plans to become an auto mechanic. He still needs to identify an auto shop where he can get his practical training. Since apprenticeships are hard to find, in particular for immigrant students, he fears he might end up in unskilled labor just like his parents.

Case 2

Twelve-year old Tanja attends an integrated class in an academic secondary school in Vienna. She has a mild intellectual disability combined with motor disorders, and at age six was diagnosed with having special educational needs. Her parents opted for one of Vienna's four hundred integrated classes in primary school. Twenty children, four of whom were SEN students, attended Tanja's class, which was provided with a head teacher and a special education teacher.

At the age of ten, the question of whether Tanja should attend a special school or an integrated class resurfaced. Her academically educated middle-class parents chose an integrated class. While most of the over

350 integrated classes in Vienna's secondary schools are in general secondary schools, Tanja gained access to one of only fourteen integrative classes in an academic secondary school. She had three SEN classmates, one with Down's syndrome, another with severe motor disorders, and a third with mild mental retardation. Her remaining twelve classmates, with excellent grade reports, were admitted to academic secondary school. At all times, there was a special education teacher in the classroom, who provided educational support to all sixteen children. Nine other teachers taught specific subjects, none of them more than one hour a day. Given that academic secondary schools do not offer integrative classes beyond eighth grade, Tanja most likely will spend her last year of mandatory schooling in a special school. Since 2001, special schools offer a vocational preparatory year in ninth grade. Tanja might attend such a class in order to ease her transition into the world of work. Unlike her previous schooling, all of Tanja's new classmates will have special educational needs.

Case 3

Twelve-year-old Milo attends a special school in the province of Lower Austria. He is a Serbian citizen and belongs to the Roma minority. At age ten, he moved with his parents from Serbia to Austria. In Serbia, where schooling starts at age seven, Milo had not attended school on a regular basis. After immigrating to Austria, his parents did not enroll him in school right away; they were unfamiliar with the school system, had no money for school materials, and because of their own low educational level, could not help him with his schooling. Eventually, Milo entered a general secondary school as an "ex-matricular student," and therefore was not graded during his first year. Milo speaks and understands some Serbian and was offered additional language support by a Serbian native-language teacher, although his first language is Romani. He also received GSL support. Given his lack of school experience, Milo was about three years behind his peers. His teachers assumed that he could not catch up to follow instruction in an age-appropriate regular classroom. He was assessed and diagnosed with a learning disability, which led to a recommendation for transfer to a special school. However, there was no native-language teacher present during his assessment. His parents were told that Milo would benefit from instruction at a special school, even though special education teachers are not trained for teaching linguistically different students. In addition, there is no native language support in Romani at this school. In Lower Austria, the ratio of SEN students in special schools to those in integrative settings is 70:30. Moreover, the likelihood that non-native speakers attend special schools is over 50 percent higher than German native speakers.[41]

FACILITATORS OF AND BARRIERS TO EQUITY AND INCLUSIVE EDUCATION

The factors that facilitate and impede educational equity and inclusion in the Austrian educational system can be identified by examining the current system against the parameters for inclusion, as previously outlined in the theoretical framework of this chapter.

Physical Placement and Access

Up until 2010, programs for early childhood education and care (ECEC) have not been mandatory, and in the recent past children of immigrants and those of low socioeconomic status (SES) have shown lower participation rates. Many provinces (e.g., Vienna) require parents to prove official employment in order to qualify for child care, and also demand kindergarten fees, thus creating barriers to access for these groups that, as evidenced by research, can benefit greatly when school readiness is promoted early.[42] Moreover, even for those who are able to gain access to ECEC, "there are also concerns about the quality of the educational and language support offer in the ECEC system, including the low educational level of kindergarten pedagogues."[43]

In Austria, compulsory schooling lasts for nine years. Pupils enter elementary schools (grades 1–4) at age six in a comprehensive *primary school*, where students with an immigrant background are taught alongside majority students. The comparatively low number of school hours in primary schools (children are dismissed around noon) favors those with access to an after-school environment conducive to learning. Those who do not have access to after-school programs may receive as little as one-half of the number of hours of structured learning.

Grades 5–8 may be attended either at a *general secondary school* or at an *academic secondary school* (lower level). Teachers at these two types of school receive different teacher training: general secondary school teachers at teacher training colleges, academic secondary school teachers at universities. Students attending academic secondary schools are much more likely to advance to higher education—upper secondary schools, colleges, and universities—while students in general secondary schools frequently advance to vocational schools and finish schooling much earlier. Tracking to either one of these two school types depends on a student's grades and teachers' recommendations in grade 4. Mandatory schooling may be completed with a prevocational year (grade 9) unless students advance to higher academic secondary schools or technical and vocational schools and colleges.

The current student ratio of German native speakers at general secondary compared with academic secondary schools is 2:1, and for students with a first language other than German, it is 3:1. Immigrant students, in particular those with a Turkish or former Yugoslavian background, are less likely to advance to academic secondary schools even if variables such as socioeconomic status and aspirations are accounted for.[44] As argued by Bacher, the Austrian educational system contributes to social inequality; advancement to higher secondary education is dependent on ascribed criteria and not on achievement only.[45]

On average, female immigrant students perform as well as or better than their male peers with immigrant backgrounds. However, in some immigrant groups, boys are more likely to stay in school beyond compulsory schooling. For example, by the ages fifteen to nineteen, about 60 percent of boys and only 50 percent of girls with a Turkish background are still in school.[46]

Limited availability of comprehensive schooling at the secondary level is irreconcilable with the concept of inclusive education. In Vienna, *cooperative secondary schools*, which were introduced to bridge the gap between general and academic secondary schools, have not prolonged the educational careers of immigrant students. In 2008, the *new secondary school*, a nationwide comprehensive school model for students in grades 5–8, was introduced as a pilot project. Currently, by law only 10 percent of all secondary schools are authorized to establish this model. As long as academic secondary schools continue to cater to higher-achieving students, this new model will have limited effects on improving the system's overall inclusiveness.

In the Austrian school system, a second tracking at age fourteen, as illustrated in the case report of Mehmet, determines if students may enter upper-level secondary education or lower tracks of vocational education. Overall, immigrant students are overrepresented in lower vocational schools and underrepresented in higher secondary schools and vocational colleges that lead toward university admission. In addition, they are less likely to gain access to apprenticeships.[47]

Students with special educational needs generally have benefited from past developments that led to more inclusion in the educational system. In Austria, the percentage of children with special educational needs is rather small compared with that of other European countries (3.6 percent of all students in grades 1–8). Even though half of these students now attend integrative schools, the rate of integration in some provinces is as low as 30 percent. Whether a SEN student attends an integrated or segregated school depends more on the local availability of integrative measures and on decisions made by professionals than on the parents' preference or choice. In particular, students with severe disabilities are more likely to attend special schools.[48]

Unlike Tanja, who attends an integrative class in an academic secondary school, most students with disabilities at the secondary level receive integrative instruction at general secondary schools. According to data from the school year 2007–08, the ratio is about 1:250.[49] In urban areas, SEN students frequently attend general secondary schools together with high numbers of immigrant students and students from disadvantaged social backgrounds. While research indicates that integrative teaching in primary schools benefits all students (i.e., those with and without disabilities), the quality of integrated education in Austria's general secondary schools is still disputed.[50]

When SEN students finish grade 8 of integrated classes, further opportunities for integrative teaching are scarce. In grade 9, some SEN students must attend a special school for the first time, as was described in the case of Tanja. Since 2003, a pilot project offers SEN students the opportunity to attend a one-year prevocational school together with nondisabled peers in order to finish mandatory schooling.[51] Efforts to extend the integrative system beyond grade 8 came to a halt after 2000, when funding for SEN students was capped at 2.7 percent of the school-age population. While some regions in Austria may just meet this quota, in urban areas, such as Vienna, the percentage of SEN children is much higher.[52] The lack of sufficient funding results in decreased staff in integrated as well as in special classes.

Students with an immigrant background are overrepresented in special schools. In 2007–08, only 1.9 percent of German native speakers but 2.8 percent of non-native speakers attended special schools.[53] Regional differences do exist; overrepresentation of students with an immigrant background appears to be more likely in rural areas and provinces where the ratio of SEN students in integrative settings compared with special schools is lower.[54] Also, the ratio of students with Turkish or former Yugoslavian background in special schools is much higher than that of other immigrant groups. For the most part, these students are descendants of labor migrants. Research indicates a high ratio of students from lower socioeconomic backgrounds in special-needs education.[55] This suggests that social and structural factors contribute to the overrepresentation of these student populations in special education. It is also critical that the ratio of male to female students receiving special-needs education is about 2 to 1. However, only small variations in gender distribution exist across all ethnic groups in special education.[56] Given a lack of data on ethnicity, evidence on school placement of particular ethnic groups is scarce. Qualitative research conducted by one of the authors of this chapter indicates that Roma immigrants are at higher risk of being placed in special schools.[57] The case of Milo exemplifies that, contrary to Austrian school law, minority students from socially disadvantaged backgrounds who cannot keep up with their peers are at risk of being transferred to special schools without clear evidence of a physical or mental disability. The fact that psychological testing and parental consent is required for such placement is thwarted by the circumstance that native-language teachers are frequently not part of the assessment team and that parents may not be familiar with the school system and their rights.[58]

Inclusive Curricula and Pedagogy

Pupils who speak a first language other than German attend the same classes as native speakers. Newcomers who enter schools with little knowledge of German are enrolled as *ex-matricular students* and are offered specific language provisions. As described in the case of Milo, such students are not graded during their first twelve months of schooling (a policy that can be extended for an additional twelve months in exceptional cases). Subsequently, immigrant students may receive GSL as well as first-language instruction. Such instruction may be offered parallel to regular instruction (e.g., in separate groups), in integrative settings (e.g., team teaching), or as additional after-school classes. Since 1992–93, GSL and first-language instruction has been provided at all levels of compulsory schooling up to ninth grade. Since 2004–05, first-language instruction has been offered at the upper secondary level as well. Since 2006–07, GSL can also be chosen as an elective course in upper secondary schools.[59]

A variety of barriers impede full inclusion and recognition of diversity. The OECD noted that a "deficit-oriented approach to the language development needs of immigrant children seems quite widespread."[60] The current policy of offering native language support in order to foster second-language development falls short in practice because of inconsistent curricula and a lack of training, status, and remuneration of native-language teachers. Furthermore, GSL provisions vary in quantity and quality across schools, school types, and geographic regions. As criticized by the OECD, "the curricula for teaching GSL in the various school forms do not distinguish between students who lack basic competencies in German and students who understand and speak the language relatively well."[61]

Intercultural learning, which aims at fostering students' understanding and appreciation of cultural and linguistic diversity and at counteracting racism and xenophobia, was introduced as an educational principle in Austrian schools in the early 1990s. With regard to its implementation, teachers are neither sufficiently educated on intercultural issues nor are immigrants and minorities represented adequately in schoolbooks and curricula.[62] For example, research on the schooling of Roma with immigrant backgrounds suggests that teachers do not feel comfortable talking about Roma in class and that they lack appropriate training on cultural topics. At the same time, they hold a variety of unsubstantiated beliefs about Roma parents' views on schooling.[63] In general, few adaptations are made that respond to the diverse groups of learners. Frequently, it appears to be viewed as sufficient if students learn to respect cultural differences and are taught factual information about different minority and migrant groups.

Curricula and instruction for students with special educational needs—in separate as well as in integrative settings—differ greatly from those for mainstream students. However, Specht et al. provided evidence that integrative environments are more conducive to learning: "Individualization and pupil-orientation, the participation of teachers and pupils in the development process of the school and intensive cooperation of the school partners were important observable characteristics of inclusive schools."[64] Contrary to the current practice of teaching general and special education curricula in integrative settings side by side, some experts call for the introduction of a common curriculum for all pupils. This would require "adapting a general inclusive curriculum to the special needs of the individual child."[65] Pledges to reform existing curricula are predominantly voiced by authorities working with people with disabilities outside of school contexts as well as by parent representatives. Teachers and administrators are generally not in favor of such curricular reforms.[66]

Educational Attainment and Achievement

There is evidence that many students with an immigrant background are educationally underserved. This is shown by national research studies and reports as well as international student assessments such as PISA, Trends in International Mathematics and Science Study (TIMSS), and Progress in International Reading Literacy Study (PIRLS).[67] Aggregated test results indicate that students whose parents have low educational levels or an immigrant background are much more likely to achieve lower scores.[68] It is stunning that results of PISA 2006 show that students with an immigrant background who grew up in Austria perform lower than those born abroad.[69]

Austrian schools rely heavily on the educational support provided by parents or privately paid tutors. Parents with low educational levels and those living in difficult social situations cannot provide this kind of support. Disparities are more attributable to social and structural factors than to specifics of ethnic subcultures.[70] However, as stated by Unterwurzacher, even when socioeconomic factors are controlled for, students with Turkish or former Yugoslavian background still perform below their peers.[71] In the decade between 1993 and 2002, immigrant students' underrepresentation in higher secondary schools as well as their overrepresentation in special schools has decreased; nevertheless, descendants of migrant laborers continue to lag behind majority students.

Research on academic achievement of students with disabilities is scarce. Studies in Germany and Switzerland indicate that students with learning disabilities show higher educational attainment in integrative settings.[72] According to Feyerer, a few studies show similar results in regard to students with mental retardation and with severe disabilities but overall this topic is underresearched.[73] One Austrian study on educational achievement of *nondisabled* students in integrative settings suggests that they not only perform just as well as their peers in regular classes but also that they show a significantly higher sense of well-being.[74] The lack of emphasis on researching the academic achievement of SEN students compared with the achievement of their nondisabled peers in inclusive settings is itself telling.

Transition to Work

Low educational attainment of students with immigrant backgrounds impedes their transition to the job market. As pointed out by Herzog-Punzenberger, most second-generation immigrants complete mandatory schooling, and their unemployment rates are comparatively low.[75] However, there is a clear ethnic segmentation of the job market, and for the most part second generation immigrants tend to work in low-skilled jobs. Schools fail to adequately prepare these students for increased job opportunities, and a rigid and partly protected labor market decreases their chances for upward mobility. A comparative study of six European countries indicates that in Austria, students from low SES and immigrant families have significantly lower chances for educational and vocational success.[76] Furthermore, a recent OECD study determined that youth with immigrant backgrounds are not only less qualified but also less likely than their majority peers to attain a job corresponding to their educational qualifications. Remarkably, this gap widens as their level of education increases.[77]

For students with disabilities, the transition phase from school to the vocational world poses numerous problems. An innovative and successful measure for young persons with learning difficulties, called *clearing*, includes a nationwide system of counseling, training courses, and work placements. However, other groups, such as adolescents with intellectual disabilities, do not benefit from this measure. Nearly all of them have no other option than to enter sheltered workshops with work or occupational therapy.

Social Integration and Participation

There is a lack of research on the social integration and participation of students with an immigrant background in Austrian schools. There is likewise an absence of studies on discrimination by peers or teachers. One study on violence in multicultural school settings suggests that majority students are more likely to be offenders as well as victims as compared with students with a Turkish or former Yugoslavian background. Turkish students tend to be less socially integrated, have fewer friends in the classroom, and are lonelier and rejected more often than other groups of students. Among other factors, the authors explain these findings as being related to racist motives by peers.[78]

As outlined by Feyerer, studies on the social integration of students with disabilities indicate a serious need for action because: (1) SEN students in integrative settings experience victimization as well as higher rates of loneliness; (2) schools make little effort to foster mutual understanding; and (3) parents of SEN students in integrative settings report reduced social contacts between their children and peers outside of school, even more so than parents whose children attend special schools.[79] Although social integration is considered to be a major rationale for educating disabled and nondisabled peers in the same class, it appears that so far this goal has not been achieved and that measures to counteract lack of integration have not been developed or implemented adequately.

Cultural and Societal Considerations

Concerted efforts to establish a more equitable educational system have been impeded by long-standing battles between the two main political parties that have alternately governed Austria, the Christian conservative People's Party, which favors the current education system, and the Social Democrats, who advocate for educational reform aimed at extending comprehensive schooling. For the most part, Austrian liberal parties combine nationalist ideologies with liberal economic policies. They frequently criticize minority group rights and immigration and support assimilatory policies. The Austrian Green Party has a more social liberal agenda, but its political influence is limited.

Among proponents of a highly selective educational system, the argument prevails that unequal intellectual abilities and merit rather than disadvantage or discrimination lead to disparate educational outcomes. According to this thinking, a differentiated school system with academic and vocationally oriented tracks will secure a high educational standard for better achievers and offer opportunities in accordance with students' interests and talents as well as fulfilling labor-market needs. This belief in meritocratic ideals explains why the current system prevails, despite the critique that "early streaming increases the impact of socioeconomic background on student achievement."[80] Contrary to the belief that a more inclusive system bears the risk of watering down educational standards, "the OECD has shown in international comparative surveys that high-quality education and equity are not mutually exclusive but can rather *reinforce one another.*"[81] [emphasis added]

Historically, in Austrian class-based society, educational and social mobility has not been contingent solely on achievement and merit but also on social status and networking. This puts immigrants at a disadvantage, particularly if they are lower-class. Until the 1980s, "immigration policy was purely seen as labor market policy" and in public view, immigrants were frequently not regarded as belonging to Austrian society.[82] At the time of writing, however, immigrants are expected to *integrate* while at the same time it is alleged that they are unwilling to adapt to mainstream culture and the norms of society. Integration is seen as a one-sided undertaking. Indeed, what is meant by *integration* is the expectation that immigrants assimilate. Only on the local level (and to some extent in schools) has it been recognized that adaptation is a "gradual process" requiring "some degree of mutual accommodation"; the fact that overall immigrants still do not enjoy full social and political rights is a sign of continuing "differential exclusion," as expressed in limited access to the labor market or the denial of dual-citizenship rights.[83]

Furthermore, neither the dynamics of nepotism and other relationship-based advantages nor the institutional barriers that determine inclusion or exclusion are openly acknowledged. Despite a long history of migration and current increases in diversity resulting from it, mainstream society has not accepted that Austria is a country of immigration. Many continue to see ethnic and cultural diversity as a temporary phenomenon. In public discourse, even second-generation youths who have lived in Austria all their lives are frequently referred to as foreigners. Their constructed *otherness* is regarded as hindering integration into society. As pointed out by Castles, immigrants' poor employment situations lead to their high concentration in low-income neighborhoods and residential segregation.[84] Following Castles, we may speak of "racialization of ethnic difference" because, "The existence of separate and marginal communities is then taken as evidence of failure to integrate, and this in turn is perceived as a threat to the host society."[85]

The dominant public perception is that immigrants do not identify with Austrian majority culture. These attitudes are reflected and evidenced in the political support of right-wing politicians and of assimilationist policies of the governing parties that also draw on these beliefs and sentiments. Contrary to this belief, as has been shown by Weiss, the majority of second-generation immigrants regard Austria as their homeland, even though they often feel marginalized.[86]

Current policies aiming for integration of immigrants are not consistent with equity policies. They specify the obligations of immigrants (learning the German language, acquiring knowledge about Austrian culture and history) rather than emphasizing their rights. Equality of opportunity, antidiscrimination, and affirmative action are not on the main political agenda despite the fact that immigrants often face racism, xenophobia, and decreased opportunities.[87] According to a recent study, 57 percent of people with an immigrant background are negatively affected by racism and xenophobia, 46 percent complain of reduced opportunities, and, among Muslims with Turkish background, 53 percent experience discrimination and two-thirds have had negative experiences with the majority population.[88]

The ability to successfully affect societal change is dependent on power relations and structures of privilege. Therefore, it is not surprising that influential middle- and upper-class parents of students with disabilities successfully lobbied for change toward more inclusive education. Descendants of lower-class immigrant families lack this kind of social capital for lobbying and support.

While improvements have been made in regard to the social inclusion of people with disabilities, many of them still face barriers; in particular, in employment. In the public view, people with intellectual disabilities are generally seen as being in need of support—that is, requiring compensation for their individual deficits and limitations in daily life. Their otherness is for the most part tolerated; however, their integration in mainstream schools or workplaces is regarded as a concession. Paternalistic attitudes prevail in Austrian society; thus people with disabilities are pitied, and calls for charity rather than equal opportunities predominate. This is symbolized by a very popular television show called *Light into Darkness*, in which donations for people with disabilities are collected at Christmastime each year. Nevertheless, there is antidiscrimination legislation, efforts to remove barriers in public life, and support for independent living and work assistance. There is widespread social consensus that integrative forms of schooling benefit all children; however, this is mainly based on the rationale to foster social integration rather than on evidence that integrative forms of schooling has led to better educational outcomes for students with special educational needs. Depending on their circumstances, people with intellectual disabilities may feel empowered to live an ordinary life or they may experience marginalization. For the most part, the arguments of advocates for independent living—namely, that limitations experienced by people with intellectual disabilities are a consequence of environmental factors rather than of personal restraints—have not entered public consciousness. Also, there appears to be lower acceptance of people with learning disabilities and behavioral problems compared with people with physical or sensory disabilities, in part, because the former are viewed as responsible for their *inadequate* social behavior.[89] From the public viewpoint, the practice of integrating children with disabilities in schools is well established. Continuing discussions on standards of inclusive education as propagated by UNESCO and the British Index for Inclusion take place primarily between progressive educators, teachers, and the staff of teacher colleges.

The report *Development of Education in Austria 2004–2007* by the Austrian Ministry of Education, which was disbursed in 2008 at the UNESCO conference "Inclusive Education—The Way of the Future," states in the preface: "'Inclusive education' signifies that areas which formerly were frequently separated, such as special education, integrative education, talent promotion, intercultural learning and gender-sensitive education, should be combined in one single educational approach.[90] However, it is notable that the remainder of the report refers to integrative and compensatory measures for separate groups of students rather than to inclusive practices that would presuppose a restructuring of the entire school system to meet the needs of a diverse student body. Accordingly, the report refers to the option of placing students with disabilities in regular schools to facilitate social integration and to remedial German language programs as well as to voluntary native language instruction for immigrants with the main aim to foster second language development.[91] Integrative measures for SEN students who are taught a special education curriculum and language support measures for migrants do not address the core issues, which impede inclusion and equity: students' marginalized social position and a highly selective school system that is inadequately resourced to teach diverse groups of learners in inclusive settings. Thus, socially disadvantaged students with an immigrant background are at a higher risk of marginalization through being identified as having learning disabilities and being channeled to school types with lower academic requirements.[92] Immigrant status and disability are treated as separate issues requiring separate kinds of policies, while in fact, as outlined in this chapter, these issues are frequently in collusion. Also, the extensive overrepresentation of male SEN students due to a higher ascription of learning and behavior problems is not addressed by any of the current policies. The policies do not account for the fact that immigrant background, social background, disability, and gender mutually interact and influence one another in processes that lead toward the formation of educational inequalities. The predominant discourse, which centers on language learning and social integration, disguises the school system's role in reproducing these inequalities. Labeling and categorizing disadvantaged students as disabled or low achievers legitimizes forms of marginalization, and thereby the meritocratic ideology can be upheld.

Overall, there is an absence of equity-related policies, a fact that was also acknowledged in a recent OECD review of migrant education in Austria.[93]

OUTCOMES, CONCLUSIONS, AND FUTURE DIRECTIONS

Various dimensions have been considered in assessing the extent to which the Austrian educational system is equitable and inclusive. To this end, access to education, the conditions for learning, educational outcomes, and benefits from the results of education, as well as social integration and participation, have been analyzed. Immigrant background and special educational needs were the two central categories under investigation; however, as exemplified by the discussion of three paradigmatic case studies, a meaningful analysis can be arrived at only if the intersections of various dimensions of difference are examined. This is supported by the results of the cited empirical studies and coincides with theories on intersectionality.[94]

The manner in which immigrant background, social background, disability, and gender interact and transform one another influences the formation of educational inequalities. Overall, results show that immigrant students are underserved and disadvantaged by the Austrian educational system. However, such a generalized assessment obscures the fact that some immigrant groups attain good educational outcomes while others underachieve.[95] Even though Austria's school system is ill-prepared to deal with diverse groups of learners, cultural and language differences per se do not necessarily lead to educational disadvantage. Social background and educational achievement correlate highly, irrespective of whether the students are immigrants or belong to the majority. Immigrant students are overrepresented among socioeconomically disadvantaged groups, a factor that in part explains their educational underachievement. However, if socioeconomic background is accounted for, children of migrant workers still lag behind their peers from the majority.

Early differentiation in school tracks constitutes a drawback for all students from disadvantaged backgrounds. Public and political discussions on whether such a weighty decision—one that determines future life chances—should take place so early in a student's school career have been ongoing since the early 1920s. Current school models such as the cooperative secondary school or the new secondary school are only compromises resulting from these long-standing discussions. The insufficient implementation of existing measures aimed at facilitating language development and intercultural learning during early childhood years and during compulsory schooling, coupled with vague and non-binding equity policies, hinders educational progress of students with immigrant backgrounds.[96]

In Austria, there appears to be broad consensus that SEN students should be given the opportunity to attend regular schools together with nondisabled peers. Individual child-centered and differentiated teaching methodologies in these integrative settings are seen to benefit all students. However SEN students and their peers are taught according to different curricula. There are no studies on learning outcomes for SEN students in integrative or in segregated settings, and studies on their social integration show worrisome results. Furthermore, the quality of integrative teaching at general secondary schools—schools in which students with immigrant backgrounds and socially disadvantaged students are overrepresented—is underresearched. In addition, integrative settings that do not span the entire length of mandatory schooling, the fact that students with severe disabilities are more likely to attend special schools, and the low availability of integrative settings in some provinces are all indicators of limited inclusive practices. While female students slightly outperform males across all national groups, two-thirds of all SEN students are males, frequently with a diagnosis in a *subjective* disability category (e.g., learning disabilities). Overrepresentation of immigrants and students of lower socioeconomic status in special needs education, in particular in segregated facilities, indicate further inequities.

Educational experts challenge assumptions regarding the sufficiency of formal equality by acknowledging that disparate educational outcomes are also due to structural and systemic factors that perpetuate inequalities. The fact that immigrants do not benefit from the results of education in the same way as members of the majority is a clear indicator that Austrian society is not offering enough opportunities for societal integration.

In response to various national and international critiques, Austrian political decision makers have pledged to improve the educational system's inclusiveness. A variety of measures to strengthen early childhood education, make secondary schooling more comprehensive, and improve the provision of language support are currently being implemented. Initiatives to foster diversity and equity could give rise to concerted efforts to make the system more inclusive, but these must be supported by the political will to overcome current barriers deeply ingrained in Austrian class-based society.

As illustrated in this chapter, immigrant students and students with disabilities do not necessarily face the same forms of disadvantage in the school system. Thus, rendering the system more inclusive calls for targeted policies taking into account that different measures are needed to improve the educational situation for each group. Still, an extension of comprehensive schooling would benefit both groups.

The repeated call for better *social integration* of immigrants is characteristic of a political discourse that tends to regard language and cultural differences, as well as attitudes and behaviors held by immigrant communities, as explanatory factors for educational inequalities. This deficit-oriented view places the burden on immigrant communities and culturalizes social inequalities. Thus, it falls short of calling for a transformation of an educational system that is inadequately prepared to teach diverse groups of learners and in which social background greatly determines educational outcomes. Instead, socially disadvantaged and linguistic minority students are overrepresented in special needs education, thus translating social and language differences into disability.

Further research is needed to investigate why resistance to more far-reaching reforms persists. The socio-historical analysis at hand may contribute to a better understanding of its underlying dynamics. To gain an even better understanding, theories of social and cultural reproduction, which provide insight about how systemic and structural inequalities are mediated within schools and incorporated by members of various groups in society, have to be consulted. If immigrant students are to attain equal opportunity, the discourse needs to change from expecting minority groups to assimilate to recognizing diversity and to identifying mechanisms of systemic discrimination. In view of a long historical tradition during which Austrian society has been class-oriented and authority-bound, coupled with pressures to conform and nationalistic sentiments, this road toward a more equitable and inclusive society will be arduous.

2

Inclusive Education and the Interlocking of Ability and Race in the United States
Notes for an Educational Equity Research Program

Alfredo J. Artiles, Elizabeth B. Kozleski, Federico R. Waitoller, and Christopher L. Lukinbeal

Inclusive education attained the status of a global movement a number of years ago, and many nations have been engaged in powerful transformations of their educational systems following inclusive agendas.[1] In the United States, for example, more than 60 percent of all students with disabilities are educated in general education classrooms more than 80 percent of their school day.[2] This number has gradually increased in the last six years, from 52 percent.[3] However, the true meanings and implications of inclusive education are located in the interstices between its universal principles and the flavors of local inclusive initiatives.[4] To complicate matters, reviews of the knowledge base on inclusive education suggest two troubling trends.[5] First, the bulk of this research narrows the comprehensive focus of inclusive education to analyses about the opportunities, experiences, and outcomes of students with disabilities. Second, systematic attention to equity issues in the implementation of inclusive education is the exception because of unexamined historical legacies both within and outside of education. For instance, in the United States, the research on inclusive education and the research on racial disparities in special education have been on parallel tracks, often published in different journals with very little attention to their potential intersections.[6] This bifurcation suggests that the time is ripe to explore how historical legacies for groups that inhabit intersecting forms of difference have informed and influenced inclusive program implementation. A concern with addressing this substantial gap in the literature guides the work reported in this chapter.

We focus on the disproportionate identification of low-income racial minority students in high-incidence disability categories—learning disabilities (LD), emotional/behavioral disorders (E/BD), and mild intellectual disabilities (MID)—as a window into long-standing educational inequities that contribute to the stratification of US society while schools grapple with inclusive education agendas that encompass a broader range of disability labels and needs. It is here, in the socially constructed disability categories that the intersections of the racialized histories of the United States and the ways that disability has been appropriated to draw distinctions between and among students that the intersections can be explored. We reframe the research conducted to date and reflect on how this perspective can strengthen future policy and research efforts. Specifically, we avoid the reliance on simplistic binary framings of the problem (e.g., is the problem due to community or within-child traits?), the privileging of individual child or teacher variables, and the primary focus on deficits of children, families, teachers, schools, and communities traditionally used in this research. Instead, we frame the analysis of racial inequities in disability categories from a cultural historical perspective.[7]

A key assumption of the proposed model is that educational inequities for racial minority children are shaped and emerge at the intersection of multiple sectors beyond education.[8] For this reason, we examine the role of school factors in the context of community forces as a means to obtain a broader, more situated understanding of educational inequities for this population. In addition, by identifying the intersections between community and school constraints and strengths, we will pinpoint factors and processes that can be used to frame community and school partnerships on behalf of these children.

We aim to provide evidence to researchers and educational leaders that defy simplistic theories of action in the design of interventions. That is, modeling a more complex view of how institutional, social, and educational factors intersect to produce inequity will compel policy makers to attend to the critical and, as of yet, seemingly invisible roles of space and time, schooling structures, everyday cultural practices in schools and communities, and regularities and contradictions in the analysis of educational inequities. In other words, this perspective calls attention to the production of educational (in)equity as mediated by sociocultural ecologies of constraints and resources in schools and neighborhoods.

BACKGROUND: THE RESEARCH AND THE CONTEXT

Before we present the assumptions of our proposed model, we outline background information on the research conducted to date and its limits.

Research on Racial Inequities in Special Education: Background and Needs

Since 1968, debates about minority students' disproportionate representation in special education remain unabated despite two reports funded by the National Academy of Sciences.[9] The more recent of these concluded that schooling independently contributes to the incidence of special needs among racial minority students "through the opportunities that it provides."[10] Research on this problem has focused largely on elementary school students and has included almost exclusively racial minority samples.[11] African American and Native American students are overrepresented in these programs at the national level. There is some evidence that Latino students and English language learners (ELLs) are disproportionately identified in certain regions and states (e.g., the Southwest) under certain conditions (e.g., the size of the group's school enrollment, presence of language support programs, and poverty level of the school).[12] NCCRESt (National Center for Culturally Responsive Educational Systems) tracked state-level data from 1998–2010 on the risk for students from six ethnic groups to be identified for special education and also tracked student risk in eight large urban school systems throughout the United States.[13] These data show that while states changed their thresholds for identifying districts with disproportionality, in a number of districts the overall risk for special education identification for African American, Native American, and Latino students increased.

It should be noted that the bulk of this research has been conducted in the last ten years despite the problem's long-standing presence, and most of it is concerned with the examination of school professionals' practices (e.g., referrals, assessment, or diagnostic decisions).[14] Many of these studies examine individuals' biases theorized largely through a cognitive lens. Attention to school contexts, (group or institutional) cultural influences, or the roles of historical legacies of oppression are noticeably neglected and theoretically narrow.[15] Another favored approach for studying this problem looks at school and community sociodemographic factors (e.g., income level, student enrollment by race and social class) and often aims to predict disability identification.[16] Conceptually, these studies tend to be framed from a "risk" perspective—that is, the search for individually rooted causes of student learning difficulties; attention to assets, cultural resources, and protective processes is virtually nonexistent.

One important consequence of using these research approaches is that school-based responses to this problem have focused on psychological (e.g., cultural competence, individual bias elimination) rather than systemic solutions that offer the possibility of understanding the sociological, political, and cultural contexts that undergird disproportionality. For instance, if neighborhoods are organized along boundaries that define immigrant nationalities, how do these monocultural enclaves impact the ways that teachers and students alike identify intellectual and cultural capital in the classroom? What group or groups are considered atypical or different, and how do these differences get interpreted in student classroom performance? If some parts of local neighborhoods are considered "unsafe," how do these perceptions affect how students from those neighborhoods are perceived, and how do students who live in those sections of town perceive themselves? Answering such questions requires attention to community and other nonschool factors so that an explicit, theoretically sound view of culture and its mediating power in human affairs (particularly in schools) can be developed.

Another consequence of traditional research approaches is that school districts and schools end up mathematizing the problem; that is, they frame and tackle it from a purely technical perspective in which constructs are quantified under abstract categories and processes are erased.[17] Thus, educators often focus solely on reducing the disproportionality indices or changing the placement thresholds that trigger state or federal audits.[18] This way, remedies become a numbers game in which placement risks can be reduced for racial minority students without necessarily improving the quality of education offered to these students or the transformation of the structures and practices that created the inequities in the first place. Another recent trend is observed in districts' efforts to change what counts as disproportionality, so that even substantially high placement probabilities (in the neighborhood of four to five times more likely) would not constitute disproportionate representation.[19] These are indeed consequential decisions with potentially grave implications.

An interdisciplinary framework to track equity in inclusive education, therefore, is urgently needed to rely on a broader unit of analysis that considers the multiple layers of this problem. More importantly, a cultural historical model will enable the research community to foreground equity analyses during program implementation and transcend the historical limits of this literature.

Assumptions of a Cultural Historical Model

We conceptualize neighborhoods, communities, and schools as interdependent spheres of influence that have the potential to advance or constrain the opportunities of the next generation of US citizens. Although the majority of racial minority children live under adverse circumstances, we broaden traditional analytical lenses so that a strengths-based, culturally responsive perspective is systematically used. In turn, we expect the knowledge gathered from this standpoint will inform the design and reform of educational programs that enhance learning opportunities and strengthen preparation for participation in a democratic society.

We use an interdisciplinary model that accounts for people's everyday practices as embedded in cultural milieus and connect local actions to larger historical/structural processes, such as race relations in racially stratified societies, and the structural distribution of opportunities along racial and other forms of difference. Moreover, a historically dynamic and instrumental view of culture informs our framework, so that culture's simultaneous pressures to renew and reproduce practices are accounted for.[20] The attention to the complexities of educational equity as embedded in larger sociohistorical processes will enable us to paint a more nuanced portrait of the educational experiences of marginalized learners.

Scholarship from urban sociology, critical policy studies, and critical geography offers important insights about the intersection of space and time in sociocultural practices.[21] Thus, a focus on the spatial distribution of opportunities at a point in time (or across time) enables us to study how educational equity is constituted by opportunities and constraints in the wider educational system and beyond. For instance, there is substantial evidence about the structuring nature of race in American society and how opportunities for valuable experiences and resources (e.g., quality teachers and schools, access to college, higher-paid employment, housing) are racially and spatially distributed.[22] And there is a plethora of evidence on the intersections of race, ethnicity, language, gender, and national status and how they mediate intergroup relations in everyday ecologies of communities and neighborhoods where schools are located that ultimately shape sociocultural processes, attitudes, and behaviors.[23] We use such analytic lens to contextualize the examination of inequities in education.[24]

Assumptions of an Inclusive Education Stance

Education for All (EFA) has influenced significant reforms in educational systems around the globe, at least at the policy level.[25] EFA has targeted inclusive education through international declarations and projects sponsored by international agencies such as UNESCO. Defined broadly, inclusive education focuses on ensuring that a variety of groups that have been traditionally excluded from formal schooling are able to access a variety of opportunities to learn in schools.[26] In spite of the press for inclusive education internationally, its agenda has some skeptics questioning who benefits from advancing a universal and standardized effort that has the potential to erase local, indigenous ways of responding to and accommodating difference.[27] How such an agenda might be accomplished and the degree to which a deep and sustained commitment to inclusiveness exists in policy and practice remains only partially examined. As the push for formal education disrupts the social fabric of communities of nomadic, immigrant, and agrarian communities, inclusive education must be examined from multiple perspectives that take into account tensions between local, national, and global scales.

Inclusive education comprises a set of ambitious reform agendas that emerged primarily from equity critiques focusing on the diluted curriculum of classrooms segregated by ability differences, the content knowledge of special educators, and the lack of opportunities to learn from and alongside peers with a range of abilities and talents.[28] Despite growing consensus around definitions of inclusive education, there are few similarities from context to context.[29] For instance, beginning in 1968, special education critics in the United States pointed to the flaws in an educational process that seemed to promise specialized treatments and interventions linked to specific needs for students who were identified in specific disability categories.[30] Beginning in 1995, a call for inclusive education in the United States found voice in the research literature.[31] Where inclusive education took hold in the United States, it benefited White children—who were more likely to be included in general education—more than their African American and Latino counterparts.[32] Although inclusive education was defined as a project for advancing a transformative agenda that focused on examining the processes and legacies that marginalized students because of race, class, gender, religion, language, and ability, inclusive education primarily focused on the construction of difference, particularly as it related to within-child deficits.[33] Oppression and exclusion because of race, language, class, gender, and complex cultural practices provided a fuzzy backdrop for the ability discourse. Yet the endemic and sustaining structure within the US education system is predicated on selection criteria that have their roots in enduring legacies of racial oppression and stratification in US society.[34] Without attention to the intersections of race and ability, inclusive education will always fail to earn legitimacy and authenticity in the eyes of minority students and their families.

Who is included, for what purpose, and in what context varies dramatically.[35] The heterogeneity of national and local sociocultural contexts dictates variances that are often unclear for researchers and practitioners working across national contexts. For the most part, inclusive education projects have failed to address deeply embedded assumptions that guard how schooling is constructed: (1) the complex process of identity formation and development, (2) the dynamic and cultural nature of practice within local schools, and (3) the institutional pressure to conform, sort, and organize along bureaucratic lines. In this chapter, we conceptualize inclusive education as a project that involves examining the nature of local and indigenous ways of interacting with what counts as "different" within a given community. How difference has been constructed and for what purposes intersects with how individual, familial, and institutional identities are constructed and sustained over time. The work of Soja and others helps to understand how spatial relationships such as proximity to physical, intellectual, and social resources; other people; and multiple languages inform, influence, and complete individual and collective narratives about what is valued, useful, and desirable.[36] Woven into these spatial narratives are historical, contemporary, and future-oriented notions of time and people's agency. These concepts function to construct and afford the degree to which difference becomes visible and subject to reinterpretation.[37] To engage inclusive education as a project of becoming, rather than a state of being, requires understanding the historical legacies that produce cultural patterns within schools and opening the possibility of reconsideration of those practices. A sociocultural framework creates the possibility of examining the affordances and constraints of inclusive education in terms of the tools, structures, and activity patterns embedded within school as well as understanding how local community culture informs and influences the ways in which difference is defined and addressed. Communities themselves play critical roles in assigning purpose and outcomes to the function of schooling. These values undergird how school is organized and for whom. In this way, a more complete understanding of who is being included, in what ways, and for what outcomes can be accomplished.

UNDERSTANDING THE RACIALIZATION OF DISABILITY THROUGH AN INTERDISCIPLINARY PRISM

In this section, we highlight some key ideas from our standpoint to examine the racialization of disability. We present descriptive evidence about the city of Chicago and one of its neighborhoods as a means to illustrate the potential value of the proposed perspective. For this purpose, we summarize broad descriptors of the state of Illinois and Chicago public schools to contextualize our analysis. Second, we describe disability as a fluid notion that is distributed across city spaces in particular ways. Third, we summarize descriptive data on a Chicago neighborhood and contextualize the racialization of disability data with evidence on sociocultural indicators of school and neighborhood life. We expect this multilevel sketch will broaden the study of the racialization of disability and compel researchers to examine this longstanding problem in its broader sociohistorical contexts.

Chicago Public Schools: An Overview

The Chicago Public Schools (CPS) district is located in the third-largest city and is the fourth-largest school district in the United States. In 2010, CPS educated 409,279 students in its 482 elementary schools, 122 high schools, and 71 charter schools. Latino and African American students constituted the largest proportion of students in CPS (41 percent and 45 percent, respectively), while White students accounted for 9 percent, Asian/Pacific Islander (A/PI) account for 3.6 percent, and Native Americans accounted for 0.2 percent of the total school enrollment.

Students from a low-income background accounted for 86 percent, and students identified as limited English proficient (LEP) accounted for 12.2 percent of the school enrollment.[38] Almost 50 percent of the teachers are White, about 30 percent are African American, and 16 percent are of Latino background.[39]

Overall, students' academic outcomes as measured by the Illinois Standard Achievement Test (ISAT) have increased over the last decade. The percentage of students in grades 3–8 meeting or exceeding standards grew from 39 percent in 2001 to over 65 percent in 2010 in reading and from 35 percent to 75 percent in the mathematics portion of the ISAT. Yet racial differences in these indicators remained throughout the decade with African American, Latino, and Native American students being outperformed by White and Asian/Pacific Islander students. The percentage of students with disabilities and LEP students meeting or exceeding reading and mathematics standards also increased over the last decade but continued to be significantly lower compared with the percentage of students without disabilities and English proficient students respectively.[40]

Similar trends are observed in the dropout and graduation rates. Overall graduation rates increased from 47.2 in 2001 to 55.8, and dropout rates decreased from 50 percent in 2001 to 41 percent in 2010. African American, Latino, and Native American students and students with either an IEP or a 504 plan had the highest dropout rates and lowest graduation rates. LEP students' dropout rates are lower and graduation rates are higher than the rates for all students.[41]

As of 2010, students with an individualized educational plan (IEP) composed a little over 12 percent of the total school enrollment, which is about the same proportion reported in 2006 (11.7 percent). If one looks at special education placement across grade levels, it is noticeable that greater percentages of students with IEP are found in the higher grades. In 2006, for instance, students with an IEP constituted 6 percent of the total first-grade enrollment, while they accounted for almost 17 percent of the total enrollment in tenth grade.[42]

Fluid Geographies of Disability: Tracing and Understanding Boundary Objects

The racialization of disability is traditionally calculated in the United States with relative risk ratios.[43] This index "provides a group's relative likelihood of identification or placement in comparison to some other group. It is represented by a ratio of the risk indices for two groups [in which a risk index is] calculated by dividing the number of group members in the disability category by the total number of those individuals in the popu-lation."[44] Thus, the relative risks for identification in the high-incidence disabilities for various racial groups in Illinois in 2005–06 are reported in table 2.1. These data suggest African Americans are the only students over-represented in MID and E/BD in Illinois. Latino and Asian/Pacific Islander students, on the other hand, are underrepresented in several disability categories at the state level, the former in the E/BD category and the lat-ter in LD and E/BD.

As we move this analysis from the state to the city level (i.e., Chicago), the aggregated data on special education placements do not show over-representation patterns for any racial category. However, the placement evidence by disability category shows that Latino and African American students were overrepresented in the high-incidence categories. African American students were almost six times as likely (5.87) and Latino stu-dents were over three times (2.41) more likely to be placed in the high-incidence disability categories than their peers (see table 2.2).

Note, however, that these placement indices by themselves do not pro-vide information about potential contributing or contextual factors. The challenge for researchers, therefore, is to use analytical tools that enable them to contextualize the identification patterns reflected in the relative risk ratios. For this purpose, we reframe some of the basic tenets typically used in the analysis of this problem. Specifically, we assume educational systems are engaged in intensive cultural work that both: (1) encultur-

TABLE 2.1   Relative risk ratio for students in high incidence disabilities (compared with all other groups) in Illinois, 2005–06*

	Intellectual disabilities	Learning disabilities	Emotional/ behavioral disorders	Speech/ language impairments
African American	3.20	1.37	2.43	0.79
Latino/a	0.78	1.04	0.46	0.74
Asian/Pacific Islander	0.52	0.29	0.20	0.67
Native American	0.76	0.89	0.92	0.98
White	0.47	0.87	0.80	1.45

Source: www.nccrest.org (based on Census count)

* A relative risk ratio of 2 or above is generally considered an overrepresentation pattern and 0.5 reflects underrepresentation.

TABLE 2.2   Disability relative risk ratio by student race in CPS and selected neighborhood school, 2005–06

	K–8 SCHOOLS		**HIGH SCHOOL**
Student race	District (n = 401,699)	Madrigal (n = 776)	Mendoza (n = 572)	Herrera (n = 1690)
African American	5.87	3.05	1.73	1.14
Latino/a	3.41	0.38	1.00	0.74
Asian/Pacific Islander	0.12	n/a	3.87	0.6
Native American	0.02	n/a	n/a	n/a
White	1.0	1.0	1.95	2.19

Source: www.nccrest.org.

ates future adult citizens to the dominant cultural codes of communities and (2) sets conditions and deploys technologies and practices that ultimately stratify those communities.[45] We further assume educational systems use notions such as giftedness, risk status, and disabilities in subtly disparate ways across social worlds to *manage diversity and cooperation* among school professionals, leading ultimately to important equity consequences.[46] For the purpose of this analysis, we conceptualize disabilities as *boundary objects*; these are defined as objects that "inhabit several intersecting worlds . . . and satisfy the informational requirements of each of them . . . [These objects] are both plastic enough to adapt to local needs and the constraints of the several parties employing them, yet robust enough to maintain a common identity across sites."[47]

We consider disability an *ideal type* of boundary object. An ideal type "does not accurately describe the details of any locality or thing. It is abstracted for all domains, and may be fairly vague" (e.g., species).[48] Thus, an ideal type of boundary object is adaptable to specific sites because of its vagueness, and these objects delete local contingencies. This notion allows us to examine the potentially changing meanings and purposes of a construct such as LD as professionals, students, parents, and administrators move through the institutional practices that lead to disability identification—from student participation and learning opportunities in the general education classroom to referrals, assessments, and eligibility meetings.[49] We are also interested in *standardized* boundary objects that are used as "methods of common communication across dispersed work groups."[50] These objects delete local uncertainties. We consider relative risk ratios a *standardized* boundary object.

Our theoretical assumptions, therefore, enable us to examine how a technical index that standardizes information (e.g., relative risk ratio) allows individuals from disparate constituencies situated in different locations to communicate about a notion that might embody rather diverse meanings and purposes (e.g., disability). From this vantage point, we broaden analytical possibilities for understanding the cultural work of disabilities.[51]

Let us take, for example, longstanding assumptions and arguments about the consequences of poverty for disability identification risk. A favored explanation in this literature is that the high poverty rate among minority families explains the disproportionate prevalence of disability in these groups.[52] This traditional explanation constitutes a major barrier in efforts to address this problem, since it could lead to the conclusion that interventions should target only families and children (given that the transformation of structural factors requires more expensive efforts over longer periods of time). In contrast, we can contextualize the association of poverty with disability identification patterns through the examination of the spatial distribution of disabilities for a particular racial group across localities with distinct socioeconomic levels. This analytical strategy can assist us to raise questions regarding the role of disability as an ideal boundary object across geographical areas.

Figure 2.1 represents the areas of Chicago where disproportionate representation was observed (red areas) for African American students in low- and high-poverty schools. Visual examination of this map suggests that African American disproportionality rates are found in areas where high-poverty schools are located, though there are also disproportionality patterns in low-poverty schools. To complicate matters, disproportionate representation levels are identified in areas of the city where *both* high- and low-poverty schools sit in close proximity. How do factors like teacher salary and attrition across districts, history of desegregation court orders, teacher perceptions of student ability, and teacher and parent perceptions of neighborhood violence and trust that can mediate parent-teacher and teacher-student interactions shape disability identification decisions? Interestingly, research suggests all of these factors are linked to equity concerns in education, some of which also bear on the disproportionate representation problem.[53] Reframing this problem from the standpoint of disability as boundary object opens opportunities to examine aspects and issues that otherwise would be ignored in the traditional research para-

FIGURE 2.1 African American student disproportionate representation in CPS's high- and low-poverty schools

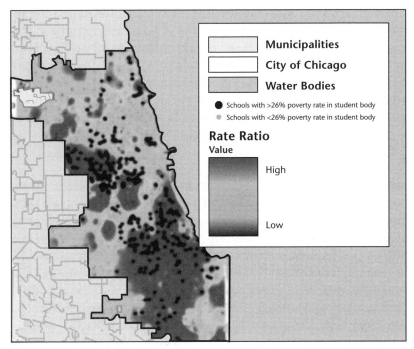

Source: E. B. Kozleski, A. Artiles and J. Klingner, National Center for Culturally Responsive Educational Systems, Office of Special Education Programs, U.S. Department of Education, Contract # H326E060001, 2004–2010.

digm used in this literature. For instance, questions that arise from the proposed perspective include the following: (1) What meanings and purposes do the notion of disability have in these schools? and (2) How do differences in the meanings and purposes of disability across social contexts shape identification rates for racial minority groups? We turn next to a closer examination of some of these issues at the neighborhood and school levels.

The Racialization of Disability in Its School and Neighborhood Contexts

We bring the analysis of the racialization of disability to the level of a neighborhood in Chicago. (We define neighborhoods as "ecological units nested within successively larger communities."[54]) This neighborhood is predominately populated by Latino residents (over 90 percent; majority Mexican), and about one-fifth of households are headed by women. The neighborhood's socioeconomic statistics portray a typical urban community in a major US city.[55] About one-third of household incomes are below $15,000 per year and over one-third of children in the neighborhood live under the federal poverty level. The median household incomes are 20 percent below the citywide level. The unemployment rate was 13 percent, compared with 7 percent for the rest of the city. Gang violence is widely considered to be second only to East Los Angeles.[56] Two-thirds of children drop out of school and almost three-quarters of adults never completed a ninth-grade education.

We reviewed patterns of disability identification for subgroups of students in the neighborhood schools and learned that Latino students were not disproportionately represented in the neighborhood schools. This is interesting, considering that Latinos were over three times as likely to be placed in special education in CPS (see table 2.2). Moreover, we found that African American, Asian/Pacific Islander, and White students were overrepresented in three neighborhood schools, two K–8 schools and one high school (see table 2.2).[57] Specifically, African Americans were over three times as likely to be placed in special education at Madrigal K–8 school. (*Note:* All school names are pseudonyms.) This risk is lower than the districtwide ratio of 5.87. In turn, Mendoza school (K–8), showed substantial overrepresentation of Asian/Pacific Islander students (almost four times as likely) and borderline levels of representation for African American and White learners (see table 2.2). Neither Asian American nor White students were overrepresented in CPS. Lastly, White learners were twice as likely to be placed in special education at Herrera High School. Note that these schools had a higher proportion of students living in poverty compared with the CPS rate (see table 2.3). In addition, compared with the district, the two K–8 schools had a higher proportion of students classified as LEP, while the high school had a comparable rate of LEP learners. Student mobility rate was lower in the two K–8 schools and higher in the high school than the CPS level. In contrast to the CPS rate, student attendance was lower in the high school and higher in the K–8 schools (see table 2.3).

Our analytic approach takes into account socioeconomic indicators in the examination of racial identification patterns in the neighborhood schools. It is not surprising, therefore, that there are patterns of racial overrepresentation in light of the poverty level and low educational attainment of most residents in this geographical area.[58] The link between disproportionality rates and these factors has been documented in previ-

TABLE 2.3   Percentage of school population in CPS and selected schools across various sociodemographic and educational indicators, 2005

		K–8 SCHOOLS		HIGH SCHOOL
Sociodemographic and educational indicators	District (n = 401,699)	Madrigal (n = 776)	Mendoza (n = 572)	Herrera (n = 1690)
Race:				
African American	48	2	4	4
Latino/a	38	96	88	93
Asian/Pacific Islander	3	0	0.7	1
Native American	0.1	0	0	0
White	8	0.3	2	2
Multiracial/ethnic	2	1	5	0.8
Limited English proficient	14	23	23	15
Eligible for free/reduced lunch	86	97	94	97
Mobility rate	24	14	10	28
Attendance rate	92	97	96	84

Source: https://research.cps.k12.il.us/resweb/PageServlet?page=schoolprofile&class=profile.SchoolProfile.

ous research.[59] However, the evidence described above also suggests the target K–8 schools had a greater demand for second-language accommodations, but also had a more stable student population and greater student attendance than the high school. What practices, policies, beliefs, and ideologies account for the differential patterns of disproportionality observed across these three schools that affected distinct racial groups? What mediated student attendance and mobility rates, and how did these factors shape special education placement patterns?

In addition, it is important that we document neighborhood and family processes and resources as a deliberate theoretical move to challenge the image of poor communities as places in which there are only despair, deprivation, apathy, and negative conditions. We aim to enrich these sources with school related data. Our goal is to examine educational equity concerns in the contexts of structures of opportunity and uses of interorganizational ties.[60] For this purpose, we rely on evidence from the Consortium on Chicago School Research about teacher and student perceptions of various aspects of school life that include professional capacity, quality of instruction, school leadership, parent and community relationship, and learning climate.[61] When relevant, we juxtapose data from a project led by urban geographers in the same neighborhood that focused on civic engagement and other indicators of community life.[62] We use these data sets in a descriptive fashion to raise key questions regarding a broader and cultural-historical understanding of disproportionality. This analytic process helps us illustrate the potential of the model proposed in this chapter to examine equity questions germane to the racialization of disabilities.

Table 2.4 reports the Consortium student perception data for the three selected schools. The evidence on student sense of support (under the parent and community relationship dimension) suggests that the three schools fell below the school district average, with Madrigal at the bottom and Mendoza at the highest level; Herrera high school fell between these two schools. This aspect of the survey instrument measured student perception of parent support for student learning and social resources in the community. We link student perceptions of social resources in the community with the notion of collective efficacy beliefs. Note that collective efficacy in the neighborhood was somewhat absent in the geographical areas where these three schools are located (see figure 2.2). Mendoza school, which had the highest level of student sense of support, was the closest to areas of the neighborhood where collective efficacy was high (see figure 2.2). Although Asian American students at Mendoza K–8 school were overrepresented, and African American and White students approached disproportionality levels, student sense of support as measured by this survey was high.

These trends are counterintuitive and raise questions about the social climate at this school and the potential influence of community efficacy perceptions. It is possible that the scores of the Latino majority in the school population are driving the average rates of these measures, thus skewing data that might be construed as contradictory with the disproportionality data. But it is also important to raise questions about what happens to students who constitute a small portion of the student population in schools where there is a strong social cohesion among the majority population. How does this situation shape their chance to be placed in special education? What would be the impact of strengthening collective self-efficacy in the community for school practices? In contrast, African American learners at Madrigal school were three times as likely to be identified with disabilities. Given that this school's students reported the lowest sense of support rates, it is relevant to question how a rather negative mood among students is associated with a heightened level of disproportionality for African Americans.

TABLE 2.4   Selected neighborhood schools' scores in the 2005 Consortium on Chicago School Research biannual survey

	K–8 SCHOOLS		HIGH SCHOOL
Dimensions	Madrigal	Mendoza	Herrera
1.1. Professional community			
a) Reflective dialogue	2[a]	4	4
b) Collective responsibility	3	3	3
c) Socialization of new teachers	3	4	5
1.2. Professional work place			
a) School commitment	5	4	5
b) Innovation	3	3	3
c) Teacher-teacher trust	3	3	4
1.3. Professional development			
a) Access to new ideas	3	3	3
b) Quality of professional development	1	3	3
2. Quality of instruction			
2.1. Engaging pedagogy and academic demand			
a) Quality of student discussion	4	3	4
b) Use of classroom libraries	3	3	n/a
c) Interactive math instruction	4	3	3
d) Student center literacy instruction	1	3	n/a
3. School leadership			
a) Teacher-principal trust	2	2	3
b) Teacher influence	3	3	3
c) Instructional debate	3	2	3
d) Program coherence	2	3	4
4. Parent and community relationships			
4.1. Participants relations			
a) Parent involvement	3	4	n/a
b) Teacher-parent trust	3	4	3
c) Teacher-parent interaction	2	1	1
4.2. Student sense of support			
a) Parent support for student learning	1	2	1
b) Human social resources in the community	2	3	3
5. Learning climate			
5.1. Safety norms and behavior			
a) Safety	3	3	2
b) Student classroom behavior	3	4	3
c) Incident of disciplinary action[b]	5	5	3
5.2. Involvement and support			
a) Student-teacher trust	3	4	3
b) Academic engagement	3	4	4
c) Academic press	2	2	2
d) Peer support academic work	2	2	n/a

Source: Consortium on Chicago School Research (2005). Improving Chicago's Schools: A report specially prepared to assist in self-assessment and long term planning. Chicago: Consortium on Chicago School Research.

a. One standard deviation below the average of CPS; 2 = One half to one standard deviation below average of CPS; 3 = One half standard deviation below to one half standard deviation above the average of CPS; 4 = One half to one standard deviation above average of CPS; 5 = One standard deviation above average.

b. This item was coded on a negative scale; thus, lower scores reflect more desirable patterns with regard to discipline.

FIGURE 2.2   Distribution of neighborhood residents' collective efficacy perceptions

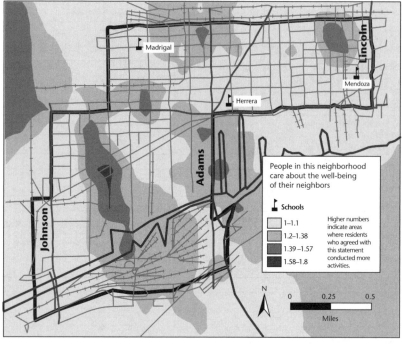

Source: Adapted from D. Fernández, P. L. Price, D. D. Arreola, C. Lukinbeal, M. Torres, and T. Ready, *Comparative Civic and Place Engagement in Three Latino Enclave Neighborhoods in Transition*, National Science Foundation Human and Social Dynamics program award number 433947, 2007.

The ratings in the safety norms and behavior aspect (under the "learning climate" dimension) show that the two K–8 schools had a higher frequency of disciplinary problems (see scores for item 5.1.c. "incident of disciplinary action") than the high school (see table 2.4). While a report from the National Center on Educational Statistics (NCES) states that there are no differences reported in incidents of violence, middle schoolers do experience more school harassment and bullying than high schoolers.[63] In fact, these schools were one standard deviation above CPS average. The high school disciplinary action score was at the district average level. Sociological research suggests neighborhood collective efficacy and neighborhood civic engagement are associated with levels of violence and sense of well-being.[64] We already noted that collective efficacy seemed to be low in the surrounding sites where the schools were located (see figure 2.2). Thus, it is possible that the disciplinary action data from the two K–8 schools reflect disorderly organizational cultures that resort to heavy use of disciplinary referrals and actions. This would not be surprising, since urban schools that serve predominately low-income racial minority students tend to adopt harsher disciplinary measures and rules.[65] It would be useful to examine teacher quality data (e.g., level of education/certification) in these schools, since urban schools serving low-income students tend to have a disproportionate number of low-quality teachers, which in turn is associated with a proclivity to refer students to special education when presented with negative behaviors.[66] Recent research also shows that teachers working in low socioeconomic and low-achieving contexts tend to underestimate their students' abilities, which increases the risk for special education referral.[67] This finding holds after data are statistically controlled for students' social and academic backgrounds.

A related aspect of the learning climate is students' perceptions of safety (see item 5.1.a. in table 2.4). The two K–8 schools reflect safety perceptions at the same level of CPS, suggesting that students feel safe inside and outside of school and traveling to and from the school. The evidence on perceptions of unsafe neighborhood spaces from local residents supports student perceptions, since these schools were not located in "unsafe" areas (see figure 2.3). Although there were neighborhood spots close to these schools that were considered unsafe, the available data on perceptions of safety do not reflect the typical image of urban neighborhoods. Although greater detail is needed about the level of neighborhood violence and safety, it is noticeable that local residents do not perceive safety problems in the immediate surroundings of the target schools. Hence, a closer examination of the organizational culture of these schools is warranted to help us understand how school contexts in which students have high disciplinary referral rates also feel safe. More importantly, this analysis should shed light on how the social spaces of these schools shape the patterns of disproportionate placement in special education for some racial groups.

Quality of instruction is a key consideration in understanding inappropriate referrals and placement in special education. As table 2.4 shows, Herrera high school was rated higher the CPS average when compared with the other two K–8 schools, though the latter were rated at the same level as CPS schools. The data on involvement and support (section 5.2 under "Learning climate") reflect a somewhat consistent pattern; Herrera high school was rated at the same level as CPS schools, like Mendoza school; Madrigal school came below the CPS average. All in all, these indicators did not show problematic trends, and it will be useful to compare them with teacher perception data. Specifically, we observe

FIGURE 2.3   Distribution of neighborhood residents' perceptions of unsafe areas

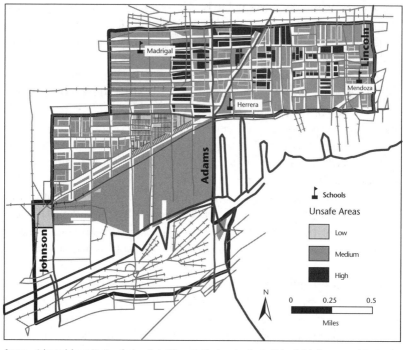

Source: Adapted from D. Fernández, P. L. Price, D. D. Arreola, C. Lukinbeal, M. Torres, and T. Ready, *Comparative Civic and Place Engagement in Three Latino Enclave Neighborhoods in Transition,* National Science Foundation Human and Social Dynamics program award number 433947, 2007.

Herrera high school had a professional workplace score above the CPS average, though the two K–8 schools were at the level of the school district. Herrera was consistently at or above CPS schools on the other measures of professional culture, such as professional community, professional development, and school leadership (see table 2.4). Madrigal school, where African Americans were three times as likely to be placed in special education, was below CPS schools in all of these areas. Although Mendoza school was at the level of CPS schools in two of these areas, it was also below the district average in the school leadership measure (see table 2.4). These data do not raise red flags for the most part, with the exception of school leadership, where both K–8 schools were rated below the district level. Hence, greater scrutiny in this domain is warranted to obtain a more in-depth understanding of the racialization of disability.

The last area we discuss is participants' relationships (under parent and community relationships). The Consortium evidence shows

Mendoza, the school with the most trouble around disproportionality, with a level comparable to CPS schools. Both Madrigal and Herrera high school were below the district average score. What seems to be affecting these scores is the rating on teacher-parent interactions (see item 4.1.c. in table 2.4). Unfortunately, racial minority families, including immigrant families from developing countries, tend to be regarded as disengaged in their children's education, particularly in urban schools—the student perception data cited above suggest the children and youth in these schools seem to share such perspective.[68] Professionals' negative perceptions can be associated with racial disproportionality in special education.[69] Although the socioeconomic and labor realities of many low-income families might get in the way of their participation in their children's education as traditionally defined (e.g., homework supervision, school volunteer work, school meeting attendance), parent-community relationships with schools can benefit from a broader analytical lens.

Therefore, a major challenge for future research on disproportionality is to examine parent and community relationships from an alternative perspective; specifically, a standpoint that taps into family and neighborhood assets. Many neighborhood effect studies have relied on national samples that aggregate a single neighborhood effect size without attention to region of the country or the presence of immigrants.[70] These are important considerations, since the concentration of immigrants in neighborhoods is associated with the presence of community resources such as small businesses, *irrespective of the level of community poverty.*[71] Similarly, the probability of having other key neighborhood resources such as public childcare centers *does not diminish with poverty level.*[72] This is a key fact, considering that "childcare centers provide important resource-access through their ties and that neighborhood poverty does not undermine this capacity."[73] The neighborhood in which we have focused in this chapter is populated by a sizable number of immigrant families. A cultural historical examination of parent-school relationships will benefit from an analysis of families' interorganizational ties at the neighborhood level in places like churches and child-care centers. These organizations serve as resource brokers to desirable social capital through their ties with state agencies, businesses, and other organizations.[74]

What resources are available in these ties that might otherwise be ignored by or invisible to school professionals? Are there aspects of civic engagement that could be capitalized on in school-family relationships? Although we do not have evidence on local civic engagement, we present a GIS image of *transnational* civic engagement that is distinctive of neighborhoods where first-generation immigrants live (see figure 2.4). The map represents residents' efforts in the last year to address neighborhood issues *in another country*. These data reflect considerable transnational engagement in the southwestern portion of the neighborhood where neither one of the target schools is located. But the most intense level of this kind of civic engagement activity is observed in the center of the neighborhood where Herrera high school is located. Questions that could guide future work in this area include: What kinds of civic engagement activities are common in this region of the neighborhood and how do they relate to intergroup relations, since White students were overrepresented at this high school? How can some of the civic engagement activities be redirected or translated into local efforts that support these children's education? Are there interorganizational ties in this geographical area that could be used to spread to other regions of the neighborhood the type of civic engagement observed?

FIGURE 2.4   Distribution of neighborhood residents' transnational civic engagement

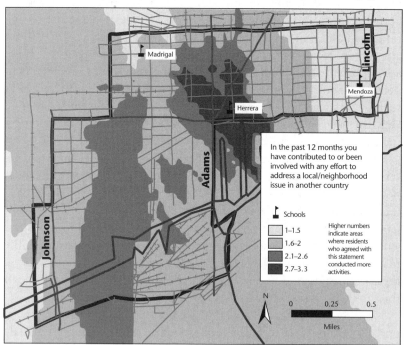

Source: Adapted from D. Fernández, P. L. Price, D. D. Arreola, C. Lukinbeal, M. Torres, and T. Ready, *Comparative Civic and Place Engagement in Three Latino Enclave Neighborhoods in Transition*, National Science Foundation Human and Social Dynamics program award number 433947, 2007.

Consider also evidence on immigrants indicating a negative association between length of residence in the United States and health status; moreover, immigrants "do better on a wide range of social indicators—including propensity to violence—than one would expect given their socioeconomic disadvantages."[75] What practices and factors explain these patterns? What cultural resources do recent immigrants bring that afford them a better health status and lower propensity to violence despite their low education level, high poverty level, and underuse of health-care resources? The analysis of inequities in other sectors, along with evidence on families' understanding and practices in these sectors, will contextualize how educational equity (e.g., disability identification practices) is explained and shaped in schools for this population.

CONCLUSION

By braiding multiple perspectives in our analysis, attention to contexts, cultural forces (e.g., perceptions), and multiple system levels (from state to city to neighborhood), we offer an approach to examining how neighborhood sociocultural ecologies and cultural assets mediate school equity processes and outcomes.[76] Because our data drew from multiple studies, we offer them not as conclusive evidence but rather as illustrative of the ways in which data can help to inform and extend understanding of complex social interactions beyond the typical institutional boundaries between school and community. The proposed framework affords the examination of evidence that is not typically used in equity research on the racialization of disability and hence the project of inclusive education. By superimposing a variety of data sets that canvas the same geographic area but address different aspects of the cultural, economic, political, and linguistic environmental contexts, researchers can inform a more complex understanding of how educational inequities (e.g., disproportionate representation of racial minority learners in disability categories) are, or are not, mediated by community contexts that have had been theorized but not substantiated as playing a role in influencing inequity. In some instances, these analyses can offer counter narratives to long-standing assumptions that endorse deficit views of these communities and hence, of their educational "worthiness." Moreover, this analysis can offer insights to guide future action to address educational inequalities.

Importantly, layering data punctuates the importance of understanding the ways in which seemingly bounded agendas, like inclusive education, are inextricably linked to multiple social phenomena not only in their genesis (e.g., "Let's fix deficit thinking"), but also in their historical links to other forms of segregation that are not typically associated. Further, by examining *patterns* within inequities, intersections are uncovered and made transparent to scholars, practitioners, community members, families, and students. Powerful convergence among these perspectives has the potential to allow change to seed and grow in ways that unitary explanations and bounded analyses are unable to capture. Through this kind of complex analysis, we hope to sustain systematic attention to the equity issues that are often unattended within the inclusive education project.

3

Inclusion, Place, and Disadvantage in the English Education System

Alan Dyson, Lisa Jones, and Kirstin Kerr

In a set of policy guidelines, UNESCO has argued that inclusion can be justified in three ways—*educationally*, in that it can be seen as a way of producing higher quality schools; *economically*, in that it can be seen as a way of holding down educational costs, and *socially*, in that it can be seen as "form[ing] the basis for a just and non-discriminatory society."[1] Without wishing to minimize the importance of the educational and economic justifications, we intend in this chapter to explore how inclusion has been understood in the English context, and to focus in particular on what kinds of social justifications in particular are implied by those understandings.[2] Our argument, in brief, is that England is anything but a *just and nondiscriminatory society*, and that it is characterized by deep injustices that are reflected in its education system. However, those injustices derive to a significant degree from the unequal distribution of opportunities and resources among different social groups and across geographical places. The field of inclusion, as it has developed in England, has, we suggest, failed to deal adequately with injustices of this kind. There is therefore a need to connect inclusion to concerns with distributive justice, and, more specifically with a spatial and territorial perspective on distributive justice.[3]

THE MEANING OF INCLUSION IN ENGLAND

As in many other affluent countries, there have long been critiques of segregated special schooling for children identified as disabled.[4] As the discourse of inclusion has become more familiar over the past decade and a half, therefore, it has often been used to denote an approach to the schooling of disabled children that is predicated on their placement in mainstream (i.e., regular) schools and classrooms. The social justification for this approach has typically been that disabled children have a right to mainstream placement, not simply because that is where they can get the best education, but because they cannot be valued equally with their peers or offered equal opportunities if they are refused access to what is otherwise a common educational institution. The Centre for Studies in Inclusive Education, for instance, which has been prominent in campaigns for inclusive education, some time ago, drew up an Inclusion Charter asserting that:[5]

1. We fully support an end to all segregated education on the grounds of disability or learning difficulty, as a policy commitment and goal for this country.

2. We see the ending of segregation in education as a human rights issue that belongs within equal opportunities policies.

3. We believe that all students share equal value and status. We therefore believe that exclusion of students from the mainstream because of disability or learning difficulty is devaluation and is discriminating.

As the inclusion movement has developed in England, the exclusion of disabled children from mainstream schools has increasingly come to be seen as simply one example of complex and multidimensional processes of exclusion in education that impact on many groups of learners. Ofsted, the national schools inspectorate, for instance, characterizes inclusion as "more than a concern about any one group of pupils such as those pupils who have been or are likely to be excluded from school. Its scope is broad. It is about equal opportunities for all pupils, whatever their age, gender, ethnicity, attainment and background. It pays particular attention to the provision made for and the achievement of different groups of pupils within a school."[6]

These "different groups," it transpires, are by no means restricted to students identified as having special educational needs, let alone to those identified as disabled. On the contrary, they include ethnic and faith groups, English language learners, gifted and talented pupils, teenage mothers, sick children, and even girls and boys. From here, it is but a small step to using the discourse of inclusion to denote a wide range of issues in educational and social justice. The English inclusion scholar and advocate, Tony Booth, for instance, explicitly distances himself from what he calls "the commonly held view that inclusion is concerned with increasing the participation of children and young people seen to be disabled or categorized as 'having special educational needs.'"[7] Such a view, he argues, is far too restrictive, and instead inclusion should be seen as "a principled approach to education and society, as the task of *putting particular values into action* . . . I see inclusive values as concerned with issues of *equity, participation, community, compassion, respect for diversity, honesty, rights, joy, and sustainability.* This list is in a state of perpetual development."[8] [emphasis in the original]

This extended view of inclusion accords well with the characteristics of an education system in which the links between disability, special education, and special schooling are weaker than in many other countries. In England, a large proportion of children—about 21 percent—are offered special-needs education, not on the grounds that they are disabled, but simply that they experience some kind of difficulty in learning.[9] Only a small minority of these—about 1 percent—are educated in segregated special schools, to the evident satisfaction of their families, and often, in any case, in a context where special and mainstream schools offer some form of joint provision.[10] In these circumstances, it is perhaps not surprising that the field of inclusion in England has not restricted itself to the question of where disabled children should be educated, but has drawn on many streams of thinking about educational and social justice.[11]

In many ways, this *perpetual development* of thinking about inclusion has made it a powerful force for the identification of multiple forms of educational and social justice. As it has generalized from the case of disabled students excluded from mainstream schools, it has, in particular, become highly effective in uncovering how the differences that define groups of learners are constructed, how those groups respond to or resist the identities that are ascribed to them, and how they can be given a voice in those constructions.[12] This has led to a view of inclusion as an exercise in what Corbett and Slee call "cultural vigilantism"—a continuing interrogation of established understandings of and responses to learner differences to uncover the ways in which they devalue or otherwise discriminate against particular groups.[13] The practical embodiment of this vigilante approach can be seen in the *Index for Inclusion*—at one point distributed by the government to every school in the country—which provides teachers with no guidance as to how to teach students with different characteristics, but instead offers them a long list of review questions through which they can interrogate their own and their school's practices.[14]

Such an approach undoubtedly has much to offer in respect of those dimensions of social justice that are concerned with what Fraser characterizes as *recognition* and *representation*—that is, with how people are accorded cultural recognition, and how their voices are heard.[15] Despite this, however, it is at least worth asking whether the cultural vigilante approach does not betray what one critic has called a certain "narrowness in the conceptualization of inclusion and the neglect of serious social inequalities" in the inclusion movement.[16] What Diniz is referring to here is the extent to which inclusion has or has not addressed the *new racisms* evident in global conflict, xenophobia, and mass migration.[17] However, we might ask more generally how fully the inclusion field has addressed the third of Fraser's dimensions of social justice—*redistribution*.[18] What does it have to say, not just about how differences are constructed and how this or that group is marginalized in schools, but about how disparities in resources, opportunities, and power occur in society, and how they are reflected in the education system?

An adequate answer to this question would require a more comprehensive review of the field of inclusion scholarship, advocacy, and practice in England than is possible here. However, what we can do in this chapter is to show how and why issues of (re)distribution are so significant in English society and the English education system, and invite readers to reflect on the contribution that inclusion has made and could make. In the remainder of this chapter, therefore, we wish to explore the relationship between children's evident difficulties in schooling, their social backgrounds, and the inequalities of English society. We wish to consider particularly the spatial distribution of social and educational inequalities, partly because this aspect of inequality is inescapable in our country, but partly also because it opens up the possibility of new kinds of responses involving schools in new kinds of ways. Finally, we wish to return to the issue of inclusive education and what these new kinds of response imply for the way in which inclusion might in future be conceptualized.

SOCIAL AND EDUCATIONAL INEQUALITY IN ENGLAND

England is a country in which goods and resources are distributed in markedly unequal ways. An assessment by the OECD points out that the United Kingdom is well above OECD norms in terms of the gap between rich and poor, earnings inequality, the proportion of workless households, the number of people living alone or in single-parent households, income poverty, and the lack of social mobility—and that childhood poverty, though falling, is still well above the levels of twenty or thirty years ago.[19] Not surprisingly, commentators on equity issues frequently reach gloomy conclusions about the country. As the Equality and Human Rights Commission recently concluded, "[A]ll too many of us remain trapped by the accident of our births, our destinies far too likely to be determined by our sex or race . . . And far too many of us are still born into families without the material or social capital to give us the right start in life . . . [W]e are not yet a fair society."[20]

Inequalities of these kinds have long been a concern of local and national policy makers. At the time of the World War II, there was a high degree of social and political consensus that the conditions in which a large proportion of the population in England lived were unacceptable, and that it was the task of the state to do something about this situation. The landmark *Beveridge Report*, published by a coalition government, identified five "giants"—Want, Disease, Ignorance, Squalor and Idleness—that stood in the way of social progress, and argued for a comprehensive and radical strategy for tackling these giants.[21] The report is generally accepted as having laid the basis for a welfare state, embodied among other things in free universal education and health care, subsidized social housing, and an extensive range of welfare benefits. Over time, the language in which Beveridge's "giants" are described has changed. *Poverty, deprivation, social exclusion, inequality*, and *disadvantage*—the terms we use here—have all had periods in which they have fallen into and out of favor, and can all be found in current use. What has not changed, however, is the sense that the unequal distribution of resources, outcomes, and opportunities is an issue that calls for some form of state action.

These (re)distributive notions have equal salience in relation to education. Not only are educational outcomes in England highly unequal, but those inequalities are strongly related to learners' social backgrounds, suggesting that the education system reproduces rather than overcomes existing social disadvantages.[22] Despite heavy national investment in education, it remains the case, therefore, that the family and social contexts in which children live are much more powerful in shaping their educational outcomes than are the characteristics of the schools they attend.[23] In particular, although the mechanisms whereby social and economic disadvantages are translated into poor educational outcomes are undoubtedly complex, social class would appear to shape educational outcomes more powerfully than other background factors such as ethnicity and gender.[24] Not surprisingly in this context, policy makers have increasingly been exercised by the relationship between social disadvantage and educational outcomes, and narrowing the gap in outcomes between learners from low income and disadvantaged backgrounds and their peers has come to be seen as a key policy objective.[25] Despite this concern, there is little evidence that the multiple interventions put in place in recent years have done more than halt the increase in these inequalities and, perhaps, bring about some marginal reductions.[26]

A SPATIAL PERSPECTIVE ON INEQUALITY

Educational and social goods in England are distributed unequally not just among different social groups, but also across different places.[27] In particular, disadvantages of different kinds—unemployment, ill-health, obesity, teenage pregnancy, illiteracy and innumeracy, poverty and welfare dependency, and unfit dwellings—tend to cluster in particular geographical places.[28] This clustering is especially marked in (though not restricted to) urban contexts. This is partly because the country's history of early industrialization produced concentrations of poverty in the major industrial cities, and partly because more recent economic restructuring has left some parts of towns and cities bereft of both manufacturing and newer forms of economic activity.[29] As Lupton observes, the long-standing spatial inequalities in England are therefore increasing: "Just as some individuals in society are socially excluded, with multiple disadvantages and few prospects, some neighbourhoods, where problems are concentrated, may also be at risk of exclusion, getting relatively more disadvantaged as other areas get richer."[30] What makes this doubly concerning is that it seems likely that the concentration of disadvantage in particular places deepens the effects of the problems that people living in these areas face.[31]

This spatial distribution of social inequalities is matched by a spatial patterning of educational inequalities. In broad terms, there are concentrations of poor outcomes in those areas where social outcomes generally are poor, and in the schools serving those areas.[32] There appear to be a number of channels through which the characteristics of place can affect educational outcomes—for instance, through impacts on learners' aspirations and self-esteem, the limited social capital and survival strategies available to families, the lack of educational resources, the lack of support services, the availability of "nonstandard" lifestyles, the poor quality of schools, and negative effects on school processes.[33] Moreover, although families are, within certain restrictions, free to choose schools for their children in any area, schools located in and around disadvantaged areas are in fact likely to attract populations of students that themselves contain concentrations of disadvantage and hence of low achievement.[34] As a result, these schools will have to work harder than others to achieve the basic conditions for their students to learn effectively.[35] They may find it particularly difficult to improve their performance—and hence the overall level of their students' achievements.[36] Furthermore, they may experience compositional effects parallel to, or as an intensified form of, those in the areas they serve, which will further depress their performance and their students' achievements.[37]

In this context, the principle of spatial—or, perhaps more specifically, territorial—justice has been deeply embedded in social and educational policy.[38] To a greater or lesser extent, policy makers have worked to ensure that (as one policy initiative in this field put it) no one should be, "seriously disadvantaged by where they live."[39] One way in which they have sought to do this is by targeting additional resources, energies, and flexibilities on the most disadvantaged places in a series of area-based initiatives (ABIs).[40] From our point of view, these efforts are particularly significant, and not simply because spatial inequality is important in its own right. As we have argued elsewhere, social and educational disadvantage are issues that, in a liberal democracy such as the United Kingdom, cannot and need not wait for an (to us) unlikely political transformation. In such a context, incrementalist and affirmative actions have an important role to play.[41] ABIs, we suggest, seem to offer real prospects for interventions of this kind, not least since they rely in large part on the efforts of local actors—including schools—and thus may be feasible within the context of *normal politics*, at least as they operate in England.

Area-based Initiatives

ABIs have typically taken the form of intervention by a partnership of central and local government, often with other local stakeholders, in particularly disadvantaged areas at the sub–local authority level. Most of these initiatives have focused on social and economic conditions with little or no reference to education. However, there is also a separate tradition of ABIs in education policy. The earliest, and in many ways most ambitious, of these were the Educational Priority Areas (EPAs) of the 1960s and 1970s, introduced in the wake of the Plowden Report on primary schools.[42] EPAs targeted extra resources and support at schools serving hard-pressed areas in towns and cities, while at the same time encouraging the development of higher levels of community involvement and inviting each area to develop innovative responses to the problem of educational disadvantage.[43]

EPAs fell victim to, among other things, a shift in education policy focus from the 1970s onward—away from equalizing resources, outcomes, and opportunities between different areas, and toward a concern for the standards of the system as a whole. However, the return of a "New" Labour (broadly, center-left) government in 1997 saw a renewed foregrounding of issues of educational equity, expressed as a concern for excellence for the many, not just the few.[44] A particular concern across all domestic policy was with groups at risk of being socially excluded because of the multiple disadvantages they experience, and for whom education potentially offers an escape route.[45] Since socially excluded people were, the argument went, frequently concentrated into socially excluded areas, area-based initiatives once again came to seem attractive.[46]

The period between 1997 and the demise of the New Labour governments in 2010, accordingly, saw the launching of a series of educationally focused ABIs; notably, Education Action Zones, Excellence in Cities, and the London (latterly, City) Challenge.[47] These initiatives differed from each other considerably in detail, but shared some broad characteristics. In essence, they identified schools serving disadvantaged populations and where measured educational outcomes were poor. They then made additional resources available to these schools and encouraged them to develop or adopt new forms of provision and practice aimed at improving outcomes for their students. To achieve this, they sought to establish governance and/or leadership structures specific to the schools involved, more or less distinct from those of the local authorities where the schools were located and involving some degree of interschool partnership.

The Impact of Area-Based Initiatives

Despite our optimism about the possibilities offered by ABIs, evidence for their actual impact, particularly in respect of their education-focused variants, is decidedly mixed. Although in each case the interventions produce some positive outcomes, impacts tend to be small-scale and to be distributed patchily across different aspects of the ABI and different sites of implementation. The problem is compounded by the fact that only the most readily measurable educational outcomes—attainments in national tests and examinations, attendance, exclusions for disciplinary reasons, and so on—seem to be taken into account in either the design or evaluation of ABIs. Nonetheless, it remains the case that there seems to be little evidence that ABIs have transformed outcomes in designated areas to the point of equalizing them between these and other areas. As one review puts it: "[T]he evidence to date suggests that ABIs continue to have limited impact and any benefits are, at best, patchy. With reference to education focused ABIs, research on England's EAZs [Education Action Zones], for example, shows that relatively few of the programme's original objectives were realized. . . . Even in terms of attainment targets, there was little measurable improvement and in some EAZs there was even a negative zone effect."[48]

While EAZs may have been a particularly badly designed intervention, evaluations of other ABIs also point to outcomes that fall some way short of transforming existing patterns of advantage and disadvantage. There is, for instance, growing evidence that the London Challenge has had significant positive impacts in raising the average performance of schools in the city and has helped narrow the gap between their performance and national averages.[49] However, it is equally clear that such improvements have not been enough to overcome the very real education problems in the city and that, in particular, the gaps in attainment between poor students and their peers remain "unacceptably wide."[50] The evaluation of Excellence in Cities reached similarly mixed conclusions, reporting some modest impacts on attainment, attendance, and behaviors, yet also concluding that the initiative probably did little to reduce the gap between more and less disadvantaged students in participating schools.[51]

These mixed findings parallel those emerging from evaluations of ABIs in other contexts. For instance, the Zones d'Éducation Prioritaires, operating in France for over twenty-five years, are similar to English EPAs and EAZs not only in their structures and practices, but also in their outcomes. While there is some indication that they may have countered the increase in educational inequalities and there may have been some impressive local successes, overall they have failed to break the relationship between social disadvantage and poor educational outcomes.[52] Similarly, a recent review of evaluations of different kinds of interventions into both educational and wider social disadvantage concludes that ABIs are no less effective than other kinds of intervention and that outcomes are often positive, but overall, the effects from *any* kind of intervention are likely to be small.[53]

Many explanations can be offered for the failure of ABIs to bring about more significant transformations.[54] Some of these are to do with relatively superficial features—for instance, the short life-span of initiatives, the problems of persuading different partners to work together, and the proliferation of ABIs with different structures and objectives. In principle, at least, these problems might be resolved through more thoughtful and sustained policy making. However, other explanations point to more fundamental issues and call into question the extent to which ABIs actually do or ever could constitute meaningful attempts to tackle educational disadvantage. It is striking, in particular, how low-geared ABIs are in relation to the issues they are seeking to address. This is evident in their short-term nature, but also in the limited amount of resources they typically are able to deploy. As Smith, commenting on the EPAs of the 1960s and 1970s, argued, "ABIs inevitably invite an unfavourable comparison between the 'puny educational resources' they deploy, and the 'major social forces' they seek to counter."[55] In the case of EAZs, for instance, the amount of funding dedicated to the initiative amounted to a mere 0.05 percent of educational expenditure in England, and generally ABIs have delivered an uplift to resources in targeted areas that is small in relation both to overall educational resources in those areas and to the apparent scale of need.[56]

This puniness is compounded by the limited scope of most ABIs—and certainly of educational ABIs. Typically, the latter are restricted to a limited range of actions aimed at improving the performance of schools and offering additional support to students in those schools. This is most evident in the City Challenge program, which is essentially conceptualized as a school-improvement initiative, focusing on "intensive support for underperforming schools," and a "city-wide leadership strategy led by school leaders for school leaders."[57] In none of the initiatives, however, has there been anything other than the most limited attempt to intervene in what might be regarded as underlying causes of poor educational outcomes—poverty, poor housing, transport and services, limited opportunity structures, or class and other social group cultures.

Finally, the impacts of ABIs are inevitably limited by their being set in a policy framework that tends to weaken the links between schools and the areas they serve. Education reform in recent years has been based on the assumptions that curriculum, assessment measures, pedagogy, and targets can be specified centrally, without regard to local differences. Meanwhile, school 'choice' policies offer families the opportunity to send their children to schools well beyond the areas in which they live, with the result that few schools serve single, identifiable localities.[58] In the meantime, governments have busily encouraged the development of autonomous academies and, more recently, free schools, which owe only the most limited allegiance to the democratically elected councils responsible for the overall well-being of the areas where the schools are located.[59]

Taking these factors together, some commentators have concluded that ABIs are based on a mistaken—perhaps willfully mistaken—understanding of the relationship between the presenting problems of disadvantage in an area and the more fundamental causes of those problems. In particular, they charge, ABIs tend to attribute the manifestations of disadvantage in an area to peculiarly local factors and to overlook the extent to which those local manifestations in fact emerge on the basis of sociostructural factors that operate well beyond the confines of the designated area. As Rees et al. argue:

> In effect, ABIs are based on the view that social and economic disadvantage is a "residual" category, which can therefore be defined in terms of remaining "pockets" of disadvantage in a wider context of increasing affluence. They do not acknowledge that, in reality, local disadvantage is a particular manifestation of the wider social inequalities which are endemic to societies such as the UK. Far from being an exceptional feature of British society, which can be tackled by special state initiatives such as ABIs, areas of social disadvantage are complex, but normal manifestations of the characteristic patterns of social differentiation and inequality in the UK (and elsewhere).[60]

In support of this argument, these critics also point to the tendency of ABIs to pathologize disadvantaged populations, blaming them rather than sociostructural factors for the problems they experience, and to misrepresent the spatial distribution of disadvantage, overlooking the uncomfortable fact that most disadvantaged people live outside targeted areas.[61]

On the basis of this analysis, our optimism about ABIs seems decidedly ill-founded, and such initiatives cannot be seen as a serious-minded attempt to create a more equitable education system and society. Instead, they demand to be read as a kind of displacement activity, the focus on the presenting problems of designated areas drawing attention away from the inability—or unwillingness—of governments to tackle underlying social inequalities. As Power et al. put it: "The state is not in a position to engage with issues of social inequality, structural shifts in the organisation of economic activity and their consequences, except at the margins. ABIs and the conceptualisations of disadvantage on which they are based reflect this. They provide a means of presenting the promise of 'active Government' within the highly restricted policy repertoire available in reality."[62]

Rethinking ABIs

Despite the power of these critiques, we believe that there is in fact an alternative explanation for the failures of ABIs—and one that leads to slightly less pessimistic conclusions. In a recent review, Lupton argues that the problem of ABIs is not in their focus on areas per se, but in their failure to develop a proper spatial understanding of the areas they target: "[W]hile particular places, as well as inequalities between places, have been to the fore in these policies, space as a concept in the education-poverty relationship is largely absent. When it is present, space tends to be seen as a surface over which educational resources are distributed— a container of people, or a site for social relations."[63] Instead, she suggests, area approaches need to view space in, "more social, historical, relative, contingent, and dynamic ways."[64] Only then will it be possible to see more clearly "that both the meaning of poverty and the meaning of education are constructed in space, and that relations between places, as well as the characteristics of particular places, are instrumental in creating educational success for some groups of young people and educational failure for others."[65]

What Lupton means becomes clearer whenever we encounter studies of particular places which, as Hubbard et al. put it, view space not simply as "a backdrop against which human behaviour is played out," but as something that is "inherently caught up in social relations, both socially produced and consumed."[66] In a study of the social distribution of educational outcomes, for instance, Webber and Butler looked beyond the familiar documentation of associations between levels of social disadvantage and educational outcomes in areas.[67] Instead, they drew on neighborhood classification systems that seek to characterize neighborhoods in terms of a wide range of behavioral characteristics of their residents rather than simply in terms of levels of economic deprivation. What they were able to produce by doing this is a richer picture of how different characteristics are associated with different outcomes. Children from some types of neighborhood, for instance—those characterized by inner-city social housing, or by Asian-background owner-occupiers—did much better than might be expected from measures of deprivation in those areas. On the other hand, children from predominantly White British peripheral housing estates in provincial cities and the new towns of the south-east of the country did significantly worse than might be expected.[68]

Webber and Butler hypothesize that the explanations for these differences are cultural in nature and are ultimately linked to how people view their prospects and what opportunities they have to encounter people with different sets of values and expectations.[69] Other studies have been able to trace these processes more fully by engaging with local people and exploring how they viewed their worlds. Living in areas of concentrated disadvantage shaped those world views, and those world views in turn shaped the areas. Green and White, for instance, point to the ways in which different places offered different kinds of educational and labor market opportunities, and, equally important, offered access to different family and peer networks from which young people learn how to interpret those opportunities.[70] In this way, the place where young people lived shapes their sense of what was possible in that place, and therefore what they try to achieve. "Geography," as the authors conclude, "matters."[71]

In the same way, Kintrea et al. focus on the phenomenon of territoriality in disadvantaged areas.[72] According to their findings, young people in such areas develop a sense of the boundaries of place within which they feel safe, but which they have to defend against others. This shapes what they believe about what they can do, where they can go, and who they are, and so serves to limit the educational and other opportunities to which they have access. There is, the authors argue: "A strong interrelationship between territoriality and disadvantaged areas. Connections were made . . . between poor housing conditions and often difficult family backgrounds and territoriality. Territoriality appeared to be a product of deprivation, a lack of opportunities and attractive activities, limited aspirations and an expression of identity. It could be understood as a coping mechanism for young people living in poverty, who were thus provided with leisure, excitement and an alternative focus of association outside their households. [73]

Analyses such as these are just a few examples of the rich understandings that can emerge when the geography—or, more accurately, geographies—of education are explored in depth.[74] What they indicate is that ABIs, as they have emerged in English education policy, are puny not just in relation to the deep structural causes of inequality, but also in relation to their understanding of, and therefore capacity to intervene in, the complex interactions of place, understandings, and behaviors. All of the ABIs we outlined earlier focused largely or exclusively on what are essentially school-improvement issues. They were concerned with how schools are organized and led, what practices are used in classrooms, and what additional support might be offered to students. They lacked the means for intervening not only in the sociostructural determinants of disadvantage, but also in local housing, transport, and labor market conditions; in the processes that congregate people from particular backgrounds in particular places; and in the cultural attitudes, values, and practices that arise in such places. As Lupton puts it, ABIs "take place in particular areas, rather than being motivated by any concern with spatial processes per se."[75]

However, this critique also raises intriguing possibilities about how ABIs might be strengthened. Specifically, what might be possible if ABIs were based on what elsewhere we have called *complex contextual analysis*—that is, an understanding not just of what the local situation is, but how it comes to be that way and how, therefore, it might come to be different.[76] What if that analysis encompassed not just the presenting problems in that situation, but also an understanding of the cultural processes at work among the people living in the locality and the material conditions helping to shape those processes? What if, moreover, the interventions marshaled by the ABI were sufficiently wide-ranging that they could address all of these factors simultaneously and in a coherent manner?

With these questions in mind, it is significant that there is currently in England a growing number of what we might call *new-style area initiatives*—new in that they are recognizably more wide-ranging than old-style ABIs and are, in some case at least, more coherent in their design and intentions. We and colleagues are currently working with a number of these initiatives, and a brief account of one of them may serve to illustrate the possibilities we believe they open up for more effective ways of tackling educational disadvantage.[77]

WESTON ACADEMY: A NEW-STYLE ABI?

Academies, in the English context, are schools that are state-funded but are established and managed by one or more private or public sponsors and are thus more-or-less detached from the framework of local authority control within which most other schools operate. Many academies serve highly disadvantaged populations and replace schools that are judged to have failed to make a sufficient impact on the relationship between the social disadvantages experienced by children and young people and their educational outcomes. Weston Academy is sponsored by the Weston Housing Trust, a major provider of social (i.e., subsidized) housing in the area that was spun off some years ago from the local authority's housing department. The Housing Trust interprets its responsibilities as being not simply to provide affordable accommodation, but also to develop sustainable communities in terms of employment opportunities, community safety and cohesion, and the well-being of residents. It sees the Academy as central to this task, offering a means of working directly with children and their families.

This means that the role of the Academy is seen by its sponsors and by the senior leaders whom they have appointed as essentially being to contribute to an overarching strategy for the development of the area it serves. One of our tasks has been to work with the Trust and Academy leaders to articulate this strategy in the form of an explicit theory of change. At the core of this work is an analysis of the area served by the Academy which suggests that it is disadvantaged by the social problems besetting many areas of social housing, compounded by the particular economic configuration of the town in which it is located. That town is part of a large conurbation where low- and semiskilled employment in manufacturing industries has been replaced by more skills- and knowledge-intensive opportunities in service, media, and arts-based businesses. The town itself has escaped the worst ravages of unemployment, but it offers for the most part only low-skilled employment with limited prospects for advancement in small and medium enterprises. To this extent, it is disconnected from the developments taking place in the wider city region, and the people who live there are becoming increasingly isolated from the opportunities available elsewhere.

In this context, the Trust and Academy leaders have pursued a twin-track approach. One track is to tackle the area's social problems head-on by supporting families, tackling criminality and vandalism, building community problem-solving capacity, and developing a sense of pride in the area. The other is to develop the skills and ambitions of local people—and particularly of young people—so that they can take more advantage of the opportunities in the city region, and so that, in time, new employers will be encouraged to locate in the town. With this in mind, the Academy offers an extensive array of support for individual students, but does so in close collaboration with the Trust's community officers, who are able to work with families and link the work done on problems in school to their own work with young people on antisocial behavior. At the same time, the Academy is developing an extensive community strategy, which involves it in offering adult learning opportunities to local residents, operating as a base for community services, becoming a hub for community activities, and involving its students in community service. In addition, it is developing a specialism in Business and Enterprise. This involves it in reviewing its pedagogy and curriculum to ensure they engage young people, but also that they equip them with the skills that are needed in the developing local economy and, it is hoped, instill a sense of entrepreneurship that might in time drive the economy further forward. Moreover, since the Trust is a major local employer, it is able not only to offer advice on curriculum development, but also to offer opportunities for vocational learning pathways into employment as young people leave school.

We would not wish to claim that the Weston Academy initiative is problem-free. On the contrary, our work with it suggests that its leaders have to manage a number of problematic issues. Chief among these is the tension between sustaining a long-term and wide-ranging strategy for area improvement and generating rapid rises in a narrow range of student attainments to meet the expectations of central government and the powerful accountability regime that the government maintains. Nonetheless, we suggest that there are certain features of the Academy initiative that give it the potential to achieve more than the ABIs of the past. Two in particular seem to us to be significant in this respect:

- *First*, whereas previous ABIs have focused largely or exclusively on schools, the Weston initiative links the work of the school with the work of a housing provider able to offer family support, community development, and economic regeneration. Moreover, although an "extended services" initiative in England has encouraged schools to enlist other agencies to work on a school-driven agenda, in the Weston initiative, it is the Housing Trust, as the Academy sponsor, that determines the strategic direction of the school, in line with its community sustainability agenda.[78] To this extent, the Weston initiative is about tackling the disadvantages facing the area as a whole, rather than simply improving the performance of a school within that area.

- *Second*, the initiative is founded on an understanding of the area that goes beyond a simple listing of problems. There is a sense of how the economic history and current economic conditions of the area relate to patterns of housing provision, family dynamics, educational (dis)engagement, and issues of community safety. There is also a sense of the people who live in the area as something more than passive victims of disadvantage or bundles of deficits. While their attitudes, values, and behaviors are certainly seen as problematic, they are also seen as cultural responses to the situations within which they find themselves. As a result, the initiative is informed by a theory of change that marshals the wide-ranging resources available into a reasonably coherent strategy, and that sees current cultural responses as malleable rather than fixed.

These two features are significant, we suggest, not simply in terms of what the Weston initiative may (or may not) achieve in its own right, but in terms of what they suggest a reconceptualized form of ABI might contribute to educational and social equity. Whatever the limitations of past ABIs may have been, it is simply not the case that such initiatives are not destined to focus only on the work of schools, nor that they necessarily lack the means for intervening in wider social and economic conditions. Wide-ranging, holistic, and strategic approaches do indeed appear to be possible where the work of schools can be brought into line with the work of other agencies and organizations tackling family, community, and area issues.

We readily concede that approaches of this kind are likely to be maximally effective when they are set in the context of progressive economic, fiscal, and social policies at national level. However, the Weston initiative also has something important to say about what might be possible here. What is happening in and around the Weston Academy is just one of a very large number of examples of similar initiatives. These include local authority–led initiatives to rethink the nature of schooling and its relationship to community development and economic regeneration, and (typically) school-led initiatives to *extend* the role of schools into areas traditionally regarded as lying beyond their remit.[79] Fundamental to such developments are consistent (though, in the scholarly education literature, somewhat underreported) strands in New Labour policy between 1997 and 2010 aimed at stimulating local solutions to social problems, reconceptualizing the role of local authorities as strategic leaders and *place shapers* for the areas they serve, and crucially, locking schools into a wider child and family well-being agenda. In the latter respect, the Every Child Matters policy played a key role, bringing together a wide range of child and family services (including schools) within integrated structures, promoting the development of common working practices, and articulating a set of shared outcomes for children which services were expected to pursue collaboratively.[80] Moreover, these integrated services are an example of the *progressive universalism* that New Labour governments saw as the basis for service delivery, in that they were intended to be available to all children, but were expected to be used most heavily by—and to have most impact on—those facing the greatest difficulties.[81] In this respect, they support and were supported by a wider raft of progressive government policies aimed at ending child poverty.[82]

The point here is not that these policies were unproblematic. Like the Weston initiative itself, they were full of contradictions, problems, and ambiguities—a situation that has hardly been improved by the return of a center-right coalition government in the 2010 general election. However, if Weston shows that ABIs can be reconceptualized in ways that are more likely to impact on spatial inequalities, the post-1997 policy context points to the possibility that local initiatives can be stimulated and supported by appropriate policy frameworks at national level. It is not the case that such initiatives *inevitably* struggle against the direction of national policy, nor that ABIs can, as Power et al. seem to suggest, simply be written off as displacement activities for governments that are unwilling to tackle underlying inequalities.[83] The picture, we suggest, is more nuanced than this implies. As we have argued elsewhere, policy regimes in relation to inequality in affluent countries such as England are typically marked by contradiction, ambiguity, and contest.[84] If, therefore, it is undeniably true that what policy makers do plays a significant part in maintaining inequities, it is also true that they can and do from time to time make decisions that are, at the very least, ameliorative. In this complex situation, there is always space for different, more equitable policy approaches to emerge. It seems to us that the progressive aspects of post-1997 policy—supporting local initiatives in which the work of schools is integrated into wide-ranging strategic efforts to combat disadvantage—form the basis of one such approach.

INCLUSION REVISITED

This chapter has taken us on a long journey from an account of the English approach to inclusion, through an analysis of the inequities of English society and the English education system, and to the suggestion that there may be ways of tackling those inequities, even within the context of a *normal politics* that leaves much to be desired. In the course of that journey, we have seen nothing that would cause us to demur from Diniz's conclusion that, for all its progressive extensions, inclusion in England has been narrowly conceptualized and has failed to deal adequately with important issues of social inequality.[85] Our analysis of the situation in England is that major issues of social justice are raised by the unequal distribution of social and educational goods between people and places, but that the dominant concern with *recognition* politics in the inclusion field means that it has little to say about these issues.

This criticism is not new. Many years ago, the disabled researcher, Mike Oliver, berated proto-inclusionists (*integration* was the preferred term at the time) for their failure to engage with what he saw as the real sources of the oppression of disabled people.[86] The problem, he argued, was that pro-integration academics believed that oppression resulted from the ways in which difference was constructed in social and institutional cultures, whereas in fact it arose from "the institutionalized practices of society."[87] In countering oppression, therefore, the focus should be on changing not "what people think" but "what people do." Without this shift in focus, Oliver argued, academic debates about integration were little more than "intellectual masturbation."[88]

While we have much sympathy with this rather damning conclusion, the starkness of the alternatives posed by Oliver does not quite accord with our own position. If, as we have argued, it is important not simply to take space and place seriously but to see them, in Hubbard et al.'s terms, as socially produced and consumed, then it is also important to take seriously the people who live in particular places and are key actors in that production and consumption.[89] As we have seen, the ways in which people understand the places in which they live and the ways in which those places shape people's understandings of their worlds are crucial factors in the processes that link material disadvantage to impoverished educational opportunities, educational outcomes, and life chances. Given the negative consequences that these understandings often have for their own lives, the processes of *recognition* and *representation* are likely to involve something more than a simple process of valuing and according equal status. Rather, they are likely to take a more dialogical form where valuing what people currently *are* does not necessarily imply accepting that they must always *remain the same*. Changing disadvantaged places necessarily involves changing both the material *and* the cultural conditions of those places.

It is at this point that a reconstituted form of inclusive education may have something to offer. As we work with area initiatives involving schools, we repeatedly find that they are driven by professionals—particularly school professionals—who, despite their evident best intentions, have little real dialogue with local people, and instead form a view as to who they are and what they need based on their own, necessarily limited, perspectives.[90] The strong welfarist traditions in the United Kingdom and the relative absence of organized community activism leaves professionals more or less untrammelled in deciding what lies in other (particularly disadvantaged) people's best interests. There is, therefore, both a need and an opportunity to rethink what the core principles of inclusion—Booth's "perpetually developing" list of values, for instance—might mean in the context not simply of creating welcoming schools, but of formulating strategic area-based approaches for tackling disadvantage. If such rethinking is not undertaken, Oliver's damning verdict on the integration movement may yet come to apply to inclusive education.[91]

4

Does Equity Exist for Immigrant Students in German Schools?

Jessica M. Löser and Rolf Werning

Inclusive education is an important part of school-development processes in terms of *equity* in educational settings. Equity issues are particularly important for immigrant students, yet their frequent and persistent overrepresentation in special education services signals the degree to which inclusive education remains in its infancy in the German education system, even though it has been a topic of discussion for more than thirty years.[1] Compared with its prominence in educational reform agendas in England, the United States, and Canada, inclusive education has not had the same traction in Germany.[2] This chapter explores the issues raised by Germany's hesitancy to embrace inclusive education and its persistent identification of immigrant students for special education.[3]

In Germany, both social and educational institutions tend to pressure culturally and ethnically diverse individuals to assimilate into mainstream German culture.[4] When individuals and groups maintain distinct ethnic and cultural practices, they are viewed and treated as different.[5] By singling out different cultural and ethnic groups, our article risks the same sort of othering; therefore, our analysis relies on more than a single dimension of difference (e.g., a cultural perspective).[6] Instead, we include multiple categories that seem to contribute to the ways in which exclusion operates within the German school system in order to offer a more detailed view of the situation.

We rely on the notion of intersectionality, because, as Crenshaw emphasized, "ignoring differences within groups contributes to tensions among groups."[7] Thus, our analysis includes the distinctions *immigrant student, gender,* and *socioeconomic background.* More specifically, we analyze immigration and gender in different states in Germany as well as the implications of immigrant status and socioeconomic background in German schools. We investigate why educational inequity for immigrant students exists and also analyze the regular and special education systems in terms of inclusive structures. This chapter is structured in four sections: (1) structural inconsistences in the German school system, (2) the process of integration to inclusion in the German context, (3) the German context for immigrant students, and (4) the inadequacy of an individual paradigm in improving the realities for immigrant students in the German school system.

STRUCTURAL INCONSISTENCIES IN THE GERMAN SCHOOL SYSTEM

To fully understand the complex situation of inclusive and exclusive structures in Germany, it is important to understand how the system is based on a long history of sorting students into homogeneous learning groups in different schools (see figure 4.1).[8]

In most German states, four-year primary schools are organized as comprehensive schools. All children between the ages of six and ten are required to attend comprehensive school. Students move from comprehensive schools into one of three different kinds of secondary school systems, which lead to unequal levels of school qualifications. The basic secondary school level includes grades 5–10. The general secondary school also offers grades 5–10, while the advanced secondary school level includes grades 5–12. Students graduating from a basic secondary school receive a less prestigious certificate than that granted by an advanced secondary school. Only a degree from an advanced secondary school enables students to enroll directly in a university.[9] Though there are a few comprehensive schools that integrate all students in educational courses, it is far more typical that secondary schools group students homogeneously. Students are required to complete the curricu-

FIGURE 4.1   Educational tracks in the German education system

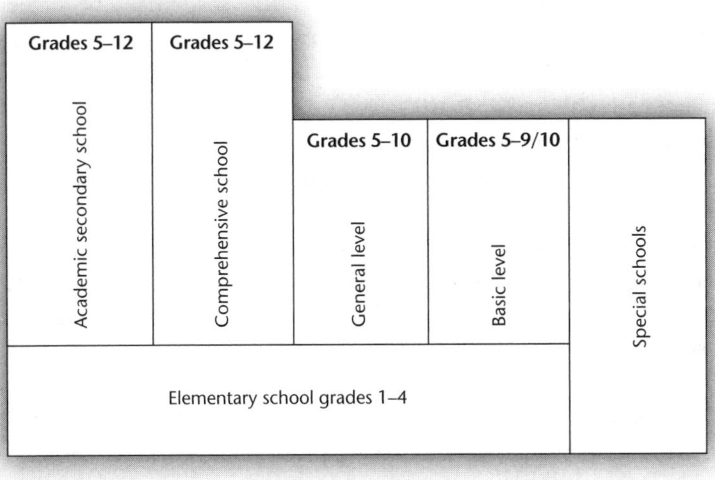

Source: Adapted from Kultusministerkonferenz: "Basic Structure of the Education System in the Federal Republic of Germany," Bonn, 2009, www.kmk.org/fileadmin/doc/Dokumentation/Bildungswesen_en_pdfs/en-2009.pdf.

lum to avoid being tracked into a lower secondary school certification.[10] It is rare for a student to move from lower- to a higher-track secondary school. In the 2004–05 school year, only 20 percent of all secondary students moved to a higher-track secondary school, while 60 percent of students moved to a lower-track secondary school.[11] Immigrant students are far more likely to attend lower-track secondary schools.

The segregated regular school system offers one explanation for why there are so few inclusive settings in the German school system. Its very structure offers few options for inclusive educational opportunities. Inclusive education practices are more likely to occur in primary schools. In addition to the constraints created in the general education system, the special needs school system is organized into eight different types of special schools.[12] In each type of school, students with similar special needs are taught in small groups by special education teachers. Some special schools confer regular school degrees such as the *basic school level degree*, but this means that graduates earn less prestigious school certificates, which in turn limits their postgraduation prospects.

Students with special needs attend different types of special schools according to their individual needs. Special school buildings are often separated from main school buildings on the same campus. As a result, students with special needs learn in segregated classrooms where they do not have contact with regular education students. The degree to which students receive appropriate supports is dependent on the schools serving them. Students can move from one special school to another if their educational needs change. For example, students may move between special schools because they need specific support in language development. The professed goal is to move students with special needs into general education schools. However, Bellenberg, Hovestadt, and Klemm documented that in North-Rhine-Westphalia, only 1,603 of the 8,831 students who were transferred to a special school were referred back to a regular school.[13] The rarity of movement from special to general education school appears to be particularly problematic for students who attend special schools because of learning difficulties.[14]

The group of students attending special schools for learning difficulties is very heterogeneous. There is no precise definition of *learning difficulties*. Most students who fall into this category have specific problems in mathematics and language development, and for various reasons, they are not able to achieve curriculum standards at the primary or basic level secondary schools. Some of them have mild intellectual disabilities as measured by intelligence tests (i.e., IQ of less than 80). The vast majority of students attending special schools for learning difficulties come from low socioeconomic backgrounds. Eighty percent of these students leave school without completing a basic secondary school certificate, which compromises their chances for obtaining a job.[15]

One of the intents of Germany's educational assessment process is to ensure that students are placed in schools that provide them with the best chance for completing a school-leaving certificate.[16] Educators are tasked with determining which schools are suitable for which students, as well as ensuring that all students in any given school are suitably matched to the curricular and learning expectations of the school. Thus *sorting*, not inclusivity, is the main focus of the system. A variety of issues complicates attempts to change this structure. Powell emphasizes that "professional interests of special educators, physicians, and psychologists have influenced the expansion and persistence of special education's organizational structures."[17] Currently, there is a new movement toward inclusive schools based on the UN Convention on the Rights of Persons with Disabilities.[18] In the following section, we examine the complexity of implementing the UN convention in the German context.

WHAT INTEGRATION AND INCLUSION MEAN IN THE GERMAN EDUCATION CONTEXT

For over thirty years a debate has persisted about whether to teach students with special needs in regular or special schools. Parent groups have tried to change the placement of their children with special needs from special to regular schools.[19] German researchers pointed out more than forty years ago that the system that segregates regular and special-needs students needed to be changed.[20] But despite rhetoric embracing more inclusive practices, most students with special needs remain in segregated schools. Inclusion is still considered to be for so-called "others." Though inclusive settings benefit all students, it is obvious that little progress has been made in applying these theories in the German context.[21] In 2006, only 15.7 percent of students with special needs in Germany were educated in an inclusive setting.[22] In addition, students with special needs achieve at a lower rate than students attending regular schools, and special needs status carries a stigma.[23] Given these factors, the chance to move from a special setting into a regular school is very low. This is especially true for students diagnosed with learning difficulties. These students are not only educated with a different curriculum, but also in separate school buildings with other students who score below average academically and intellectually.

In Germany, inclusive education deals with a pedagogical antinomy or mutual incompatibility. On the one hand, every student is unique and has to be treated individually. On the other hand, all students must be treated equally. This contradiction is insolvable if equality is conceptualized as the same treatment or opportunity for everyone. Clearly, the personalization or individualization that is required to meet the unique language, intellectual, emotional, sensory, and cultural needs of each student demands differential treatment. If students get access to different supports and scaffolds, are they being treated equally? Educational systems around the world face the same challenge to treat all students equally while providing individualized treatment.

School systems must develop structures to deal with this challenge. Each student has the right to be both equal and different. In Germany, the debate about inclusive education has become more dominant lately, due to the UN convention. In international research debates about inclusion, defining the breadth of inclusive education has been a major focus of discussion. There is a strong argument that the term *integration* refers to placement or mainstreaming, whereas the term *inclusive education* implies a broader structural change in schools; that is, for inclusive education to occur, curricula should be adapted—schools should be changed. All students should be taught in one school without segregated settings.[24]

There are differing perspectives regarding the terms *inclusion* and *integration* in Germany. Some authors, such as Hinz, distinguish between integration and inclusion as described above.[25] These authors support using the term *inclusion* because the ideas of integration have been insufficiently put in practice. According to Hinz, a new concept might give new motivation to change structures and habits.[26] Other authors, such as Reiser, point out that the German debate regarding integration within the German school system has already included changing the curriculum and accepting differences within the regular school setting.[27] Many of these ideas, combined within the concept of inclusive education, had been included in the integration debate, but the implementation of these ideas has not reached either the political or the school levels. There is a tendency to use the term *inclusive education* mainly in relation to special education or special needs. This parallels its usage in countries like the United States and England.[28] In the 1990s, the German discourses on inclusive education began to extend to other types of diversity and to explore the intersection between markers of difference as described by Crenshaw (e.g., gender and race).[29] This influenced not only the theoretical debate, but also the political and educational discussions and implementation. In this article we use the term *inclusive education* to include different groups of students—not only those with special needs. We believe that different types of minority groups should be included in this definition of inclusive education.[30] Furthermore, this definition should address the intersections of various markers of difference.[31] According to McDermott, Raley, and Seyer-Ochi, "one cannot belong to a race, class, or disability group alone; they are all relational terms, and everyone in the culture is somehow involved in their expression."[32] The interaction between the social context and students who embody several markers of difference leads to differential outcomes for students within the educational system.[33]

IMMIGRANT STUDENTS IN THE GERMAN SCHOOL SYSTEM

An examination of various markers of difference within the German school system reveals that certain groups of students appear to be particularly disadvantaged. For example, the segregated nature of the German school system is problematic for immigrant students. This becomes obvious when the regular school system and the special education system are scrutinized.[34] The Federal Statistical Office shows that students without German citizenship are likely to achieve a much lower level graduation certificate than German students.[35] For example, only 10 percent of students without German citizenship achieved the academic certificate, the most prestigious school certificate, while 29 percent of German students obtained the same certificate. In addition, more than twice as many students without German citizenship (16 percent) left school without a basic school graduation as compared with German students (7 percent).[36] Regarding the academic competencies of students from immigrant backgrounds, the first PISA study shows that out of the 20 percent of fifteen-year-old students whose parents had immigrated to Germany, only 2 percent achieved high levels of reading proficiency, whereas a full 50 percent did not even achieve a basic proficiency level.[37] Disparities are also evident in school enrollment. Table 4.1 shows the percentage of students from immigrant backgrounds across the different types of German secondary schools.

As the table shows, immigrant students are overrepresented in special schools and lower academic secondary schools. Diefenbach defines this phenomenon as *ethnic segregation*, and notes that immigrant students are more likely to attend schools that offer less-prestigious school certificates.[38] Students with and without immigrant backgrounds are unlikely to learn alongside each other in the same classrooms and school settings. Often, they do not live in the same neighborhoods.[39]

Other minority groups, such as students from lower socioeconomic background, are also strongly challenged and segregated in the current school system.[40] Students' immigration and socioeconomic backgrounds

TABLE 4.1   Percentage of students without German citizenship in German schools, 2007–08

Type of secondary school	Percentage
Advanced level	4.30
General level	7.90
Basic level	19.40
Special schools	15.3
Special schools for students with learning difficulties	19.9

Source: Data drawn from Statistisches Bundesamt (2008) and Kultusministerkonferenz (2008).

overlap to some extent. Students with two foreign-born parents are more likely to come from lower socioeconomic background than students with German-born parents.[41] Because the German school system sorts students on these pivotal dimensions, the structure of the system itself is designed to result in inequitable learning opportunities for students from immigrant and low socioeconomic background.

Table 4.2 shows that Serbian, Italian, and Turkish students are more likely to attend special schools for learning difficulties.[42] Serbian students, most of whose parents are refugees of the Kosovo war, have by far the highest relative risk ratio. Italian and Turkish students, whose families came to Germany as immigrant workers during the 1960s, have had limited opportunities to attend advanced secondary schools. Italian students, interestingly, who are seen as being culturally closer to the German culture than Turkish students, have a higher risk for attending special schools than their Turkish counterparts. Greek and Spanish (also immigrant worker groups) students achieve significantly better results.[43] The data indicate that educational disparities still remain for foreign students.

Educational outcomes disparities in and among immigrant students also vary across German states. Immigrant student performance on assessments is higher in some states (such as North Rhine-Westphalia) than others (such as Bavaria and Baden-Württemberg).[44] Similarly, the risk ratios of immigrant students for being placed in schools for students with learning difficulties vary across states.[45] For example, in 2008 Baden-Württemberg had the highest relative risk ratio, at 3.5, whereas Berlin had a relative risk ratio of 1.2 and Bremen 1.6 (see table 4.3). In addition,

TABLE 4.2   Relative risk for different ethnic/national groups to attend a school for students with learning difficulties

National origin	Relative risk ratio
Serbia	6.1
Italy	2.9
Turkey	2.1
Greece	1.9
Croatia	1.8
Poland	0.9

Source: Data drawn from Statistisches Bundesamt (2008); calculations done by the authors.

TABLE 4.3   Relative risk ratio for students with learning difficulties across German states

States	Percentage of German students	Percentage of immigrant students	Relative risk ratio
Baden-Würtemberg	1.5	5.1	3.5
Lower Saxony	2.1	6.2	3.1
North Rhine-Westphalia	1.8	4.4	2.7
Bremen	1.0	1.4	1.6
Berlin	1.8	2.1	1.2

Source. Data drawn from Statistisches Bundesamt (2008); calculations done by the authors.

in Baden-Württemberg and Lower Saxony, foreign students are nearly three times more likely to attend a special school for students with learning difficulties than those in Berlin or Bremen. These data emphasize the need for change in the German school system in order to achieve equity for minority groups. In the following section, we interpret these results and their impact on educational equity in more detail.

Reasons That Immigrant Students Experience Educational Inequity in German Schools

Certain groups of students experience more disadvantages than others in the German school system. German policies constrain access to education for immigrant students on a variety of dimensions. For instance, the school system assigns immigrant students to homogeneous learning groups in segregated schools.[46] The results of this policy disadvantage students who are still learning the language and culture of mainstream Germany, since they have little or no access to models for typical German academic and social language usage nor opportunities to learn cultural practices from peers in school. Male immigrant students from a low socioeconomic background are particularly disadvantaged, since their presence alone challenges a broadly held notion of Germany as a homogeneous society.[47] Without access to meaningful participation in the German school system, immigrant students lack the opportunities to learn that are experienced by typical German students.[48]

Often, the school failure of immigrant students is attributed to the students themselves or their family background. The problem with individually based and deficit-oriented explanations is that they cannot account for the complex placement patterns observed across the federal states (see table 4.3) and across students' national origin (see table 4.2). One cannot say, as McDermott et al. pointed out critically, "Fix the children, and race and class barriers can be overcome one person at a time."[49] In the German educational context, it seems that language problems are often redefined into learning difficulties.[50] A similar trend is found in the United States.[51] McDermott et al. note that in the US context "social activities of noticing or labeling a person, say, Latino, increase the chances of labeling the same person poor and/or LD [learning disabilities]."[52] The deficit point of view does not include a wide enough "comprehensive analysis of problems and solutions."[53]

Data reviewed in this chapter highlighted how immigrant students with the same performance levels in elementary schools are likely to be referred to different types of high schools, depending on the school system or state in which they reside.[54] These referrals cannot be attributed to the intelligence of immigrant students, their family background, or the abilities of their teachers, but rather to the result of the different educational policies of each state.[55] For example, Bavaria and Baden-Württemberg's school systems have rather rigid structures that make moving between different types of schools more difficult. In contrast, North Rhine-Westphalia has comprehensive schools that facilitate student transfer between low- and advanced-level secondary schools.[56]

Moreover, special education placement differs across different German states. In Berlin and Bremen, inclusive education settings are more common. These settings necessitate support systems for students with special needs within regular schools, which are lacking in other states that retain and invest in segregated special education settings. The risks of placement in special educational settings are higher in systems that maintain segregated schools than in inclusive systems. Furthermore, there appears to be a connection between systems that offer comprehensive schools and a reduced reliance on a secondary school structure that segregates students into particular kinds of curriculum, denying some students a challenging curriculum and opportunities to earn advanced graduation certificates.

Placement in certain types of school cannot be attributed to a student's ability level. Research shows that even if students' performance on their grades 1–4 report cards is equivalent, immigrant and foreign students often do not get the chance to attend advanced secondary schools. The rationale is that the students' German-language skills are not sufficient for advanced academic learning or that they are not supported adequately by their families.[57] Researchers in the United States emphasize that "race and class problems in school replicate social structural problems so closely that educators should not drop children too quickly into success and failure piles and then explain them as a product of race and class difference."[58] This same logic can also be applied to the German situation.

The overrepresentation of immigrant students in special education settings must be examined in the broader societal context. We emphasize that Germany is not as culturally/ethnically homogeneous as it is often described in the context of a European nation state.[59] Despite the increasing multicultural nature of German society, there is a strong tendency among the dominant cultural group to set apart groups of students whose language, customs, and cultural patterns are seen as different in the German context.[60] Because policy assumes that Germany is an ethnically/ culturally homogeneous nation, the government does not offer many support systems for multilingual students. A comparison of the Canadian, Swedish, and German school system shows that German schools offer less second language–acquisition support than Canada and Sweden.[61]

In German schools, having an immigrant background is equated with experiencing difficulties in schools. The social construction of *cultural difference* seems to be a common argument that teachers use to explain why students from immigrant backgrounds are not as successful as students without immigrant backgrounds.[62] Gomolla and Radtke point out that the high rate of immigrant students in special schools can be interpreted as a form of institutional discrimination.[63] Their study shows that school professionals have justified the placement of students from immigrant backgrounds in special schools by alluding to individual attributes (e.g., mental stress, individual learning problems, generalized language problems, cultural differences and/or conflicts). Educational research in Germany shows that the category *culture* should be unpacked so that nuanced information can be shared and better understood.[64] Artiles and Dyson state that "the power dimension of culture enables us to understand how a cultural boundary—i.e., the objective presence of cultural difference—can be transformed into a cultural border, which is defined as a social construct that is political in origin."[65] Cultural borders seem to lead to negative consequences for ethnic minority students in the German context. This brief insight into the German school situation shows that the current structure of the school system leads to unequal educational opportunities for foreign students who attend regular or special schools.

CONCLUSION

The German education system struggles to accept students' differences and diversities.[66] Being different in terms of culture, language, or abilities often leads to educational exclusion. In the individual paradigm, the failure is the *student's fault*. We hope, with this chapter, to have contributed toward overcoming the individual paradigm. Our analysis of the intersections of migration status and country of origin, migration status and gender, migration status and socioeconomic background, and migration status and state residency shows that the individual paradigm does not explain the complex patterns of exclusion related to this intersections. This chapter offers new insights on why there is educational inequity for immigrant students in German schools.

The analysis of the regular school system and the special education system in terms of inclusive structures has led to a deeper understanding of the changes that must be made in the German education system. We have demonstrated that students' abilities are not always the main reasons for transferring students to a different level of high school or a regular school setting, but that educational disparities must also be interpreted as the result of expectations of society and the educational system. To reduce exclusion, changes should address not only teachers' attitudes, but also inequities in the entire school system (e.g., school, states, and educational policies) and broader social inequities.[67] Support systems seem to be missing for immigrant students. We conclude that reducing the number of selection criteria in the education system and the enhancement of support and assistance offered (e.g., second language–acquisition support in primary and secondary schools) might be one promising way to improve this situation. A more inclusive system would offer higher flexibility. Of course, one cannot say that more heterogeneous grouping would necessarily solve every problem described above.[68] There might still be some form of discrimination and inequity, but most likely it will be a step toward to a more equitable society.

5

Challenges and Responses to Inclusive Education in Sweden
Mapping Issues of Equity, Participation, and Democratic Values

Girma Berhanu

It is difficult to grasp the complexity, multidimensionality, and problematic nature of the concept of inclusive education without confronting its practical ramifications. In a special education graduate seminar in Sweden, I raised the notion of inclusive education with my students. A heated debate ensued. Until that moment, I had no idea that the concept could be conceived in so many different ways, or that the whole agenda was of such a sensitive, controversial, and problematic nature. Among my students were a principal and five teachers with many years of experience as general or special educators. Three of the teachers were also parents of children with disabilities or children with special educational needs. In that discussion I noted the overlapping concerns of parents, teachers, and school leadership.

Five key concerns emerged that I summarize here. First, what are the implications of choice? Parents have choices about school placement in Sweden, and these choices include selecting segregated school settings for their children with disabilities. Since choice is a cornerstone of the Swedish education system, maintaining segregated schools seems unavoidable. Second, what about the wishes and voices of children with disabilities? What if children want to mix with other students with similar special needs or disability? Whose choice should prevail, the child's or the parent's? As some of the participants noted, "This human need for solidarity and connectedness cannot be neglected." Third, can students who need to have calm and highly structured settings learn in association with children with profound disabilities and severe behavioral and emotional problems? What about the ever-increasing number of hyperactive and violent students? What kind of support services can be available in an ordinary classroom? Under what circumstances should individual rights trump common interest or vice versa? Fourth, how are we going to deal with the *common frame of reference* which has been and *is* still Sweden's fundamental value, a cornerstone of social justice, in the face of a strong trend towards difference, individuality, competition, and freedom of choice spearheaded by the neoliberal political agenda? And fifth, what do equity, equivalence, and equality mean in educational practice in the face of shifting political discourses and rhetoric? Although our arguments were intense, the word *inclusion* remained an ideal.

My purpose in this chapter is twofold. First, I map out the challenges and responses to inclusive education in Sweden from a cultural historical point of view, because a country's educational system and its core values emerge from historical contexts to reflect national characteristics. Second, I analyze core concepts that bear on how we conceive and implement the inclusive agenda. As an offshoot of this general investigatory theme, I describe how constructions of inclusive education are mediated by the purposes and goals of Swedish public education and by collective, country-specific understandings and educational responses to sociocultural differences.

This analysis incorporates the political intentions, rhetoric, and praxis of government reports, research materials, and commissioned evaluations. Sweden's current political and educational discourses reflect contradictions and dilemmas between community and individual, utility and culture, public and personal, economy and welfare, and individual agency versus collective and political action. The analysis, therefore, is based on the assumption that policy and practice decisions involve dilemmas.[1] Billig et al. noted that dilemmas arise from a "culture which produces more than one possible ideal world."[2] Given the tensions that can arise from different values, "dilemmas are a condition of our humanity."[3] Special needs education is also a specific, socioculturally situated response to the dilemmas of dealing with a modern education system for fundamental education.[4]

This chapter is organized into four major sections. The first deals with the general context of the Swedish education system; the second addresses inclusive educational policies and practices; the third deals with democratic values and participation in school and society; and the fourth explores on issues of equity, equivalence and equality.

EDUCATION POLICY IN SWEDEN: THE GENERAL CONTEXT

In 1842, a policy called *allmän folkskola* (folk school) came into force. Before this, education was reserved only for middle- and upper-class society. The intent of the folk school policy was to provide schooling for all citizens, although in practice two parallel school systems evolved: one for poor and disadvantaged people and the other for privileged people. Even so, the policy's intention was revolutionary, and we can still trace Sweden's long tradition of comprehensive, compulsory, and equivalent education to the folk school policy.

At the same time, special-needs education established its roots as a two-track system (i.e., special education or regular education settings). In the special education track, the so-called "problem-child" was categorized using a nomenclature that included such categories as *idiot, poor, feeble-minded, imbecile,* and *dullard.* In the mid-twentieth century, these categories were redescribed as *intellectually disabled, learning disabled,* and *mentally retarded.* During the last two decades, such students became *pupils with special needs,* and a new culture of diagnosis based on neuropsychiatric methods, such as ADHD, DAMP, autism, or Asperger's syndrome emerged. This continued tuning of terminology illustrates how such classification and categorization has been an activity "as old as schools themselves."[5]

Education can be described as one of the cornerstones of Sweden's modern welfare state. Strong Labor parties were able to secure broad support for their policies during the interwar period and after World War II, when *solidarity, community,* and *equality* became keywords. There were high hopes that uniform, free-of-charge education for children from all social strata would contribute to equality and justice and promote social cohesion. Although the belief in the potential of education in this respect may have faded, education is still regarded as one of the major methods of preventing unemployment, social exclusion, and poor health outcomes.[6] Thus, "contemporary policy for equity is very much a latter day echo of the social democrats' age-old concept of the *'peoples' home'.*"[7]

Sweden's reputation for successfully combining effective economy and social welfare measures is still unscathed in many ways. By OECD measures, Sweden is an affluent, healthy, and well-educated society. Its population is about 9 million, and approximately 20 percent are from an immigrant background. The unique combination of social equality and equity measures, underpinned by high levels of taxation and public spending based on redistributive policies, and a regulated capitalist economic system, has contributed to Sweden's reputation for achieving a high quality of life for its citizens. Overall, educational attainment is quite high. At least 80 percent of the population has attained at least an upper secondary education. The average life expectancy is 82.8 years for women and 77.7 for men. Furthermore, the country has one of the highest OECD employment-to-population ratios, with 74 percent of the population working. This is third only to Switzerland and Denmark. Sweden also has one of the highest OECD employment rates for mothers, second only to Portugal. Seventy-eight percent of all mothers of children under age seven were working in 2003.[8]

Most of the modern history of Sweden is characterized by collective action spearheaded by a social democratic welfare state that favored full employment and focused on minimizing differences, social alienation, and exclusion as opposed to individual responsibility and market solutions.[9] This political and cultural background has been instrumental in creating an early and fertile platform from which to criticize the historical exclusionary approach used in special education and to formulate concepts such as normalization, integration, and mainstreaming.[10] The Swedish backdrop fostered awareness of social inclusiveness in general and resulted in organizational changes such as closing large institutions for intellectually disabled persons and building community-based residential, learning, and working environments. These policies were a remarkable achievement by any standard. Citizenship, social integration, social equality, and democracy were placed on an equal footing with the economic agendas that also drove education not only in Sweden but also in Scandinavia as a whole.

The slogan "A school for all" (*En skola för alla*) embellished most of the policy documents and government-commissioned reports and propositions from the 1960s through the late '80s. In 1962, the Curriculum for the Compulsory School System (Läroplan för grundskolan, or LGR), a nine-year unified compulsory school program for all children ages seven to sixteen, was introduced. As part of the framework of a school for all, this compulsory curriculum emphasized that pupils belong at the center of the learning process and that their development should be multi-faceted. Current Swedish educational policy documents recognize that students are *different*, which has important implications for how schooling and the learning process are organized as well as the avenues for reaching educational goals. The LGR specifically states that "consideration should be taken of the different abilities and needs of the students. There are different ways to reach the goal . . . Hence teaching cannot be designed in the same way for everyone."[11]

While postwar Swedish educational policy measures are characterized by comprehensiveness, equity, and inclusion, as represented in the slogan "A school for all," the policy did not stop the differentiation, classification, categorization, and segregation of children. In fact, paradoxically, the amount of special education, as Emanuelsson, Haug, and Persson have noted, has increased steadily.[12] Vast differences have been observed in how pupils with special needs are actually defined and registered in different municipalities. This is, of course, partly the consequence of a decentralized education system that manifests itself in divergent local practices.[13]

INCLUSIVE EDUCATIONAL POLICIES AND PRACTICES

Sweden has signed the UN Convention on the Rights of the Child, the Standard Rules on the Equalisation of Opportunities for Persons with Disabilities, and the UNESCO Salamanca Statement and Framework for Action.[14] These are all powerful tools to prevent exclusionary practices in the school sector and make a strong case for inclusion. These documents have shaped a number of important government reports, directives, and policies and worked to place inclusive education firmly on the agenda. Political expression, however, has not matched practice.[15]

The government's role in providing appropriate services to special needs children within a regular school framework was outlined in the first (1962) LGR, where "the contents and organization of special education were carefully specified and the accompanying proposal was for a system of coordinated special education as alternative to remedial and special classes."[16] However, it was not until the 1969 national curriculum was implemented that increased emphasis was given to integrating children with various forms of disability into regular education. The discourses in the 1969 curriculum have many similarities with the current inclusive agenda, although the term used then was *integration*. One significant perspective shift in the curriculum and official reports of the time and through the 1970s was the statement that the school's environment represents a possible cause of children's difficulties in school.[17] Consequently, the discourses of the *categorical* versus the *relational perspective* evolved.[18]

The Categorical Model Versus the Relational Model

The *categorical* model described in several Swedish reports corresponds to international research that addresses the *within-child* model, the *medical* model, the *psycho-medical* model, the *discourse of deviance*, the *defect* model, and the *pathological* model.[19] In this model, school failure is ascribed to some defect, pathology, or inadequacy within the student. In the *relational* model (variously referred to as the *social* model, the *sociopolitical* model, the *sociopolitical paradigm*, and *the deficient system* model), the term *students with difficulties* was challenged and began to be replaced by *students in difficulties*.[20] Fierce criticism against the traditional and categorical special pedagogical perspective has brought about a paradigm shift and a policy deeply ingrained with a relational perspective (which is more environment oriented) as a guiding principle for educational services. However, the categorical perspective, which is associated with historical, segregated, and exclusionary approaches, has not given way to the relational perspective. In fact, the categorical perspective reemerged in the 1990s and has since dominated both special education research and praxis in Sweden. The recent growth in categorization, identification, and classification under the guise of "redesigning regular education support" to facilitate inclusion has been strongly criticized by Emanuelsson, a prominent Swedish professor of special education.[21]

In one recent study, special-needs students reported that in segregated settings or special units, the demands put on them by the special teachers are minimal and expectations are generally low.[22] Studies have also challenged the reliability of diagnostic categories and the notion that diagnoses have important implications for educational processes. In addition, studies underline the stigmatizing effects of diagnoses and segregated educational arrangements. On the other hand, parents express relief when their children's "problem" is diagnosed and receives a medical label.[23] The sense of relief has also been experienced by some of the pupils interviewed in the above-mentioned studies. This is another dimension of the dilemma of categorization versus individuality. Unfortunately, there are too few comprehensive studies that examine levels of participation and the extent of inclusiveness experienced by children with disabilities in the ordinary school system in Sweden. Additionally, too few studies offer comparisons of pupil development in special and regular education.

What Happened in the 1990s?

Many of the social and educational changes that took place in the early 1990s were dramatic. Key was the ascent to power of the right wing in 1991 and the coalition government headed by a liberal conservative Carl Bildt from 1991 to 1994. The country was in a deep recession, employment rates fell, followed by a sharp decrease in social expenditures and a move toward further socioeconomic inequalities. The situation abated in the mid-1990s. As a consequence of the shift in power to the conservatives, education was increasingly regarded as a private rather than a public good. Policies governing state-sponsored education shifted from an emphasis on collective values and social community to individual rights, academic progress, and choice. A new financial system was introduced that moved control of resource allocation from the national to the local level. Local control was combined with a new type of steering and control mechanism.[24] Relocating control to the local level mirrored increasingly conservative fiscal policies worldwide. This era of "late modernity" and capitalism emphasizes effectiveness, competition, standardization, freedom of choice, individualism, and elitism.[25]

The impact of the decentralized educational policy on equity has been pervasive. Paradoxically, in the footsteps of the introduction of inclusive education, the number of pupils labeled as having special needs increased dramatically. Teachers found themselves incapable of dealing with diversity in the classroom and meeting individual student needs.[26] One in five compulsory school pupils in Sweden are judged to be in need of special-needs education.[27] This means that approximately 200,000 pupils in Sweden receive some kind of special educational support during the school year. At the same time, the number of pupils enrolled in special schools for the intellectually disabled (*särskolan*) has increased from .9 percent to 1.4 percent during the last five to six years, and "from 1992 to 2001 the number of students registered in schools and classrooms for students with severe learning disabilities has increased by 67 percent."[28]

In the beginning of the 1990s, a national special education curriculum to prepare teachers was launched that had a significant impact on the praxis of special/inclusive education in Sweden. The curriculum aligned with a relational or system-based perspective of educational difficulties. In addition to a focus on particular kinds of teaching tasks, the curriculum described the roles that special educators would implement in their regular practice: supervising, consulting, and counseling of regular teachers to help them meet the needs of all pupils. Accordingly, all teacher trainees studied special-needs education within the so-called "general field of education" and could also study this field of knowledge within an eligible field of study or in specialization courses. The curriculum was institutionalized broadly until 2007. At that time, a new conservative government came into power and discredited it. In 2008, the government introduced a new special teacher course of study in which trainees are expected to work directly with individual pupils, not through their general education colleagues. Special educators now learn to focus on the student, not the system, a dramatic shift from the previous perspective. Currently both curricula exist side by side, are offered at an advanced level, and qualify graduates for specialist tasks in schools.

Inclusion Versus Integration

Integration and *inclusion* have been used interchangeably in Swedish educational discourses. Most people are familiar with the former term. The term *inclusion* has been difficult to translate into Swedish, and this difficulty has contributed to considerable ambiguity about its use. In the first Swedish translations of the Salamanca Statement, *inclusion* was translated as *integration*. As in many other countries, confusion and controversy developed around the semantics of inclusion, demonstrating how problematic terms can be when they are borrowed from other cultures. Many have questioned whether the new word is merely a terminology shift or signals a new agenda. Although conceptual problems remain, the difference between integration and inclusion has been sorted out and defined by the research community.[29] *Inclusive education,* as outlined in the Salamanca Statement, has now begun to permeate the Swedish language, at least in official documents. The social model of disability and the relational nature of disablement have been officially accepted, which implies that schooling "is more or less disabling or enabling."[30] This in turn places the burden on schools to restructure and adjust their learning environments, pedagogical methods, and organizational arrangements.

Policy documents, propositions, and official evaluation documents have, in different ways, begun to incorporate the core elements of inclusion. Yet, the term *inclusion* has been hollowed out as a result of neoliberalism's political intransigence. One mechanism that drains inclusive education of its social significance is positioning it in novel contexts that result in "simplification, condensation and elaboration and refocusing."[31] Since the term *inclusion* has positive connotations, other fields have appropriated the term. In the process of appropriation, the original meaning of inclusion is changed. This appropriation of the term could be why some pessimistic academics argue that the commitments to a philosophy of inclusive education may be stalled, if not in retreat. Progress toward more inclusive education in Sweden has certainly slowed over the past few years despite positive policies and intentions at different levels of the education system.[32]

It is clear that there are large differences between municipalities and their approaches to inclusive education. Most reports on inclusion practices indicate that inclusion is happening. However, neither up-to-date and reliable time series data nor data on the number of pupils who are included in the ordinary classroom are available nationwide. Further, data that track the number of exclusionary special units (classes) are not available. Even the definition or construction of *special needs* is shifting and is fluid. There seems to be no effective mechanism to monitor inclusive/exclusionary processes at regional and national levels, which makes it difficult to document equity in inclusive education.[33]

Ethnic Minority and Socially Disadvantaged Pupils

The Swedish education system has been strained during the past two decades by massive migration. The ethnic landscape has changed dramatically and ushered Sweden into an era of multiculturalism and globalization. This rapid demographic change has also brought ethnic segregation and inequalities, particularly in large cities. These pressures are layered on top of the existing inequalities between municipalities and social groups resulting from decentralization and competition.

Sweden explicitly adopts multiculturalism and cultural diversity in an atmosphere of mutual tolerance; however, terms such as *ethnicity*, *color*, and *race* remain obscured in official taxonomies, educational policies, and school practices.[34] The complex relationships that exist between ethnicity, socioeconomic factors, special-needs education, and gender have only recently become a subject of research interest.[35] The fragmentation of educational policymaking witnessed in the past two decades has negatively affected already vulnerable groups, such as people with disabilities, ethnic minority students, and socially disadvantaged segments of the population. Over the next decade, Swedish society will become increasingly multiethnic and multilingual, and the number of disadvantaged children will increase substantially.

A recent report by Gustafsson concluded that from 1992–2000, a consistent increase in school segregation occurred on the basis of immigration background, educational background, and grades.[36] A national tracking system compares achievement among groups of students. Students with foreign backgrounds receive lower average grades, are less likely to qualify for higher education, and have a higher dropout rate from upper-secondary education than their peers with Swedish background. There are also differences in achievement between girls and boys. Girls receive higher average grades in the majority of all subjects in compulsory and upper-secondary school.[37]

Some recent Swedish studies indicate that immigrant students are overrepresented in special schools and classes.[38] These students were categorized in diffused, vague, symptom-based, and pedagogy-related terms such as *concentration and behavioral problems, speech and language difficulties*, unspecified *"poor talent,"* or *developmental retardation*. However, there is a need for a coherent cumulative body of disproportionality research in Sweden; extensive and longitudinal studies have yet to be carried out.[39]

DEMOCRATIC VALUES AND PARTICIPATION IN SCHOOL AND SOCIETY

Democracy is a cornerstone of both Swedish curricula and educational legislation. Fostering democracy and raising democratic citizens are key functions of schools. However, the reality of the past two decades—characterized by competition, efficiency, standardization, and devolvement of responsibilities to local authorities—has introduced divergent educational access and outcomes that, in turn, threaten the long tradition of equity, equality, and solidarity. Increased opportunities for school choice and increased residential segregation have contributed to growing disparities and differences between groups, not only in equality of access but also in social outcomes.

Student advocacy groups, such as the Pupils Welfare Committees, that were once features of Swedish democracy in action in schools have been marginalized by the neoliberal agenda. As Arnesen and Lundahl correctly point out: "One may ask to what extent schools can afford pupils' democracy at a time when performance and competitiveness is a major priority."[40] The extent to which inclusive education can be realized in such a context is in question. Many studies indicate that the number of special-needs education pupils has increased, particularly in large cities, and different forms of segregation have expanded. For instance, the Skolverket (Swedish National Agency for Education) found that poorly executed assessments coupled with unreflective educational plans have led to many students being viewed as derailed from the "norm."[41]

As more and more reports indicate that pupils are entering special educational placements within the regular school framework and in special schools, the government is financing a number of projects to examine the processes that lead to exclusionary measures in an attempt to mitigate the situation and therefore enhance full participation of pupils with special needs in all aspects of school life. Other studies have aimed at identifying factors and good examples at different educational levels that contribute to participation and equality.[42] These studies have identified the problematic nature of the term *participation*. Some of the major findings are identified here. Participation is context bound, multidimensional, and has subjective dimensions. For instance, adult support can hinder the development of peer relationships. The presence of special teacher assistants in classrooms, which is designed to help students with special needs, can instead create barriers to social inclusion—their proximity to students with special needs marks those students as different and, by working alongside students, the assistants inhibit interactions with other peers. Participation appears to be more related to autonomy and interactions with significant others than to disability type and general environment.[43] Tension exists between having security in a small group with similar disabilities and the desire to be like somebody else and belonging to the collective unity; at the same time there is fear that the general public has negative stereotypes against specific groups of people. Another aspect of the dilemma is the need for institutionalized support, individualization, and flexibility. The ties between participation and democracy converge in considering how to balance these aspects and who should make those decisions. Social learning and development of friendships and solidarity are as important to the development of the whole person as the acquisition of knowledge.

Although the situation in Sweden in terms of pupils' participation and democracy is gloomy by Swedish standards, internationally, Sweden is among the few OECD countries that have maintained such features as comprehensiveness, limited tracking at lower and upper secondary levels, comparatively lower segregation and marginalization, highly networked human rights, gender equality, and so forth. At the same time, the balance between social democratic ideals and liberal components of Swedish educational politics is far from stable at present.[44]

One exemplary action in Sweden in relation to monitoring participation and inclusive/segregative processes is the recent establishment of a Forum for Inclusive Education by Örebro University and the Swedish Institute for Special Needs Education. The main goal of the forum is to enhance knowledge on inclusive and segregation processes in school and identify good examples that promote participation in general education.

THE ISSUE OF EQUITY, EQUIVALENCE, AND EQUALITY

The purpose of this section is not to explore and analyze these three complex and overlapping concepts. It is, rather, to map out some aspects of the concepts in relation to inclusive education and the extent to which they enhance inclusiveness, and to describe changes of their meanings in different periods of Swedish educational policy making. Since the early nineteenth century, when elementary school was regarded as a basic school for all, equity has been and is still a central element in the Swedish educational policies, ordinances, and directives. "Equity is a general term indicating 'fairness'; for example, that principles of justice have been used in the assessment of a phenomenon."[45]

Equity in the school is guaranteed by the Swedish Education Act 1§2: "All children and young people shall, regardless of gender, geographical residence, and social or economical situation, have equal access to education in the public school system for children and young people."[46] The act stipulates that consideration must also be afforded to pupils with special needs. The school has a particular responsibility for those pupils who, for different reasons, experience difficulties in attaining the established educational goals. The links between education and the rest of society are widely recognized, and one task of the school system is to foster in children a spirit of equality and democratic values.[47]

The main question is how this critical equity issue can be addressed in a relatively recently decentralized educational system. How can we guarantee those values without an effective system of indicators to measure and monitor equity? What does follow-up and evaluation look like? I do not claim to provide a complete description of this complex research area. I do, however, provide some examples that bear on inclusive practices both negatively and positively.

The Swedish constitution recognizes equal human worth and respect for the freedom and dignity of the individuals. The principles laid down sources for the curriculum's goals and objectives. In that respect, as Wildt-Persson and Rosengren note, "an important principle in achieving equity has been and still is the compensatory principle, i.e., that the state should not remain neutral in issues relating to equal opportunity.

Differences among geographical regions, social or economic groups must not be attributable to any form of discrimination that would indicate that the principle of equality has been neglected."[48]

Equity carries a particular significance for children with special educational needs. The majority of these children are integrated into regular child-care activities, compulsory schools, and upper-secondary schools. There are, however, eight special schools for pupils with hearing/vision and physical disabilities, as well as some schools for students with intellectual disabilities. A total of 1 percent of all pupils in the compulsory and upper-secondary school levels are in such segregated settings.[49] This is minimal by international comparison.[50] Nonetheless, since the early 1990s, the situation has deteriorated. The number of pupils placed in educational programs for learning disabled students has increased dramatically. The influence of a number of background factors significant to educational attainment, such as parental social position, cultural capital, type of community and gender, may have diminished over the last century yet, in pernicious ways, they remain a troubling artifact of the Swedish system of categorizing its students.[51]

Evaluating Equivalence

Although the concepts of equity, equality, and equivalence are inextricably intertwined, they do not convey exactly the same meaning. As I understand the concept, the term *equivalence* represents or encompasses the other two in Swedish discourses, although this is a bold statement. Englund notes that the concept of equivalence has undergone significant changes and has been given different authoritative interpretations:

> Viewed from a longer-term perspective, the concept has undergone a displacement whereby its substantial meaning and the contextual criteria involved in it have changed from consisting of types of goals such as unity, common frames of reference, and equal value of continued studies, to a situation where supplementary goals have been added; these are often vague and in total opposition to the original objectives. These new goals can accept difference and individuality independently of shared frames of reference. They have also become equivalence's link to freedom of choice and parents' rights.[52]

Equivalence is used to mean "of equal worth" and does not imply a strict criterion for comparing two objects, but it does assume comparability.[53] Educational paths, for example, can be equivalent but do not necessarily have to contain identical courses and subjects to have the same value. In line with this, the idea of one school with a common curriculum for all can be problematic if not totally questionable. Lindensjö notes that the "reforms in Sweden have led to the insight that it is difficult to attain true equality without promoting uniformity, which in turn is seen as negative. Therefore, the term equivalence has become central in the Swedish Education Act and has thus come to replace equality as the adjective describing the principles of equity."[54]

The principle of fair education as embedded in the concept of equivalence has been operationalized in the Education Act (chapter 1, §2), which stipulates that the education provided within each type of school should be of equivalent value, irrespective of where in the country it is provided. The new curriculum introduced in 1994, written under a conservative government, states: "National goals specify the norms for equivalence. However, equivalent education does not mean that education should be the same everywhere or that the resources of a school should be allocated equally. Account should also be taken of the varying circumstances and needs of pupils as well as the fact that there are a variety of ways of attaining these goals. Furthermore the school has a special responsibility for those pupils who for different reasons experience difficulties in attaining the goals that have been set for the education."[55]

Further, this curriculum states that education is to be adapted to each pupil's circumstances and needs. However, that does not mean that results should be equal. *Quality* is also a crucial term used inseparably with equity, equality, and equivalence in government reports, because the quality of services at all levels of the educational system can have serious implications for equivalent education. A conceptual model of equivalence has been developed by the Skolverket to enable it to monitor equivalence and it is currently being applied (see table 5.1). This elegant model encompasses three critical areas: *equal access, equivalent education*

TABLE 5.1 Equivalence in schools

Prerequisites	Process	Results
Equal access to education regardless of gender, geographical location, social and economic circumstances.	Equivalent education within every type of school wherever in the country a school is run.	The equal value of an education with respect to further studies, society, and working life.

Source: Adapted from A. Wildt-Persson and P. G. Rosengren, "Equity and Equivalence in the Swedish School System," in *In Pursuit of Equity in Education: Using International Indicators to Compare Equity Policies*, ed. W. Hutmacher (Hingham, MA: Kluwer Academic Publishers, 2001), 288–321.

and the *equal value of education.* These can also be described as *equal opportunity strategies, equal treatment strategies* and *equal outcome strategies.* These critical areas are structured within three general areas: prerequisites, process and results.

It is through this indicator system that the participation and learning progress of pupils with special educational needs and culturally and socially disadvantaged segments of the school population can be monitored. A summary of the general trends according to these indicators includes the following points: growing inequalities and varied results between schools and pupils; an increase in special educational placements; and an increase of labeling students as special needs (e.g., dysphasia, autism, ADHD, socioemotional problems). However, there is still a huge information gap on equity in inclusive education with respect to pupils with special needs education including children with immigrant status. It is critical to include specific categories within the indicator system in order to gather information on inclusive and exclusionary processes and on the participants, in particular within the regular education system.

Furthermore, the term *equivalence* is highly problematic. Some scholars advocate framing the term as a notion that encompasses both equity and equality. This discourse might lead to the possibility of accepting segregation from a common or collective identity—much like the U.S. history around *separate but equal.* The use of the term requires close scrutiny as it has serious implications on how we conceive and implement inclusive education. Although there is little discussion in the literature about the term's hidden or tacit message, this application of the term might strengthen the "separate but equal" discourse. This could be one reason why progress in Sweden, with regard to inclusive education, has slowed over the past few years despite positive policies and intentions at different levels of the education system.

Evaluation and Assessment: Learning Outcomes

The new grading system (LPO) that came into force in 1994 has also been a source of debate about equity in Sweden.[56] According to this system, grades are to be given according to nationally formulated criteria denoting certain qualities of knowledge and skills corresponding to the syllabus for a given subject. The possible grades are *pass, pass with distinction,* and *pass with special distinction.* When a student in compulsory school fails to meet the criteria of the syllabus, no grade is given; in upper secondary school, the grade *fail* is given. The criteria, however, are to be based on curricula and syllabi, without reference to the accomplishments of a pupil's peers. This system of grading is referred to as absolute in comparison with its predecessor, a relative system, in which grades were awarded on a Gauss curve denoting the normal performance for a given age group of pupils. The possible grades had been 1, 2, 3, 4, and 5, with 5 denoting the best performance.[57]

Issues of accountability as described above (and coordinated by the Skolverket) are exerting some pressure on schools to document not only equal access and equivalent education, but also effectiveness in terms of outcomes. This emphasis on accountability represents a significant shift from issues of access and quality of services. Systems of assessment, monitoring, evaluation, and documentation of effectiveness in terms of learning outcomes and equity in inclusive education remain lacking and need attention.

Sweden has very few examinations, grades, or certificates in comparison with many other European countries. Until recently, no grades were awarded for subjects before grades 8 and 9 in the compulsory school. Mandatory tests in Swedish, English, and mathematics are administered at the end of comprehensive education. At upper secondary levels, tests are compulsory in the first course of study in core subjects. Generally, teacher assessments are viewed as having more values than tests.[58] This limited use of testing and grading is commendable; however, the culture of testing has entered the school system and the center-right coalition government is pushing for more nationally administered tests even at lower grades (e.g., third grade). Currently, the assessment system has reached a crossroads concerning whether or not formative-summative assessment should be or could be combined. The tension is fresh at the time of writing. The impact of this decision on inclusive practices is obvious.

While there are signs that inclusive education as envisaged in the Salamanca Statement is being exercised at different levels, gaps in research and follow-ups are most noticeable in this area. Finally, an over-representation of minority pupils in special educational placements and significant gender differences in specific disability categories, as well as in general learning outcomes and methods of testing and assessment, are areas of grave concern that require further studies.[59]

Democracy is a fundamental value of the Swedish society, but in itself does not guarantee inclusiveness. The principles governing democratic processes are important. As a result, we encounter different models of democracy, although representative democracy is basic and shared by differing models, whether law-governed democracy (the New Right) or participatory/deliberative democracy (the New Left); as Nilholm describes them, "The former stems from the liberal tradition and the latter from a Marxian, pluralistic tradition."[60] Law-governed democracy puts the individual at the center, minimizing the impact of the state on public life. Law-governed democracy appears to be the order in Sweden, although not in its extreme form. There are already signs, however, that this is becoming detrimental to the goals of inclusion.

I now return to the five dilemmas outlined in the introduction of this chapter. These questions do not have simple answers. The answers may lie partly in how we conceive social justice. It has been indicated earlier that the justification for inclusive education is based in part on the ideals of social justice, and that these social justice goals and inclusive education are inextricably intertwined. However, social justice views in inclusion discourses vary. As Artiles, Harris-Murri, and Rostenberg note, "Social justice views can be classified as individualistic or communitarian; both perspectives permeate the discourses on inclusion."[61] The authors argue that we must move from a traditional social justice discourse in inclusive education (individualistic/communitarian) to a transformative model of social justice. The values involved relate to a vision of a whole society, of which education is a part. Issues of social justice, equity, and choice are central to the demands for inclusive education. This vision concerns the well-being of all pupils, and making schools welcoming institutions through, for instance, examining ideological and historical assumptions about difference, critiquing marginalization, debunking merit based cultures, deliberating/negotiating program's goals, tools and practices, and so on.[62] I also believe that a fundamental change in our educational system and core of educational practice may mitigate the dilemmas.

CONCLUSION

I attempted in this chapter to map the challenges and responses to inclusive education in Sweden, in particular at organizational and systemic levels, from a cultural historical point of view. Core concepts such as equity, equality, and equivalence that have bearing on inclusive education have been discussed. The analysis incorporated government reports and research findings and has been conceptualized in terms of the assumption that policy and practice decisions involve dilemmas and contradictions and are situated in a historical, social, and cultural context. That holds true for policies and practices of education in general and special/inclusive education in particular.

In comparison to even many well-developed countries, Sweden is one of the most successful at combining equity and social inclusion with high economic efficiency. The tradition of universalism and comprehensiveness with minimization of streaming and tracking has been the hallmark of its education system. Redistribution policies underpinned by high levels of taxation and public spending still appear to have strong social consensus. At the same time, Sweden has undergone a dramatic transformation within the past two decades. The changes are framed within neoliberal philosophies that place greater emphasis on devolution, marketization (driven by principles of cost-containment and efficiency), competition, standardization, individual choices and rights, development of new profiles within particular school units, and other factors that potentially work *against* the values of diversity, equity, and inclusion.

National evaluations and OECD reports indicate that differences in a number of aspects (e.g., socioeconomic factors, educational achievements, and resources) have increased between schools and municipalities, as well as among pupils. The number of children who are placed in special educational settings—and, in particular, in *särskolan*—has increased. Notably, "growing ethnic inequalities are probably the Achilles heel of the present-day Swedish education system."[63]

The paradox is that all these trends that work against inequity are happening while the rhetoric advocating a school for all and inclusive education have become policy catchphrases. As a consequence of massive immigration, the education system has come under serious pressure during the past two decades. Swedish society's response to this rapid demographic change has brought ethnic segregation and inequalities. This presents a major challenge to policy makers in terms of social integration and educational inclusion. Targeting positive discriminatory measures is a way to address these challenges. Such measures, however, are anathema to Swedish policy principles.

A number of government-funded studies have been conducted in the past five years to investigate the participation and inclusion of students with disabilities at different levels of the education system, in particular at the individual, classroom, and school levels. In addition, conferences are being held to discuss these studies. There is therefore some hope that the studies will reveal micro- and meso-level activities that hinder or enhance full participation of students with special needs and problematize further real-world dilemmas, including the growing culture of diagnosis.

On the positive side, there are still commendable activities and policies in Sweden that promote social inclusion. Acclaiming Sweden's past achievements, an OECD report has stated that "the tools to achieve equity in Sweden have not been added as corrections to the education system—they are at the heart of the Swedish model."[64] There is, however, a cause for concern for how long Sweden's positive reputation will persist, given the drastic changes that have taken place within a short span. Caution is needed if the traditional model is to survive.

6

Ability Construction, Deficit Thinking, and the Creation of an Inclusion Gap for Students of Color in the United States
Views from Suburban Schools

Roey Ahram and Edward Fergus

Based on findings from a New York State Education Department (NYSED)–funded project on special education disproportionality, this chapter focuses on two specific conditions within schools that contribute to the informal and formal racial barriers to inclusive education—the deficit-based thinking of school personnel to explain the disproportionate representation of students of color in special education and inadequate early intervention services to support struggling learners.[1] In doing so, this chapter explores the complex way in which the beliefs of individual school personnel about students of color and the school structures designed to support struggling learners are implicated in the production of special education disproportionality. *Special education disproportionality* is the phenomenon of overrepresentation and underrepresentation of students of color in a particular disability classification, given a classroom placement, or receiving a particular treatment compared with other students. As such, disproportionality provides a broader lens to understand the issues around inclusion—looking at the full spectrum of ability classifications assigned to students.

Mehan et al. posit that student ability and disability are not necessarily facts in their own right, but rather are constructed (produced) within the context of schools.[2] That is, teachers' assessments of student are, in part, the result of social constructions that are predicated on the interactions between teachers and students within and shaped by the educational institution (as defined by the context factors of education). This identification process is, in part, subjective in that it is based on teachers' individual perspectives but at the same time is grounded in a more objective reality defined by the school context—the policies and practices within schools and within the classroom. At the same time, research on disproportionality shows that students of color are both more likely to be classified with a disability compared with all other students and, among those students who are classified with a disability, are more likely to be placed in more restrictive classroom environments, isolating them from their peers in general education classrooms.[3] Losen describes the harmful effects of racial imbalances in special education as placing students of color in triple jeopardy—first in their increased likelihood of being misclassified as disabled, then in their greater likelihood of being placed in the most restrictive settings (classroom settings with the little of no interaction with general education students), and then in their greater likelihood of receiving poor-quality services within those settings.[4]

By looking at how educators explain the disproportionate placement of students of color in special education, this chapter focuses on this construction process, elucidating how children's opportunities to learn are affected by teachers' perceptions of their students' ability—particularly Black and Latino struggling learners—and how schools' support services and programs fail to meet the needs of their struggling learners.[5] We show how such perceptions of race, class, and culture are superimposed on ideas about ability making them part of the ability construction process, and also how school structures reinforce or legitimize these perceptions. Additionally, we use case studies to demonstrate that the root causes of disproportionality are complex and multifaceted; even when considering a district's racial/ethnic makeup and size, racial disproportionality results from a confluence of factors, and not a single explanation.

INTRODUCTION TO THE CASES: TWO SUBURBAN DISTRICTS WITH DISPROPORTIONALITY

In examining disproportionality, this chapter focuses on Carroll and Hannover School Districts (pseudonyms), two small school districts in New York State. Both are located in suburban communities outside of large cities, making them typical of the school districts that were identified by the NYSED for disproportionality under Chapter 405 laws of 1999 of the New York State education law. After identification, Carroll and Hannover volunteered to take part in a five-year project conducted by the Technical Assistance Center on Disproportionality (TACD) at New York University's Metropolitan Center for Urban Education (Metro Center). TACD provided intensive technical assistance to these districts to identify the root causes of disproportionality there, followed by professional development and additional technical assistance to address the identified causes.

The TACD project compiled district demographic data as well as special education classification data. These data were reported to the Metro Center by participating districts as well as from NYSED, and included (1) the total district enrollment by race/ethnicity, (2) the total enrollment of students classified as disabled by race/ethnicity, and (3) the total enrollment of students classified in each of the Individuals with Disabilities Education Act (IDEA) disability category by race/ethnicity. In addition to the quantitative data, a large amount of qualitative data was collected over four years (2005–2009). These data consisted of observation notes, focus group and individual interviews with school based personnel and district administrators, notes from technical assistance meetings with individuals from a twenty-member district team, surveys of teachers and administrators, and analyses of documents related to district policies and practices. By examining these data to understand how the districts positioned disproportionality (how they initially explained its occurrence) and how they sought to help struggling learners, this chapter hopes to provide a more textured understanding of how racial lines are drawn around ability and how school structures such as faulty intervention programs and special education placement policies and practices reinforce these lines.

Carroll

The Carroll School District is a small school district serving twenty-five hundred students. Districts in New York state range in size from nine students to over 1 million (in New York City). The mean student population is around five thousand, and the mode is 1,051 when New York City is removed from the calculation. The Carroll district comprises predominately White students, who, at the start of the project (2004–05), accounted for nearly 75 percent of the student population. Black students were the next-largest demographic group (20 percent) followed by Asian/Pacific Islander (3 percent) students and Latino students (2 percent). In the 1998–99 school year, however, White students comprised over 90 percent of the student enrollment, while the Black student population comprised less than 7 percent. Thus, in the time leading up to its involvement in the project, Carroll experienced a significant demographic shift—a decline in its White student enrollment accompanied by increases in its Black and Latino student enrollment.

In the 2004–05 school year, Carroll began the project with an overall classification rate of 13.56 percent, meaning that over 13 percent of the overall district population was classified as disabled. Moreover, Black students were 1.24 times as likely to be classified disabled compared with all other students, and Latino students over 1.70 times as likely (see table 6.1).

Looking specifically at what are commonly referred to as the *judgmental* or *soft* categories—emotional/behavioral disorder (E/BD), learning disability (LD), and speech or language impairment (SI)—over 9 percent of Carroll's district population was classified as ED, LD, or SI.[6] Black students were 1.31 times as likely to be classified ED, LD, or SI compared with all other students, and Latino students 2.23 times as likely. This indicates that much of the disproportionality in Carroll comes from the judgmental categories of disability.

Hannover

The Hannover School District is a medium-sized school district serving eighty-five hundred students. At the start of the project (2004–05), White students comprised nearly 50 percent of the student population. Latino students were the next-largest demographic group (35 percent), followed by Black students (12 percent), and Asian/Pacific Islander students (3 percent). The relative stability of district demographics over the previous school years did not reflect a larger community demographic shift in the town of Hannover—a sizable growth in the Latino population from seven thousands residents in 1990 to an estimated twelve thousand residents in 2006.

From a disproportionality perspective, Hannover began the project in the 2004–05 school year with an overall classification rate of 15.74 per-

TABLE 6.1   Classification rates and relative risk ratios in Carroll

	All students	Black	Latino/a
Classification rate (risk)			
All disability categories	13.56%	16.05	23.08
LD	6.70%	9.67%	13.46
Judgmental categories	9.72%	11.99%	21.15
Relative risk ratio			
All disability categories	—	1.24	1.73
LD	—	1.63	2.05
Judgmental categories	—	1.31	2.23

Note. The classification rate, or risk, answers the question, "What percentage of students from a specific racial/ethnic group is classified as disabled, classified as learning disabled, and classified disabled in a judgmental disability category?" The basic equation for calculating risk is: Number of students from racial/ethnic group in disability category ÷ Number of enrolled students from that racial/ethnic group × 100. The relative risk ratio or risk ratio answers the question, "What is a given racial/ethnic group's risk of being classified as disabled, classified as learning disabled, and classified disabled in a judgmental disability category compared to the risk for all other students?" The equation for calculating the risk ratio is: Risk for racial/ethnic group for disability category ÷ Risk for comparison group for that same disability category.

For more information on how to calculate risk, see the Data Accountability Center's "Methods for assessing racial/ethnic disproportionality in special education: A technical assistance guide" (www.ideadata.org).

cent—significantly higher than New York State's average classification at the time. Moreover, Black students were 1.29 times as likely to be identified for special education services compared with all other students, while Latino students were only slightly more likely (1.11 times) to be so identified (see table 6.2).

In the judgmental categories, over 12.78 percent of the overall district population was classified as ED, LD, or SI. Similar to Carroll, the relative risk of Black or Latino students increased when ED, LD, and SI classifications alone were considered; Black students were 1.34 times as likely to be classified ED, LD, or SI compared with all other students, Latino students 1.21 times as likely.

Causes of Disproportionality Across School Districts

Through a series of technical assistance workgroups with the twenty-member district team (see table 6.3 for a breakdown of team participants)

TABLE 6.2   Classification rates and relative risk ratios in Hannover

	All students	Black	Latino/a
Classification rate (risk)			
All disability categories	15.74%	19.70%	16.87%
LD	8.04%	10.45%	8.65%
Judgmental categories	12.78%	16.52%	14.39%
Relative risk ratio			
All disability categories	—	1.29	1.11
LD	—	1.35	1.12
Judgmental categories	—	1.34	1.21

Note. The classification rate, or risk, answers the question, "What percentage of students from a specific racial/ethnic group is classified as disabled, classified as learning disabled, and classified disabled in a judgmental disability category?" The basic equation for calculating risk is: Number of students from racial/ethnic group in disability category ÷ Number of enrolled students from that racial/ethnic group × 100. The relative risk ratio or risk ratio answers the question, "What is a given racial/ethnic group's risk of being classified as disabled, classified as learning disabled, and classified disabled in a judgmental disability category compared to the risk for all other students?" The equation for calculating the risk ratio is: Risk for racial/ethnic group for disability category ÷ Risk for comparison group for that same disability category.

For more information on how to calculate risk, see the Data Accountability Center's "Methods for assessing racial/ethnic disproportionality in special education: A technical assistance guide" (www.ideadata.org).

that focused on determining the causes of disproportionality in their districts, as well as analyses of district early intervention and special education referral policies and practices, it became evident that the lines around student ability were, in part, constructed around *deficit thinking*— thinking is characterized by the beliefs that students' negative achievement or behavioral outcomes are inherent to them or their families, not in the social ecology of the school, grade, or classroom.[7] This is not an uncommon stance. When asked about why Black and Latino students perform academically at lower levels, teachers often exhibit cultural deficit thinking, citing deficiencies in those students' home lives, socioeconomic status, or culture as impediments to those students' ability to learn.[8] In many cases, disability is a socially constructed category and the decision to refer to special education is informed by biases related to race and class (i.e., racism and classism) and formalized by the types of interventions and services provided to students who are perceived to be struggling— particularly inadequate institutional safeguards to prevent referrals and to

TABLE 6.3   District team membership

Superintendent or designee

Curriculum and instruction director

Special education director

Intervention coordinator(s)

Union president

Board member (optional)

Teachers (general and special education) from each schools

Parent members from PTA

Parents from racial/ethnic group experiencing disproportionate representation

Child study team members

School administrators

provide teachers with assistance in meeting the needs of struggling learners. We describe these themes in the following sections.

CULTURAL DEFICIT THINKING IN ABILITY CONSTRUCTION

When asked why a disproportionate number of students of color enter the special education system, school personnel tend to explain disproportionality through cultural deficit thinking, applying it to both their students and their families.[9] This pattern is evident in how district personnel in Carroll and Hannover talked about the root causes of disproportionality.

In September 2005, during an opening session, the district personnel in attendance were asked to write down the factors they felt contributed to the disproportionality citation—we labeled these as their district *hunches*. Practitioners in both Carroll and Hannover overwhelmingly identified poverty or conditions related to poverty as underlying causes of the patterns of disproportionality. Hunches included the following.

- "Low-income status"
- "Lack of books at home"
- "Lack of belief in education among the students and parents"
- "Connections in achievement gap between lower socioeconomic and higher groups"
- "Correlation of Head Start students and special ed.–classified"
- "[There is a] correlation of poverty to classification"
- "The federal statistics of programs given through the administration for the disenfranchised poor. When the Bush administration funds programs for poor and children, some issues will disappear."

- "They bring ghetto to the school"
- "They don't speak English"

The finding that educators discussing disproportionately tend to locate its root cause in student poverty echoes similar research.[10] The school personnel in both Carroll and Hannover as well as the school personnel in Skiba et al.'s study explain student ability and disability in much the same way—by attributing students' failure to presumed deficiencies related to their socioeconomic status, families, and cultures.[11] These beliefs are often part of teachers' *a priori* judgments; for example, Harry, Klingner, and Hart found that teachers held negative views about students of color from income backgrounds and their families without ever having justification or evidence for these beliefs.[12] The responses of the Carroll and Hannover school personnel may either indicate prior notions of students or deficit-based interpretations of student behavior—in either case, identifying the students' learning difficulties as inherent or part of the student rather than as the result of poor instructional practices.

This belief about the role of poverty in special education classifications is somewhat perplexing and troublesome. Although the district team members in Carroll and Hannover were typically unable to articulate how poverty might cause a learning disability, they readily cited it as a cause. This indicates that their cultural deficit thinking may be grounded in broader and previously unchallenged or unexplored cultural conceptions about student ability. Moreover, staff members were typically reluctant to attribute the cause of disabilities to race, instead using socioeconomics and culture as a form of coded language. These behaviors were similar to the findings of Lewis, Pollock, and Artiles, Klingner, and Tate around teachers' reluctance to talk about race.[13] There were fears that discussing race explicitly would lead charges of racism or expose beliefs about whether inherent biological differences related to race and intelligence exist. Despite these concerns, the overwhelming majority of those who had been referred to special education were low-income children of color. The conflation of race and class therefore made it nearly impossible to avoid the question of race, but made it equally easy to avoid speaking about race. As one Carroll staff member explained, the majority of the barriers associated with recognizing and addressing disproportionality had to do with the attitudes of staff because there was "a lot of resistance to acknowledging that there was a race issue."

This tangled combination of cultural bias, racial stereotyping, confused logic concerning the relationship between poverty and learning disabilities, and fear of being accused of racism contributed to the difficulties each district experienced in confronting the issue of disproportionality. The relationship between teachers' beliefs about students, education policy, and teacher practice is central to understanding how notions of academic ability are constructed and how these in turn contribute to the overrepresentation of racial/ethnic students of color in special education. In other words, every district constructs and employs notions of what it means to be academically successful in that district; however, these notions are also rooted in cultural frameworks that are based on the experiences of the dominant group. Special education disability labels placed on students who do not meet those norms legitimize difference as deficit, and can lead to the exclusion or segregation (either through labels or physical space) of students of color from the general education curriculum and high-quality educational opportunities.[14]

Othering of Students and Families

While school personnel revealed deficit perspectives as they discussed the root causes of disproportionality, conversations also revealed an an *othering* of students of color, exemplified in the ways school personnel characterized a perceived disconnect between schools and their community—i.e., how schools set themselves apart from students of color. In both Carroll and Hannover, the presence of bias in constructed notions of ability was not problematic until the presence of Black and Latino students increased substantially. This othering was continuous and at times driven by the overriding and growing presence of Black students, which turn justified a separation between Black students and the school. A focus group with teachers from Carroll, highlighted the fear that developed as a result of the mere presence of Black students; as one Black teacher in the focus group explains:

Teacher: And I think the fear is still there. I mean, you have to figure the kids are just as big a fear. I mean, that's—

Researcher: So teachers are fearful?

Teacher: Exactly, the teachers.

Researcher: Okay.

Teacher: There's a fear. There's a fear of an overload of Black people at one time, too. You know, if there's too many in one setting, the fear sets in. I mean, it's like—and then I'm the only Black teacher. So it's "Oh, my God, what do we do?"

Many of these fears are tied to practitioners, particularly White practitioners who have not previously engaged in conversations about race and class and face a changing student demographic. This perceived challenge from shifting demographics is discussed in the following quotations by teachers in Hannover. During a focus group at the end of the first year of implementing their action plan (2006–07), members of the Hannover district team described the frustration with some of the fear expressed by their colleagues, while at the same time acknowledging the ever-present impact of racism:

> I think . . . poverty is a big issue in America—it's not just Hannover, it's America—and it's getting worse, and we all know that. So, these issues are not going to go away, and I think what has happened . . . is, the school environments like this where you used to get good kids with good parents and a few losers here and there. And the teachers can do their thing on the board and the groups get along . . . So now, you kind of can't be that same type of teacher, and so that's one issue. The other issue is the racism issue. . . . I have never heard anyone bring that up, but . . . that is something that the 405 [the original New York State law that required school districts to examine special education disproportionality] has kind of brought up—[How does] racism play into it? And I think that is something that is difficult for a White person to stand in front of a White staff and say, "Are any of ya'll racists?" when we know people to this day use the N-word still. I saw a girl crying in the hallway. I've seen situations at my high school because I'm in that hallway, and I guess my point is, that, inside of all this where teachers can't teach, there is still that resentment of what's going on today. I do believe that if 405 weren't here, it would just grow the resentment.

The prevalence of this fear and inability to talk about race made the presence of our project welcome news for staff members who struggled with the elephant in the room—race.

At the same time, this inability to talk about race created a sharp divide between the school and the students:

> Black parents, poor Black people are frustrated with [Branch] schools.[15.] They know their kids aren't educated . . . When I look into the classrooms at Hannover, and I see Black kids working, I am, like "Praise the lord!" So, I know people are frustrated, but at the same time, as a community, isn't it better to have them educated than robbing you? . . . [A]nd it's not just Black kids, there [are] a lot of poor White kids who are uneducated here too and poor White parents who don't do the right

thing and aren't available. So how do we, as middle-class educated people, create a system for people we are not really familiar with? And I don't think that discussion would be had in that way without 405 here.

These notions of disconnect from and fear about students of color and students from lower socioeconomic backgrounds also appeared in the ways in which district personnel assigned the cause of disproportionality to parental involvement. Educators voiced frustration in their inability to understand families of color. In a focus group at Carroll, several teachers began talking about their struggle to understand why the Black families kept moving in and out of the district; apparent in their discussion of this mobility is the inability to understand that interactional form:

> I mean I can't imagine, I can never ever in my life put myself in their shoes because I have never had the opportunity to experience a life like they're experiencing, when we have them leaving in November and coming back in March. I was in one school, this school, my entire life— my entire education was here at Carroll and it's one of those things where I can't relate to that. That's one of those barriers that I know that I am not the only teacher who is having a hard time with the whole 405 idea, because we can't put ourselves in their shoes. We can try to be as sympathetic, empathetic as we possibly can, but we can't put ourselves in those shoes to understand why they are picking up and leaving, why can't they make a conference, why, you know, we have our priorities and our things that we have to do, but my God, I can't even begin to think what these families, sometimes I need my social worker to put my head back on straight, because I am throwing a fit about the conference that snipped me for the fourth time, while she had just got a daughter who just moved back home from a rehab center who just had a baby and now she is taking care of the baby and she has no car— yes, ok, now I understand. But again, that's the initial way that I think, because I have never been in that situation. So that's a change that I know that I'm not the only one in this district that's attempting to deal with [it], that's where the staff development, that's where hearing personal experiences, that's where all that comes into play.

These educators fail to recognize or attempt to understand the meaning behind these families' interactional forms—they set themselves up as standard-bearers of the norm and characterize the families of their students as aberrant. Harry and Klingner lament that getting to know families requires only a few visits and conversations, yet this inability to understand families and recognize their strengths can result in "disdain and disinterest" on the part of school.[16] In Carroll and Hannover, the inability to understand families of color often resulted in the blaming of parents of struggling students as key culprits in the minimal academic ability of their children. In a teacher focus group, one participant talked about "getting caught up" in the blaming of parents:

> The one thing I will say [is] that we talk at the elementary building . . . [And] I get caught up in it. And it is, What do [parents do with their children] at home? You know, that's the problem that we have . . . if education is a priority at home, I mean, that's your most important resource. And if they're not buying into it, if they're not telling them at home, "You need to do this, you need to do that," how are you going to make that [happen]? That's one thing we do hear from our teachers in the elementary level. So they're not taking ownership of their child's education.

This teacher goes on to state that some of these parents have also had bad schooling experiences or "ghosts in the classroom" and it is their job as teachers to make them believe in education:[17]

> I still say that's a huge important part. Because my whole thing is that I think some of these students that have difficulty in school, I'm not saying all of them, but some of their parents come from that type of situation themselves. They're not coming in because school's a bad place. They don't want to go back to a bad memory . . . And they do not want to go back to something like that. [We need to] try to get them to understand that, "You know what? You know, it's not a bad place. We're here to help you. We're not here to judge you, say that you're doing wrong. We want to show you what you can do to make it better for your child." Because we always sit there and say "God, you know, why wouldn't you want your child to have a better life than you, right? Wrap your brain around that" . . . Sometimes—it's not the easy yes or no, like they're trying to do this on purpose or they don't care. They just don't have the avenue or the way to get the job done. And how to get them into school is the big thing.

Thus, even when teachers seek to engage parents in their students' education, as seems to be the intent of the teacher quoted above, in not attempting to genuinely understand their students families and instead speculating about their educational experiences, a dynamic of *us* and *them* can be created. This dynamic is predicated on the need for students of color to assimilate to norms of schools—i.e., white, middle-class norms—without valuing any particular or different norms that students might arrive with.[18] In other words, the presence or arrival of families of color was also framed as a need for them to adopt the culture of the district; otherwise, they were not seen as an "us." One teacher exemplified this notion in the following statement:

> Black parents have a trust issue with the school district, which, I think is kind of hypocritical, because you're thinking, why would you move out here if you're afraid or don't trust . . . administrators or just the teachers? Or, if you don't have the trust there, why would you go to their district? However, I think that we have to really try to do more things to get . . . the parents here. And in on a positive note, instead of when they're coming to pick up their child because their child is in trouble . . . [Because] it's very unfortunate . . . for the high school, most of our behavior, um, you know—maybe violent attitude—it's from our Black population. So it's like, you would love to try to keep doing things to get the parents involved so that they're not coming to pick them up that day . . .

Thus, even though Harry and Klingner "could not document a pattern of individual ethnic bias," there is evidence that, in Hannover and Carroll, *othering* emblemizes ethnic bias and and (mis)informs teachers' collective cultural deficit thinking about students and families is present in schools.[19] The cases of these two districts demonstrate that cultural deficit thinking around students is imbued in the construction of student ability. The construction of *disability* that initiates the special education process (prompts teacher referrals to special education) takes on a more pernicious racial and socioeconomic bent, thus resulting in disproportionality. Moreover, the evidence of cultural deficit thinking revealed in the districts' schools experience of disproportionality informs how Blanchett's "subsystems of American public education" are mirrored within schools districts through a translation of race (and class) into ability.[20]

Our findings on how school personnel construct notions of student ability show how cultural deficit thinking around students' ability is seemingly an easy and comfortable stance—one that school personnel in both Carroll and Hanover unabashedly held at the start of this project—and, as the research demonstrates, how this stance can impact student outcomes. Research on the social construction of academic ability has demonstrated that teachers form judgments about student ability by interpreting student behavior relative to cultural norms of schools (and the interpreting teacher). Moreover, these interpretations are often based on superficial interactions with students, rather than on analyses of their academic work. [21]

Mehan explains that in order to be considered competent, students must have both academic knowledge and engage in appropriate behaviors—what he calls "interactional form"—to demonstrate this academic knowledge.[22] Teachers interpret students' interactional forms, but their interpretations are by no means neutral or objective assessments. Rather, the judgments teachers make about students are informed by their own perceptions of what they regard as appropriate classroom behavior—i.e., teachers' cultural beliefs and the culture of schools. The cultural significance of these interpretations is inherent in both the formal and informal aspects of the assessment process and invariably influences how teachers perceive students from culturally and linguistically diverse backgrounds.[23] A substantial body of research has shown that teachers can easily misinterpret interactional forms of students, thus failing to recognize the funds of knowledge these students possess and ultimately misinterpreting these students' academic knowledge and ability.[24] As a result of this incongruence between academic knowledge and interactional form, Black and Latino students who possess academic knowledge and ability but do not display it in the manner deemed appropriate by their teacher may be more likely to be viewed as incompetent, incorrigible, or learning disabled.

The interpretation of interactional forms take on even greater significance, given that teachers often judge students' ability in part on nonacademic criteria and after only limited contact with the students they are assessing; this can produce inaccuracies in the assessment of students' ability that disproportionally affect students of color. Teachers construct notions about students' ability based on benign student characteristics. These can be physical traits: for instance, being big for one's age increases a student's likelihood of being thought of as having lower academic ability; or cultural—for example, the way that a student walks may influence the extent to which observers perceive that student as aggressive.[25] Ray Rist's analysis of teachers' grouping of students by perceived ability highlights how students' ability are determined by teachers' perceptions of nonacademic characteristics.[26] His observations of an elementary school classroom showed that the teacher identified students for different reading groups based on the students' dress, behavior, verbal ability, and social status relative to their teachers' normal reference, before any significant interactions between the teacher and students took place. While some of these beliefs may have academic implications, several provide no real grounding for understanding academic knowledge or interactional form. Rist further explains that the process of grouping begins with teachers having preconceived notions of what characteristics a student must possess in order to be successful. Similarly, Irvine's study of teacher assessment of student ability showed that teachers assessed students' ability after only limited contact with the teacher (as they did in Rist's study), and these teachers' assessments were frequently inaccurate for Black male students compared with their assessments of other students.[27] Similarly, paired sample studies have demonstrated that when teachers are presented with similar cases of students—the only difference that in some cases the student was identified as White males, while in others the students was identified as Latino males—teachers were more likely to refer the Latino student case for E/BD and MID (mild intellectual disabilities) special education placements than the White student.[28] While arguments can be made that the research on teacher's racial bias in determining student placements is inconclusive, it cannot be dismissed entirely; given the specific studies that have demonstrated its presence, it should be considered as a plausible root cause of disproportionality.[29]

This interpretive process is highly problematic, considering that the processes of identifying students as having one of the high incidence disabilities are ambiguous and subjective.[30] The combination of cultural biases in the interpretation of student ability and the ambiguous and subject nature of formal classifications may result in racialized ability constructions. Within Carroll and Hannover, the normalization of ability around white , middle-class interactional forms created systems whereby being non-White (oftentimes also viewed as poor) precluded students from being "normal" and thus not as "able" as their White peers. When these perceptions are coupled with lower academic knowledge, such students are thus situated even further away from the norm toward a disability classification. This creates de facto racial segregation in these districts, masked in more palatable (though at times equally troublesome) ability segregation.

Poor Institutional Safeguards for Struggling Students

In the cases of Carroll and Hannover, the interpretations and deficit beliefs of teachers alone did not create the disproportionate outcomes. The special education process itself contributed to those outcomes. The process requires that students pass through several institutional safeguards that support struggling learners before a determination as to whether special education classifications and placements are appropriate. Given that Black students are disproportionately referred to early interventions and assessments for special education compared with White students, and moreover, that a large proportion of students who are referred to special education are eventually classified with a disability, it is important to look at how school policies around early intervention for struggling learners can either mitigate or exacerbate disproportionality. When these intervention programs are developed around or fail to challenge deficit thinking, they can become segregatory.[31]

Carroll and Hannover both created various programs based on these notions, but each was implicitly based on the need to separate out groups of students—particularly students of color—from the general education based on perceptions of these students' abilities, and formalized in the structures developed to support these students. For example, Carroll created a transition program for students entering the district from other schools who appear to be "behind" relative to other students, with the result that students in the transition program tended to be Black students from a local urban school district. The transition program was well-intended: that is, Carroll wanted to help in the acculturation process of Black students by reviewing with them the expected conduct and educational practices of successful students in Carroll. The stumbling block of such programs, however, is their failure to examine the difficulties Black students were experiencing beyond the perception that "the Black students just don't know how to code switch," as one teacher lamented. The transition was focused on getting the Black students to "fit in" to Carroll's system and at times a faster rate, as another teacher explains:

> We are testing every child that comes into our building, and . . . yes, we are seeing what's going on, but just within the last year or two, our building, our administration has finally opened up to the idea that they are coming into us a grade level behind, two grade levels behind, and yes, they are coming from a fourth-grade class . . . just because that is what we are dealing with most of the time. But, they need to be in a third-grade class just to get these basic skills down. [T]hey are attempting with the transitional piece, that is something that not only needs to be done but needs to be perfected because we have actually talked about the fact that we have kids—I had two new children that came into the district this year, that ended up having, they were in my room for about two and a half to three weeks and [Sandy, the head of intervention services for the district] developed a testing [system] . . . there was no special needs, per se, at that point in time. They tested below

grade level, but it was two and a half to three weeks after being in room, getting the school supplies, getting to know the kids, then it was decided between us and the parents and the administration that they needed to go back to third grade. Why did three weeks pass by?! That's what we are attempting to avoid right now. We are saying that we actually need some sort of, two to three days, whatever we need to do, and we don't have it in the works. We have a lot of brainstorming going on right now, but instead of just saying, "Ok, you are coming from a fourth grade, we are going to put you in the fourth grade, we are going to test you in the process, and if you need to go back, we will put you back," we are saying, "We are not putting you in a grade right now, we are going to bring you in, we are going to teach you about the school, teach you about the expectations, teach you about everything that needs to go on around you" and then . . . at the end of those two or three days [students would return to typical class schedule].

In regard to students identified as having learning difficulties, both Carroll and Hanover were plagued with inconsistencies in basic safeguards and structures, such as common referral forms within a district, a range of interventions for struggling learners, misaligned or lack of core reading programs, etc. Such inadequacies in programming tended to be framed as unintentional. In Carroll, a breakdown in support for students with learning difficulties came to light in the spring of 2006. After examining the achievement data regarding all special education students, the Carroll team realized the overwhelming majority of students with disabilities were attaining a level 1 (below proficiency) on the New York State English language arts exams. It was during this analysis that the coordinator of Academic Intervention Services, a program outlined by the NYSED to provide academic services to struggling students, stated, "our training is focused on moving level 2 students into level 3 (proficiency); we haven't been trained to move level 1 students to level 2." Though intentionally focused on supporting the academic growth of students below proficiency at level 2, the school system had been operating in such a way that it did not know how to structure itself to serve the neediest learners. These level 1 students become expendable or beyond the pale of help and, in the case of students in Carroll, ended up classified as disabled. It is relevant to note that such an instructional focus is not uncommon among school districts in the current climate of accountability; districts have recognized the importance of raising the performance of particular subgroups in efforts to demonstrate adequate yearly progress. Figlio and Getzler offer evidence that the use of high-stakes testing, such as state performance exams, increases the likelihood that low-performing students and students from low socioeconomic background will be placed in special education. Moreover, they suggest that these placements are often done by school districts to "game the system"—manipulate student classification to achieve the best possible accountability standing for the school district.[32] This gaming is often in the guise of helping students meet established state and national performance standards but at the same time, perpetuates artificial notions of ability and disability.

Additionally, in both Carroll and Hannover, these failures to support struggling learners were embedded in their instructional support team (IST). ISTs can significantly reduce the overall number of referrals to special education and have been shown to diminish levels of disproportionality in a school district.[33] In Hannover and Carroll, ISTs were present in each school building and served struggling learners, but at the same time were also a pivotal institutional factor in maintaining disproportionality, and the inconsistencies in IST operation and membership within and across these districts also demonstrated the lack of institutional safeguards. In 2005–06, we gathered from each school the list of interventions provided to struggling readers, sample referral forms, types of benchmarks and assessments used to identify struggling learners, and the number of students referred to the IST. The interventions list included some of the following: Read 180, Reading Recovery, move child seat, small group instruction with reading specialist, reading book series, peer-to-peer tutoring, after-school services, graphic organizer, etc. Closer examination showed that these interventions varied in application. For example, in one elementary building in Hannover, struggling readers in grades 2–4 would receive small-group instruction as a pull-out service (students were removed from their classroom to receive interventions and services); yet in another building the same population would receive push-in service (services were provided in their normal classroom). When asked about the differences between the buildings, district levels cited the "comfort level" of the staff in determining which type of service would be offered. Meanwhile the IST referral forms differed from building to building within the district. Of a random sample of eighty-six students with disabilities in Hannover, not one record contained IST referral forms with complete information (e.g., types of interventions provided to students, dosage and length of intervention, types of progress students have made as result). The following are examples of interventions noted by teachers and IST members: "moved child seat to front so they can behave better"; "told parent to read more books at home"; "paired child with a stronger reader." Although such strategies may provide some benefit in conjunction with more prescriptive interventions, they tended to be listed singly, implying that teachers attempted only one intervention with the student. In 2005–06, both districts varied in the number of students being referred to the IST; the rates ranged from 5 percent to 20 percent across similar school levels within a district. And in some buildings, the IST members described being overwhelmed by the sheer number of students. In the aggregate, the inconsistent framework surrounding the interventions, the referral forms, and the differential patterns of students being referred to IST demonstrated how this one element of the special education referral process without the proper safeguards operated as a tipping point in causing disproportionality in these districts.

Additionally, the ISTs in both districts had common patterns of operation that included an unbalanced membership team making up the committee on special education (CSE—the members of the district team and in the list of groups from which qualitative data was gathered), poorly maintained records of interventions and effectiveness of intervention, and a failure to use benchmark or screening tools to identify students in need of interventions. It should be noted that while the flaws and failures of the ISTs in Carroll and Hannover clearly show the capricious nature of special education classifications, they do not appear to be affected by the race or ethnicity of the students involved. An analysis of the rate at which students were referred to special education through the IST process showed no bias with regard to race, indicating that once students entered the special education referral process, they had similar probabilities of being classified. Thus, the failure of the ISTs proved to be a compounding factor in the perception that the racial outcomes of special education classification were legitimate. Overall, then, the academic intervention services and instructional support teams were critical institutional elements perpetuating disproportionality in these districts.

School personnel's beliefs about students create relatively implicit statements about student ability, but at the school level context layer, implicit labels are made explicit as they are "refined by the institutional machinery" through a formal identification, referral, and classification process.[34] This institutional machinery takes the form of early intervention policies and practices, meant to support struggling learners, and CSEs or child study teams (CSTs), whose job it is to evaluate the student to determine what if any disability a student may have and—if the student is determined by the team or committee to have a disability—what services and classroom placements should be provided to the student.

Early interventions have been shown to reduce the number of students who are referred to committees on special education and special education placement; moreover, the instructional consultation (IC) model of early interventions has shown success in reducing disproportionality in schools.[35] The IC model is designed around supporting classroom teachers. It looks at the instruction content and centers on collaborative data-driven problem solving and the reflective relationship between the student and teacher, thus minimizing the need to refer students to early intervention programs. When implemented properly, early interventions not only provide students with additional support to meet their learning needs, but also provide teachers with new and better instructional practices to help meet the needs of struggling learners.[36] Moreover, as Knotek explains, strategies like IC provide teachers a way to look at data on student achievement and their own instructional practices, and to shift their perceptions of students' difficulties from being within-child to being related to instructional practices.[37] This demonstrates the importance of early intervention processes on effecting change in the classroom context.

CONCLUSION: BRINGING TOGETHER DEFICIT THINKING AND SCHOOL STRUCTURES

In examining Carroll and Hannover educators' explanations of disproportionate placements of students of color in special education and the intervention structures in the districts to support struggling learners, the evidence suggests that perceptions of race, class, and culture are superimposed on ideas about ability, and that school structures reinforce or legitimize these perceptions. It is apparent in these instances that the causes of disproportionality are complex and multifaceted; even within a specific context, racial disproportionality results from a confluence of factors, not a single explanation. This is because the concept of ability and the labeling of student's ability are not completely constructed by any one individual within a school; ability, instead, is constructed constitutively within schools at multiple levels and through the confluence of various policies, practices, and beliefs. As Mehan et al. posited, educational handicaps and learning disabilities are culturally constructed within the context of schools:

> Learning disabilities are more like touchdowns and property rights than like chicken pox and asthma. They are defined as real by a complex set of legal and educational practices and governed by school rules and

policies. They are objects that are culturally constructed by the rules of schools, laws, and daily educational practices. Just as the rules of football constitute touchdowns, so too the rules of special education constitute learning disabilities and educational handicaps . . . [W]e do not deny that some students have difficulties in school . . . We are proposing that educational handicaps and learning disabilities are institutional facts and not brute facts; they cannot exist without an institutionally established machinery to recognize and identify them. Once we recognize educational handicaps and learning disabilities as institutional facts, then the absence of an empirical basis for teachers' referrals and the variability in teachers' interpretations of students' behavior is not surprising.[38]

Thus, when teachers refer students to special education, they are engaged in an institutional practice whereby they, operating within the constitutive rules of school, identify behaviors in students that warrant referrals to special education. This identification process is in part subjective, in that it is based on a teacher's individual perspectives, but at the same time is grounded in an objective reality defined by the structures of the school; teachers' cultural deficit thinking around students and parents is cemented by structures (or lack of structures) around early intervention. By looking at the classroom with an attentive eye toward student and teacher interactions, research has demonstrated that teachers' perceptions of their students' behavior, actions, and even looks influence their judgments about their students' ability. These judgments can become the trigger to turn a struggling student into a disabled student. What we do know about the placement of students in special education is that it begins with the practices and beliefs of several individuals who, in informal evaluation of students, construct notions of student ability. In examining teachers' beliefs around the causes of disproportionality within the context of teachers' perceptions of Black and Latino students, it becomes apparent that teachers' perceptions of student ability (and disability) are mediated by racial and cultural factors, specifically by cultural deficit thinking. This does not mean that teachers are either overtly racist (though there may be instances where this is indeed the case); rather, bias may be operative at a less overt, less conscious (and even institutional) level.

The mere fact that the race and class of students are often predictors of the likelihood that they will be referred to special education to remedy a perceived cognitive or behavioral problem suggests that subjective judgments related to the race and class of teachers may be a factor informing perceptions. Moreover, as the cases presented in this chapter show, these constructions of ability cannot simply be defined as misalignments between teachers' (and schools') cultures and those of their students—i.e., the misinterpretation of interactional forms. Rather, the disproportionate representation of Black and Latino students in special education in Hannover and Carroll suggests a convergence of two distinct conceptualizations that occur in school districts—cultural deficit thinking and an unclear or misguided conceptualization of providing academic services for struggling learners. Through their use of cultural deficit thinking, teachers begin to attribute their students' academic troubles to the students' socioeconomic status, family, and culture. In this respect, cultural deficit thinking has the effect of pathologizing academic and behavioral discrepancies of low-income students and students of color relative to White middle-class students, labeling them as disabled.

The use of cultural deficit thinking also highlights teachers' unclear and misguided conceptualizations of disability and their application in providing academic services for struggling learners. This is most evidently viewed through the lens of the Individuals with Disabilities Education Act, which clearly states that children who have learning problems that are the result of "cultural or economic disadvantage" do not have learning disabilities.[39] Yet cultural and socioeconomic reasons are used by school personnel to explain the root causes of disproportionality.[40] Moreover, for teachers working with struggling learners, special education becomes an emergency cord that teachers can pull to get students additional services.[41] Nevertheless, although the confluence of deficit thinking and misuse of special education placements can have a detrimental impact on students, this impact can be ameliorated to some extent by school processes.

School processes such as intervention services and CSEs can either serve to echo teachers' initial judgments about student ability or guard against them. Echoing is often the result of inefficient or relaxed student support services, essentially allowing struggling students to remain struggling until they are eventually classified. Once the district leaders in our two case studies began to take an active role in shaping district programs to address the needs of their struggling learners, they were able to move from the passive echoing to a more active role supporting student growth. To this end, both districts reported intensifying their efforts to provide academic support for their struggling learners, including new program models such as response to intervention (RtI) and ISTs to provide early and effective interventions for struggling learner; trainings to develop educators' professional capacity to raise the achievement of struggling learners; and data monitoring to ensure program fidelity and track student progress.

Ultimately, these programs demonstrate the fuzzy and socially constructed line that separates ability from disability, showing that the position and shape of this line is not fixed, but is determined by school professionals, and therefore can be moved and reshaped to create a genuinely more inclusive education for all students. Nevertheless, while the presence of these programs and procedures did appear at the very least to ameliorate the effects of teachers' beliefs around student ability, they were not able to change their beliefs.

PART II

Equity Issues in Second-Generation Inclusive Education

7

Equity in Inclusive Education in South Africa

Petra Engelbrecht

In 1994, the newly elected democratic government in South Africa introduced a Constitution that not only transformed the governmental system but also the lives of all South Africans. The final adoption of the Constitution of the Republic of South Africa of 1996 included a Bill of Rights that safeguards and entrenches the rights of all South Africans—regardless of race, gender, sexual orientation, disability, religion, culture, or language—to basic education and access to educational institutions.[1]

Government policy has required that the democratic principles enshrined in the Constitution and Bill of Rights undergird every education policy initiative since 1994. Key education policy documents and legislation such as the White Paper on Education and Training, the White Paper on an Integrated National Disability Strategy, and the South African Schools Act stress the principle of education as a basic human right as enshrined in the Constitution.[2] This principle defends the equality, quality, and relevance of schooling and education and implies that all learners have the right to equal access to the widest possible educational opportunities. This acknowledgement of the right to education paved the way for the recognition that both abled and disabled children have these rights.

The synchronicity of the establishment of a democratic society and an equal education system with global changes in politics, society, and culture and local social reconstruction processes has deeply affected education policies, practices, and schools in South Africa.[3] The development of inclusive education can serve as an example. In 2001, White Paper 6, *Special Needs Education, Building an Inclusive Education and Training System*, was published.[4] It acknowledged the failure of the education system to respond to the diverse educational needs of a substantial number of children, and called for the acceptance and understanding of the difference between children with barriers to learning and development rooted in organic/medical causes and children whose barriers are rooted in systemic difficulties, including poverty and underresourced schools. Inclusive education, as defined in White Paper 6, is based on the ideal of freedom and equity as set out in the Constitution. It is seen as a single system of education within the South African context dedicated to ensuring that all individuals are enabled to become competent citizens in a changing and diverse society.[5]

Whether key education policies and the establishment of inclusive school communities—especially with reference to the implementation of inclusive education—have indeed enhanced equity in and quality of education (as the overall goals of education policies) remains questionable, since access, participation, and outcomes continue to be differentiated along a number of demographic, linguistic, and psychological dimensions. This chapter therefore seeks to explore how South African schools are dealing with the challenge of inclusion, with specific reference to the given historical legacies of apartheid, be it race, class, language, or ability.

EQUITY AND EQUALITY IN THE SOUTH AFRICAN CONTEXT

Equality, according to Adler, implies that by being human, people are all equal—equal as persons and equal in their humanity.[6] Formal and substantive equality therefore both emphasize the constitutional and human values of social justice and fundamental human rights and requires that people receive equal treatment in spite of their differences.[7] Formal, or legal, equality can be achieved (and has been achieved in South Africa) through the repeal of discriminating laws and the adoption of formal desegregation policies.[8] Substantive equality demands that people be treated exactly the same, irrespective of individual differences, in situations where their essential likeness as human beings outweighs their merits as individuals. Substantive equality therefore celebrates human dignity by focusing on the attributes that humans invariably share.[9]

Equity, on the other hand, is more difficult to conceptualize and implies more than equality. According to Beckmann, the term is invoked when the removal of formal barriers to equality is not enough to ensure fairness and justice in the light of historical and other contextual factors—in South Africa, those that remain within the social fabric of communities because of years of purposeful discrimination under the apartheid government.[10] Invoking equity shifts the debate from equal treatment to access, respect for diversity, and the capacity to address the complex and multidimensional aspects of inequality and difference in education.[11] Fairness, justice, and other human rights values, as well as the development of skills, are integral parts of the concept of equity and can be seen as a transformative recognition of difference and a principled basis for redistribution.[12] Equity in inclusive education in South Africa is, like equality, framed within a human rights approach and is closely tied to the ability of the education system to foster equity on physical, educational, and social levels. Given this background, the following conception of equity in inclusive education is used in this chapter: *Equity refers not only to access to equal educational opportunities in education, but also to the full participation of all learners in an education system that embraces difference and acknowledges the concepts of rights, within and through education, to participate meaningfully in society.*

EDUCATION IN SOUTH AFRICA: A CULTURAL HISTORICAL ANALYSIS

The government's aim has been to restructure the entire education system from a fragmented system based on segregation and racial inequality to a single nondiscriminatory, democratic system that endeavors to offer equal education opportunities to all students. Since 1994, there have been three broad phases in the policy cycle. The initial intense focus on policy formulation was followed by a period of concerted implementation. Efforts in the current phase concentrate on reformulating or revising policies, as there is general popular consensus that, although the sentiments behind certain policies are admirable, they tend not to be sufficiently focused on the transformation of the actual conditions in school communities.

In this single education system, schooling takes place in primary schools (grades K–7), secondary schools (grades 8–12) or combined schools (grades K–12), Mondays to Fridays from 7 a.m. to 1 p.m. for primary school learners, and 7 a.m. to 2 p.m. for secondary school learners. The student numbers fluctuate between eight and seventy in one classroom, depending on the type of school and the area in which the school is situated; classrooms tend to be more crowded in less-resourced rural schools. The new school year starts in mid-January and ends early in December, with breaks in April (2 weeks), July (3 weeks) and September (1 week); and the school year must have a minimum of 180 school days.

White Paper 6, while it focuses on the development of an inclusive education system, still distinguishes between learners requiring low-intensive, moderate, and high-intensive educational support as well as those with mild, moderate, severe, and multiple disabilities.[13] According to this document, mainstream schools should provide services for students who do not need intensive levels of learning support. At this level, learning support is guided by daily teaching strategies, changes in culture in the school, and development of appropriate attitudes within school communities. Full-service schools, on the other hand, should provide support for students with moderate learning support needs (the first thirty full-service schools in South Africa were established only in 2007). Existing special schools/resource centers provide support for students who need high levels of support; for example, students with specific disabilities, such as deafness or hearing impairment, blindness or visual impairment, physical disabilities, and severe intellectual disabilities. These schools are equipped with technical equipment as well as professional support teams, and therefore also need to develop their role as resource centers for all the schools in their districts.

It is claimed that this structure developed for inclusive education reflects the country's determination to promote equality and prevent any form of discrimination, regardless of its basis, in all spheres of life. In a review of national policies for education in South Africa, a report by the OECD emphasized that the implementation of inclusive education as proposed in White Paper 6 moves beyond mere access to education; it is part of the nation's promotion of diversity, citizenship, and economic and social well-being.[14] Despite these claims, it must be stressed that, as mentioned earlier, the inclusive education approach as formulated in the policy framework still distinguishes and excludes people on the basis of identified needs for support, severity of disability, and barriers to learning and development.[15] While it should be acknowledged that White Paper 6 has gone a long way in the development of a more inclusive education system, key questions remain regarding the construction of special schools/resource centers/full-service schools in a system that claims to be fully inclusive. Furthermore, researchers point out that despite the fact that these policy visions have a role to play in displacing the social engineering of the apartheid government; they are idealistic texts that are not rooted in the realities of schools and are not responsive to complex contextual social conditions.[16] It has become increasingly clear that the education system still bears many profound and enduring remnants of apartheid inequalities; some dominant practices have remained essentially the same and these continue to constrain the rights of groups within and through education.

However, one aspect of implementation that seems to be achieving results is general access to education in South Africa, which is now close to universal for basic education (96.6 percent enrollment for seven- to fifteen-year-olds in the period 2000–2005) (see table 7.1).

TABLE 7.1   Learner and teacher numbers in schools and other educational institutions in South Africa, 2002–2005

Type of schools	Learners	Teachers	Institutions	Teacher-student ratio
Public schools				
Primary	7,588,987	224,439	18,857	33.8
Secondary	3,769,255	120,377	5,668	31.3
Combined	385,018	12,857	674	29.9
Intermediate	159,056	4,997	371	31.8
Total	11,902,316	362,670	25,570	32.8
Independent schools				
Primary	92,337	4,518	403	20.4
Secondary	59,450	3,570	183	16.7
Combined	163,662	11,375	436	14.4
Total	315,449	19,463	1,022	16.2
Total schools	12,217,765	382,133	26,592	32.0
Other				
Adult education	269,140	17,181	2,278	15.7
Special education	87,865	7,394	404	11.9
Further education Colleges	377,584	6,407	50	58.9
Early childhood	246,911	9,000	4,815	27.4
Higher education	737,472	15,315	23	48.2
Total other	1,718,972	55,297	7,570	31.1
Grand total	13,936,737	437, 430	34,162	31.9

Source. Adapted from OECD, *Reviews of national policies for education: South Africa* (Paris: OECD, 2008).

Yet despite the fact that education has undergone fundamental transformation and that indicators show equity with reference to general access, the right to basic education, with specific reference to equal educational opportunities, remains problematic. If we define equal educational opportunities not only in terms of general access and equal educational outcomes for a diverse student population, but also in terms of the quality of education offered in the schools they attend, historical disparities become more apparent.[17] Huge disparities, for example, in basic resources (including proper sanitation or electricity), effectively trained teachers, and adequate leadership still exist between former advantaged and disadvantaged schools, especially those in rural areas. These rural school communities are characterized by poverty in all its manifestations, and this can be singled out as the most salient characteristic of the schools in these areas. In the Eastern Cape, for instance, 40 percent of schools, most of them in the rural areas, are assessed as being in poor condition.[18] Figures indicate that children who live in rural areas are more likely to live far from the nearest primary and secondary schools (19 percent and 33 percent, respectively) compared with, for example, 8 percent and 10 percent of children living in more privileged urban and semi-urban areas.[19] National research conducted in 2007 indicates that only 7 percent of all schools in the country have adequate libraries and 68 percent of all schools have no computers, posing some serious challenges in this digital age.[20]

One report on education in South African rural communities argues that the historical development, contours, and consolidation of political and power relations between urban and rural areas and within rural areas have resulted in neither formal (general access to education) nor substantive (experiences, quality, and outcomes of education) equality.[21] The enabling conditions for the right to education to be translated into formal and substantive equality include those that enhance substantive freedoms through the redistribution of resources. Access to schooling in rural areas is compromised by poverty and school-related financial demands (for example, school fees and uniforms).[22] The direct and indirect (or opportunity) costs incurred by families, especially in rural areas, have a huge impact on education. The direct costs of food, fees, uniforms, and transport have immediate consequences for inhibiting participation in education. Parents are also affected by the opportunity or indirect costs if they withdraw their children from the labor market and send them to school.

Disability is an additional poverty-related issue that influences access to education. Having a disability increases one's chances of living in extreme poverty and having limited access to education, since the majority of people with a disability in South Africa are excluded from the mainstream of society. People with disabilities belong, for the most part, to the lowest income categories, as they are also more likely to be excluded from employment and would have no income without social assistance grants (e.g., disability grants [DGs]). According to the survey on social security recipients' profiles, the median monthly household per capita income of DG recipients in 2005 was ZAR 320 (about US $30) per month, including all income sources.[23] Regarding access to education, the last official national census reveals that people with various forms of disabilities, which include in the South African context vision, hearing, communication, physical, intellectual, and emotional disabilities, had fewer opportunities to access education than their nondisabled peers.[24] For instance, 29.8 percent of people with disabilities had no schooling, 34.6 percent had only primary education, and 29.5 percent secondary education; only 2.9 percent had attended a higher education institution.[25]

Using the World Health Organization benchmarks, White Paper 6 estimates that, in 2001, between 260,000 and 280,000 children with disabilities were out of school.[26] However, these learners' access to education seems to have improved from about 2003 onward. In the early post-1994 period (1995–2003), school attendance for seven- to fifteen-year-old students with disabilities fell by about 24 percent, and for sixteen-to eighteen-year-olds by about 28 percent.[27] Since 2003, however, rates of learners with specific disabilities (e.g., intellectual impairments) enrolled in special education programs rose from 0.52 percent (64,604 of all South African learners) in 2001 to 0.68 percent in 2005, with the greatest increase in the Western Cape Province (from 0.96 percent to 1.5 percent), Gauteng Province (from 1.62 percent to 1.93 percent), and the Free State Province (from 0.40 percent to 0.72 percent).[28] While the attendance rate at preschools and day-care centers rose very slightly, the rate of learners enrolled in regular schools grew from 0.16 percent in 2001 to 0.26 percent in 2005. It is also important to note that although gender disparities have decreased; female students remain disadvantaged compared with their male counterparts. For girls and young women with disabilities, the struggle for access to education is made worse by the fact that they have fewer a priori chances to participate in or complete education and find work. The 2001 census revealed that women with disabilities are more likely to have less formal education (32.1 percent with no formal education) than their nondisabled peers (15.4 percent with no formal education).[29]

It is clear that the government's focus still seems to be on physical access, but improving the quality of educational provision for children with a wide variety of educational needs demands more attention. Implementing inclusive education requires intensive information and capacity-building efforts to help provinces and schools to regard inclusive education as a way of achieving equitable educational opportunities for all learners and on facilitating the acceptance of difference.[30] Research conducted on inclusive education in South Africa to date clearly indicates that the focus has largely been on the pragmatic aspects of access to equal educational opportunities.[31] Against this backdrop, it is important to acknowledge that the government and the wider education system are aware of issues regarding equity of access and equal educational opportunities. Specific strategies are therefore being developed or have already been put in place to make the education system more physically and pedagogically receptive to the inclusion of children with diverse learning needs, including those with disabilities.[32]

EQUITY IN THE IMPLEMENTATION OF INCLUSIVE EDUCATION

Despite the advances noted above, when equity in relation to participation in inclusive education in South Africa is qualitatively examined (in contrast to access to education, for which quantitative indicators are used) in the larger context of cultural histories and practices that affect how our society treats difference when race, class, socioeconomic contexts, language, and ability intersect, progress seems rather dismal. Any definition of equity in education must recognize that education serves a crucial function of binding people together in democratic societies, and this is especially so in the case of South Africa, where society is still struggling to come to terms with its past and present.[33] Although there are various policy documents aimed at altering the apartheid-era status quo by acknowledging human rights, difference, and inclusivity in a diverse society, the *acceptance* of such within communities, including school communities, is critical if there is to be any meaningful participation in inclusive education. Without interrogating how dominant practices have possibly remained as they were (illustrated in the case study below), whether one talks of race, social differences, language, or ability, the ultimate vision of equity in inclusive education (as a strategy that contributes to building a democratic equitable society) cannot be attained as long as the intentionally inequitable system of apartheid continues to contaminate relational dynamics.[34] In the context of rising poverty and growing protests over school fees and other substantial barriers to equity of access and participation to the poor, Spreen and Vally have grasped a fact that seems to elude politicians and education policy analysts: *progress or the lack thereof in schools cannot be divorced from existing realities regarding poverty, school violence, and its consequences.*[35] There is a growing convergence in the literature about the importance of social relational constructs—including students' sense of relatedness, belongingness, caring community, and positive teacher-student relationships—as contributors to success in inclusive school communities. Traditional conservative attitudes, however, still prevent the establishment of communities of practice that define normative ways of belongingness and caring teacher-student and peer relationships in which participants embrace particular identities that signal inclusive membership.[36] Research indicates that negative and conservative attitudes abound even among those who were subject to such discrimination during the apartheid era. Racially entrenched attitudes and discriminatory practices toward "outsiders" and those who are "different" affect the way communities regard "difference."[37] Most people seem unable to grasp that their own attitudes and actions in regard to difference contradict basic human rights and equity in inclusive education, and that they precipitate social exclusion and negative teacher-student as well as peer relationships. Soudien clearly states that that inclusion/integration in education in South Africa is arguably a process of accommodation or assimilation in which the values, traditions, and customs of the dominant group frame the social and cultural context of a school.[38] It must be stressed once again that, despite the definition of various forms of educational needs in White Paper 6 and its implicit suggestion of exclusion regarding support, the implementation of inclusion in educational settings in South Africa implies more than a different understanding of where and how special education should take place and who the target population should be. Inclusive education instead implies a different understanding of the purposes of education and different assumptions about how best to develop communities of caring responsible citizens.[39]

In view of the above arguments, the challenge posed for implementing inclusive education is to develop mainstream schools as environments where dialogue takes place on multiple levels and difference is accepted and dealt with in ways that allow all the members of the school community to experience a sense of belonging and meaningful participation. Howell stressed that a new set of social relations that values differences is an important benchmark for evaluating the effectiveness of the reconstruction of an inclusive education system.[40] The question is whether social relationships in school communities create the opportunities for students, teachers, and parents to experience acceptance, despite differences in language, race, socioeconomic status, and abilities.

A case study that illustrates the ways in which relational dynamics influence meaningful participation in inclusive education will now be discussed briefly. This case study challenges the fundamental, traditionalist notions of dictating the implementation of inclusive education on a pragmatic level, and argues for a shift, as suggested by Sayed, toward a closer consideration of who is doing the excluding and including, who is endorsing the excluding and including, and how these processes of inclusion and exclusion are being facilitated.[41]

CASE STUDY

In a subproject that formed part of a UNESCO-funded project on piloting the Index for Inclusion in three schools, researchers focused on understanding the world of the school through the eyes of students.[42] An initial analysis in the overall research project of the implementation of inclusive education in the school as part of the national policy on inclusive education indicated that teachers' negative attitudes toward difference are a critical barrier to the establishment of a caring and supportive school community.[43] Furthermore, research results of the first two trial phases of the overall project indicated that discrimination, disrespect, and bullying among students were rife in one specific school.[44] In order to further explore possible exclusivity and inclusivity among students in this school, a case study using visual research as methodology was decided on.[45] The school is in a rural area and has certain underutilized assets relative to more affluent schools in the vicinity. It was established in 1912 by a mission church for children with mixed racial backgrounds (so-called "children of color" under the apartheid government). The school has 644 students aged between six and fourteen years. Afrikaans is the language of instruction, as the school is situated in a traditionally Afrikaans-speaking "colored" community. There are also a small number of English and Xhosa speakers in the school, due to the fact that there is no school with English as language of instruction in the vicinity. The current school buildings were erected in 1988. Since 1994, student numbers have dwindled because after all schools in South Africa became racially integrated, parents were no longer forced to send their children to specific neighborhood schools, As a result, more affluent parents who can afford to transport their children to schools now have a wider choice of schools.

A group of nine Afrikaans-speaking students in grade 7 (six girls and three boys) was identified (at the insistence of the principal, they were identified by the teachers) to participate in the case study, after permission was obtained from the educational authorities, the school staff, and their parents. A discussion on social inclusion and exclusion was held, facilitated by the researchers; the group was then randomly divided into two. An experienced researcher (Afrikaans-speaking) accompanied each group, and the students indicated where photos should be taken—of what they saw as the best and worst places in the school, situations where they were comfortable and uncomfortable, and where they felt welcome and unwelcome—in order to illustrate exclusion and inclusion. After the children reviewed the digital photographs, they identified why they wanted the specific pictures taken. They then selected the most important ones and discussed what these pictures meant to them in detail. Photos were coded, and the discussions taped, transcribed, and analyzed using content analysis.[46]

Disabling relationships as key barriers to meaningful participation and social inclusion of peers in inclusive education were identified as the overall theme (see table 7.2). In this instance, social exclusion was conceptualized as a process of nonparticipation in the social, civic, and economic norms that integrate and govern the school society in which an individual resides.[47] Furthermore, positive social peer relationships were defined as providing students with the emotional security necessary to engage fully in learning activities and scaffold the development of key social, behavioral, and self-regulatory competencies needed in the school environment.[48]

Socioeconomic Barriers

As mentioned earlier, the inability to pay school fees or buy school uniforms, together with coping with hunger, mean that the experience of

Table 7.2   Disabling relationships as barrier to meaningful participation and social inclusion

Theme	Categories
Disabling relationships	Socioeconomic barriers (e.g., inability to pay school fees or buy school uniforms and coping with hunger)
	Prejudice and negative attitudes regarding race, class, language, ability/disability

schooling is often associated with exclusion in rural schools.[49] The school meal scheme for children living in poverty, for example, is seen by the government as an important incentive for ensuring school attendance and as an example of inclusion. The National Treasury provides funding to provincial departments of education to improve food-related infrastructure at schools in order to provide balanced meals to students who need it.[50] There is, however, evidence of teasing, bullying, and exclusion of children who needed the food, borne out by the following excerpt: "Some children do not collect the bread even though they are hungry because they do not want to stand out as poor." (Student B)

Visual images of the meal scheme at the school for children from poverty-stricken households also illustrate how learners who do not make use of the scheme ridicule some of the children who do. Children who do not wear a school uniform because their parents cannot afford it are labeled as "poor"—a clear illustration of the impact of poverty on children's meaningful participation in schooling. One student, for instance, stated, "They don't wear the correct school uniform . . . Most poor children do not wear shoes to school." (Student E)

Prejudice and Negative Attitudes

Although South Africans tend to demur at the reductive and essentializing discourses of race, class, and language, we cannot but acknowledge the important part these forces play in everyday life.[51] In relation to socioeconomic barriers, including social division, prejudice as well as negative and harmful attitudes toward difference in South African society clearly remain a critical barrier and influence the establishment of positive student-teacher as well as peer relationships. In the visual images and follow-up discussions with students, discriminatory attitudes resulting from prejudice against peers on the basis of race, language, class, and disability are clearly identifiable. For example, children whose home language and race differ from the majority of the children in the school are subjected to discrimination and bullying—a continuation of the arbitrary ways in which the mark of stereotype was assigned to people under the apartheid government.[52] One student in our research study told us, "They are teased because of their skin color . . . because they are darker." (Student A) And another student said, "Xhosa-speaking children sound funny." (Student C) Regarding attitudes toward disabilities, specific children with learning disabilities are, for example, seen as "not trying because they do not want to" and "are always causing problems in class . . . They do not behave themselves." (Student F)

Thus, our study of how students themselves construct and react to difference suggests that normative notions of difference permeate not only adult judgments but also those of students. It is no wonder that legislating inclusivity is only one step toward developing a society in which difference is accepted and valued for the contribution it makes to expanding understanding and generating knowledge.

CONCLUSION

Exclusionary practices in school communities indicate a lack of acceptance of difference and are thus cause for grave concern, since they militate against the development of an equitable inclusive education system in South Africa. As discussed earlier, the *intended* outcomes of the government that won South Africa's first democratic elections in 1994 were to reverse policies of overt inequality and inequity in education and to reconfigure dominance in relation to race, class, language, and ability in order to establish effective inclusive school communities.[53] The acceptance of White Paper 6 set in motion a movement away from segregation and exclusion toward equity in educational participation.[54] Inclusive education is, however, based on a comprehensive educational policy that aims to transform all spheres of activity in educational systems, and should therefore be active not only in the political sphere but in the transformation of all spheres of education.[55] The findings of various research projects and the case study suggest that policy makers tend to erroneously believe that decisions made to bring about change will automatically result in changed institutional and societal behavior.[56] However, although dominant practices have adjusted to changing conditions and the presumptions on which they have been premised, most of them have essentially remained unchanged, whether one is talking of race, class, language, or ability/disability.[57]

Equity in inclusive school communities is a dynamic process and co-constructed in the everyday interactions between the members of the school community and the building of collective histories. It cannot be achieved merely by policy or facilitated through a physical and pedagogical receptiveness for inclusion or a general change in the attitudes of educators. Furthermore, the importance of dialogue on multiple levels in the development of inclusive school communities capable of accepting difference should be emphasized. This suggests that inclusion and integration in education in South Africa should be a process of accommodation in which particularly previously excluded groups are not subordinated or merely assimilated in the dominant groups within school communities but enabled to fully participate.

It is evident that an understanding of the complexity of the coconstruction of inclusive school communities is a necessity if equity, not only of access but also of full participation, is to be taken seriously. To facilitate equity in inclusive education in South Africa, we therefore need to challenge the tendency to focus primarily on equity of access and equal education opportunities while ignoring the importance of meaningful participation in inclusive school communities. A shift toward the enhancement of equity of participation, with an emphasis on dynamic interactive relational processes in school communities, is urgently needed. The implication is that the understanding and recognition of the political dynamics; the strategic occupation of space-agency by groups, particularly previously excluded groups; and the strategic yielding of space by others are of the utmost importance.[58] This shift will, it is hoped, contribute to the development of relational dynamics that can create more equitable inclusive school communities in South Africa and international scholarship through the penetration of the complexities of our local practices and the discernment of regularities amidst diversity, taking us beyond the stereotypical ways in which difference is understood.[59]

8

Inclusive Education in India
The Struggle for Quality in Consonance with Equity

Nidhi Singal and Roger Jeffery

There was a teacher from Ramgarh, who said that we should enter Karan in school so he will learn counting. We enrolled him in school. But because he was blind, the other children used to trouble him, used to fight with him, so we withdrew him . . . He never completed any class; it was just for a few days. Then the teacher asked us to take him away, saying that he fights and all the children chant, "The blind kid has come, the blind kid has come." (Interview with the mother of a boy with visual impairment, February 2008)

Kanchan: On my own I got myself enrolled in the school. Since I was the eldest in the family [aged about nine at the time], I went with the neighborhood girls who were already enrolled and got my name registered in the school . . .

R: So why did you leave studies after class 5?

Kanchan: It was not in my father's capacity to send me. Also, the higher school was two kilometers away. And poor people are scared of higher-caste people; that is why they did not send me to school. Once when I was heading for school, the son of the head of the village approached me and pulled my plait, threatening me not to go to school. (Interview with a young woman, March 2007)

The clichés that bedevil writing about India—such as that India is the largest democracy in the world and that India proves that democracy is compatible with widespread poverty, illiteracy, and the lack of a genuine national language—have recently been joined by those hailing India's "shining" future, as it emerges as a global economic powerhouse. Many argue that India will soon return to the thriving economic and political position it occupied before British imperialism. For some, sixty years of independence have allowed India to overcome two hundred years of exploitation and neglect. But others see India as an economy that will remain divided and dual, with many attendant dangers. On the one hand, we are presented with images of a vibrant middle class and of sophisticated scientists in great demand worldwide; but they come from a society where many people remain ill-fed, anemic, and vulnerable to major communicable diseases like tuberculosis and malaria.

In schooling, for example, there are some pupils who hardly ever leave an air-conditioned environment, moving seamlessly from home to school and back again without having to engage directly with even the world outside their buses and schools, where English is the only language likely to be heard. Others, by contrast, find what is available is limited to a one- or two-room school, perhaps a half-hour's walk from their home, with no certainty that there will be a teacher ready and willing to teach them when they arrive. Beyond these simplified extremes, which are the paradox of every society—both in developed and developing economies— some people in India belonging to certain groups have been systemically marginalized. In this chapter, we set out some of the bases of those exclusions and their impacts. We pay most attention, perforce (given the available data), to issues of *access*, but where possible we go beyond physical enrollment to consider participation in the curriculum and culture of the classroom. Less information is available about the *quality* of schooling that marginalized children can access and the educational *outcomes* of their schooling experiences, but we refer to this material where possible.

In line with the focus of this volume, we then turn attention to the concept of *inclusive education* and how it is being made sense of in the Indian context. We focus on the developments in educational policies and how these have shaped practices, especially with reference to the education of children with disabilities. We conclude by discussing two dominant themes emerging from these debates, namely the tensions inherent in attempts to address unique needs without perpetuating inequalities, and the narrow conceptualization of educational equity in terms of access and resources rather than equality of participation.

OVERVIEW OF THE INDIAN EDUCATION SYSTEM:
SCOPE, NATURE, AND PURPOSE

As in most countries, in India the official statements about the purpose of education tend to be vague and noble-sounding but inadequate guides to action by themselves. As one commentator summarizes the official positions: "A significant aspect of educational development in India during the post-independence period has been the continuous and sustained efforts to evolve a system of education relevant to the life, needs and aspirations of the people."[1]

Over time, the Indian government developed clearer statements on the aims and purposes of education, laying these out in a series of reports and educational policies. Plans for social development are formulated every five years in agendas ("Five-Year Plans") along with short-term annual plans. These plans are formulated by the Planning Commission, a high-powered central agency constituted in 1950 to prepare a blueprint for the development of the country. This agency assesses the resources of the country and draws up plans for their use. Thus, these plans are the guiding paths for the nation's development and provide information on the government's vision for development over the next five years.

At different times, issues such as education for development, for nation building and national unity, and for overcoming historical and inherited disadvantages and inequalities have been given political salience. Until the 1980s, these efforts often showed considerable continuities between colonial and post-independence educational systems, and political leaders often held an ambiguous relationship to some of the goals they espoused; for example, "an intellectual adherence to egalitarianism co-existing with its denial in the realm of education in practice."[2]

The National Policy of Education (NPE) is often regarded as a seminal document.[3] It stressed removing disparities and equalizing opportunities, and the late 1980s and early 1990s saw a series of public-sector initiatives (most notably *Shiksha Karmi* and *Lok Jumbish* in Rajasthan) and non-governmental ones (e.g., establishing compensatory programs for dropouts to reenter formal schools[4]). The NPE and the associated Program of Action also stressed issues of social justice and, for the first time, brought action with respect to the educational needs of children with disabilities into educational policymaking as an issue of equity.[5]

India has had a long-standing constitutional commitment to universalization of elementary education (UEE). During the constitutional debates in the late 1940s, the significance of education for overcoming historic patterns of exclusion were highlighted, and in the Directive Principles of State Policy, attached to the Constitution of 1950, there was a commitment that "The State shall endeavor to provide, within a period of ten years from the commencement of this Constitution, for free and compulsory education for all children until they complete the age of fourteen years." (article 45). This commitment was "nonjustifiable"—no one could be held to account for failing to deliver on this commitment—and on several occasions the time limit was extended, taking notice of failure to deliver but doing very little about it. In December 2002, owing to pressure from activist groups, elementary education was made a fundamental right through the 86th Constitutional Amendment. The new article 21.a reads: "The State shall provide free and compulsory education to all children of the age of six to fourteen years in such manner as the State may, by law, determine." However, the phrase in "such manner as the State may, by law, determine" has attracted the hostility of activists, as it seemingly gives power to the government to control or dilute the scope of provision. The exclusion of early-years education (children three to five years old) has also been criticized. Additionally, it is still not clear whether the courts (especially the Supreme Court), which have been proactive in many spheres (e.g., labor rights) can achieve in education what political pressure has so far still not managed to do.

India has by far the largest number of school-aged children in the world. The population aged six to ten years was 146.4 million in 2005, whereas the comparable figure for China was only 108.9 million.[6] Unfortunately, nearly 7.5 million primary school–age children (2.8 million boys, 4.7 million girls) were not in school, according to UNESCO 2005 estimates. However this number does not account for those who repeated years or had disrupted schooling attendance: only 63.5 percent of those who started primary schooling completed five years of schooling in 2001–02.[7]

Since 2000, under the *Sarva Shiksha Abhiyan* (Program for Education for All, or SSA), concerted efforts have been made to improve the number, location, and facilities of elementary schools across the country and to monitor progress on each of these indicators. In 2006–07 it was noted that there were1,018,808 schools offering primary schooling (grades 1–5) and a further 175,696 providing upper primary schooling (grades 6–8); some upper primary schools also offered schooling in higher grades.[8] Of the schools offering primary schooling, 83 percent were managed by either local, state, or national levels of government; the remaining were under private management, but about 30 percent of this remainder received some direct government aid.[9]

Typical Indian Classroom

There are considerable variations in terms of a model classroom across the country, so it is unwise to generalize. In Indian terminology, the *primary sector* is grades 1–5, with admission to grade 1 usually around the age of five (admission is often delayed to age six or seven, or accelerated at age four). Since birth registration is not universal, pupils may be given a birth date when they first attend school, often one or two years later than a real birthday. This gives the child more time to pass the final school exams (which have an age restriction) and to take part in competitions for public-sector jobs. Upper primary schooling comprises grades 6–8: these two together constitute elementary education. Not all Indian states (which have constitutional priority in educational matters) follow this pattern; however, the mean number of classrooms in schools can range across states from 2.2 (in Bihar) to 5.7 in Kerala. In Bihar, 63 percent of all primary schools have only one or two classrooms; in Uttar Pradesh, only 23 percent of schools fall into this category, whereas in Kerala, the figure is 1.5 percent. In Bihar, there are ninety-two children per classroom, compared with twenty-six in Kerala (nationally, the figure is forty).

However, this picture can be somewhat misleading, as teachers may be innovative in how they use the space available to them. In winter, especially in rural schools, classes are held in the open or, as the temperatures rise, in the shade of a nearby tree. Furthermore, multigrade teaching is common in many rural schools across the country.

Pattern of Schooling

Nationally, primary and upper primary schools are expected to be open for teaching for 208 days in a year, but the figure varies from around 160 days (in Delhi and Haryana, for example) to over 230 days (in Punjab, Himachal Pradesh, and Chandigarh). The major difference seems to be whether the school week is five or six days. Some schools (e.g., *madrasas* and *gurukuls*) may run according to different, religious calendars and observe different holidays. A standard day may be six hours, from 10 a.m. to 4 p.m., in government schools in north India, for example. But there is considerable variability in the daily routines. Some of this is attributable to seasonal variation: during the heat of April–May, schools may open and close much earlier than in the rest of the year; schooling may also be disrupted by monsoon rains where classrooms are not weather-tight. Also, variations may be common because of teacher absenteeism: a 2003 World Bank study found that 25 percent of government primary school teachers were absent from work, and only 50 percent were actually engaged in the act of teaching when at work.[10]

Teachers

In 2002, there were 3.18 million elementary school teachers in India.[11] National trends indicate that 40 percent of primary school teachers are female, but this varies from 28 percent in Bihar to 70 percent or over in Chandigarh, Delhi, Goa, Kerala, and Tamil Nadu. Teachers in India, as Rao, Cheng, and Narain argue, are typically regarded as transmitters of knowledge rather than facilitators of learning, with emphasis being placed on the completion of a vast and rigid curriculum.[12] Thus teaching tends to be curriculum oriented and examination driven, with high pressure on achievement of good grades.

Educational Exclusion

Despite the early commitment to UEE, India is still struggling to achieve universal school access and completion. Furthermore, in relatively few parts of the country can it be claimed that equity in participation and outcomes across diverse groups has been achieved. A recent UNESCO document provides the following account of the bases of educational disadvantage: "Chronic poverty, social exclusion, and inequalities linked to gender, race and ethnicity, conflict, location, and disability can interact to lock disadvantaged groups into extreme educational disadvantage."[13] All of these dimensions are important in India, but they have received very different priorities in policy development; and the interfaces—where multiple disadvantages overlap—are even more difficult to overcome.

In India, educational exclusion has most often been considered in terms of caste or membership in so-called "tribal" groups. The Constitution recognizes a list of castes (those previously regarded as "untouchable") and tribes in one of its attached schedules (hence the legal terms *Scheduled Castes* [SC] and *Scheduled Tribes* [ST]). SC (16.2 percent of the total population) and ST (8.2 percent of the total population) groups are also known as *Dalits* and *Adivasis*, respectively. SCs can be found throughout the country, often in segregated hamlets away from main villages, whereas STs are concentrated in more remote parts of central India and

the northeast. India has also had an early and highly visible commitment to gender equity.

The NPE's restated commitment to the "removal of disparities," along
with an attempt "to equalize educational opportunity by attending to the
specific needs of those who have been denied equality so far" led to a targeted approach in which different ministries and/or departments have
launched their own schemes and programs.[14] We provide a brief overview of the official approach and current educational status in relation to
those marginalized groups that have been prioritized by the government.

Caste and Ethnicity

Since independence, the government has taken affirmative action and
expanded mandatory reservations to respond to exclusion based on caste.
The Directive Principles of State Policy (enshrined in the Constitution)
note, "The State shall promote with special care the educational and economic interests of the weaker sections of the people and, in particular, of
the Scheduled Castes and the Scheduled Tribes, and shall protect them
from social injustice and all forms of exploitation."

States have increased provisions through reservation of seats for such
students, offering financial schemes and scholarships, building special
hostels (especially for STs, who often live in small dispersed communities), reducing or abolishing school fees, providing grants for books, and
offering remedial coaching and also through recruitment of teachers belonging to these communities.[15] Some success has been noted as the social gap has narrowed. An increase in SC enrollment has been noted at
the primary level from 18.9 percent in 2002 to 21.3 percent in 2006.
Similarly, ST enrollment has also increased—from 10.3 percent in 2002
to 11 percent in 2006.[16] However, success in terms of improved quality of
learning and on the nature of positive educational outcomes for children
from these disadvantaged groups has been limited.[17]

An additional dimension that must be acknowledged here is that
of religion. The Muslim minority in India has low educational indicators, while other sects, notably the Christians, Jains, and Sikhs, have
high educational achievements. Drawing on the National Family Health
Surveys of 1992–1993 and 1998–1999 data sets, Bhalotra and Zamora
calculate that the disadvantages of SC/ST children are still very visible,
especially for lower-caste Hindus, and the rates for Muslim boys are
much the same as those for SC/ST boys.[18] Muslim girls show higher attendance rates, but the differentials from SC/ST girls narrowed over the
six-year period between surveys. In 2004, the government established

the National Monitoring Committee for Minorities Education to address many of these issues, such as modernization of madrasas, but evidence of achievements on this front is not forthcoming.

Girls' Education

Since the mid-1970s, increased attention has been paid to issues of gender. On one hand, the aim has been to make the education system responsive to the needs of girls (through structural and curriculum changes); on the other, efforts are aimed at generating a community demand for girls' education. As table 8.1 shows, considerable progress has been made in enrollment over the years. The gender parity index has improved from 0.91 in 2004–05 to 0.93 in 2006–07 at the primary level (DISE). Additionally, it is suggested that once girls are in the primary school system, they may be more likely to stay the course and complete five years: UNESCO data for 2001–02 suggest that 63.5 percent of girls survive to grade 5, whereas only 59.7 percent of boys do so.[19]

Issues of Location

The differences in Indian education by caste, religion, and gender are overlaid by exclusions on the basis of location, which takes three forms. First, there are differences between rural and urban India, with rural areas significantly more likely to have higher numbers of children out of school. The rural population in 2001 was 72 percent of the total. Second, there are regional variations, with the large north Indian states particularly likely to have poor educational access, quality, and outcomes. For instance, nearly half of all children aged six to eleven who were not in school in 1999–2000, according to the NSS data, were in Uttar Pradesh and Bihar, with a further 11 percent in Madhya Pradesh. There is further

TABLE 8.1   Enrollment and literacy ratios in India by gender, 1990–2007

	1990	2000	2007
Ratio of female to male primary enrollment	.77	.85	.96
Ratio of female to male secondary enrollment	.60	.71	.82
Ratio of female to male enrollments in tertiary education	.56	.54	.66
Ratio of young literate females to males (ages 15–24)	.67	.80	..

Source: www.worldbank.org.in/WBSITE/EXTERNAL/COUNTRIES/SOUTHASIAEXT/INDIAEXTN/0,,menuPK: 295609~pagePK:141132~piPK:141109~theSitePK:295584,00.html.

geographic concentration at the village level. Just 10 percent of villages in India account for nearly 50 percent of all out-of-school children aged six to eleven, while 20 percent of all villages—generally smaller, more distant from access roads and often predominantly SC, ST, or other low-caste populations—account for 75 percent of all out-of-school children.[20]

Quality of Education

While enrollment levels in the Indian education system have greatly improved, concerns abound about the quality of provision. It is widely acknowledged that a substantial majority of students coming out of the education system, whether at the school or the first degree stage (an additional three years of college education after finishing twelve years of schooling), are leaving with little or very low competency levels. For instance, even after ten years of school education, many young people are unable to write a letter correctly or articulate their thoughts clearly. Secondary data from government statistics draw attention to the alarming rate of alienation from school education resulting in high dropout rates. Here children from groups already highlighted are heavily overrepresented. Achar argues that these children are very often not dropping out voluntarily or out of ignorance but are either walking out in conscious protest or simply being pushed out.[21] These children are deeply alienated from the school system, which continues to delegitimize and denigrate local community-based knowledge, reinforces gender and caste stereotypes through curriculum and curricular transactions, and renders local knowledge invisible and unavailable as a pedagogic resource in the school curriculum. It is against this backdrop that we discuss issues of equity in debates around inclusive education in the Indian context.

ADDRESSING THE EDUCATIONAL NEEDS OF THOSE WITH DISABILITIES

While multiple forms of inequality—market inequality (poverty), status inequality (caste), and spatial and sexual disparity—have rendered certain social groups incapable of achieving freedom from illiteracy and innumeracy, in this chapter, we will discuss issues of equity in education in relation to a group of people who have until very recently been systematically marginalized from mainstream participation—those with disabilities.[22] Differing combinations of structural factors (such as caste, gender, religion, poverty, etc.) intersect with disability, resulting in varied individual experiences, but the broad commonalities that shape the lives of people with disabilities in India transcend these divisions. A recent study by the World Bank, for example, noted that children with disabilities are five times more likely to be out of school than SC or ST children, and that if children with disabilities stay in school, they rarely progress beyond the primary level, leading ultimately to lower employment chances and long-term income poverty.[23] Government documents also describe marked variations in the provisions envisaged for different marginalized groups. Historically, SC/STs have had a strong political lobby since independence, and this is reflected in the provisions made for them. Whereas article 46 of the Constitution makes a straightforward commitment to promoting their "special care and education," article 41, referring to children with disabilities, proclaims: "The State shall within the limits of its economic capacity and development make effective provision for securing the right to work, old age, sickness and disablement."

The clause, "within the limits of the State's economic capacity and development," greatly reduces the expectation of urgent action that is seen in article 46 with respect to the SC/ST population. Such caveats have had important implications in the national planning process. Majumdar, analyzing the provisions for various disadvantaged groups across different states, sums up the scenario of children with disabilities: "Apparently, nothing is available other than a few government scholarships, facilities in the form of a couple of institutions for boys and girls and institutes for training teachers for the disabled . . . for the mentally disabled, no conscious developmental scheme is focused on by any of the states."[24]

Even though there are serious concerns regarding the accuracy and reliability of data on people with disabilities, according to the 2001 census, they constitute 2.13 percent of the total population.[25] A similar total (but with different distributions among disability categories) was produced by the National Sample Survey Organisation (NSSO) 58th round survey (conducted in July–December 2002), which also suggests that about 45 percent of people with disabilities are literate (compared with 65percent of the total population).[26] The survey also suggests that 25 percent of the literate population of people with disabilities had received education up to the primary level and 11 percent up to the middle level, while a mere 9 percent continued up to or beyond the secondary level. In other words, only about 4 percent of those identified as disabled had received an education that included more than eight years of schooling.

However, estimates differ greatly with regard to the participation of children with disabilities in the school system. Here figures range from anywhere between less than 1 percent, not more than 4 percent, and 67.5

percent.[27] While these differences could be attributed to different definitions of disabilities, differences in what is considered as "education," (whether enrollment or attendance data are used, and so on), the lack of elaboration in these sources makes it difficult to assess these claims.[28]

Our major reason for focusing on the educational concerns of those with disabilities is to enable a critical examination of "inclusive education" discourses as they are being perpetuated in the Indian context. Even though the term is widely used in academic circles, government texts and popular media, it is rarely defined; rather, it is assumed to be a given. The term has gained much international currency, and hence there is a danger that it may distract people from exploring the realities of practice. In India the concept of *inclusive education* has become synonymous with the education of those with disabilities in almost any form at all, without an exploration of the purpose and the quality of education being delivered.

INCLUSIVE EDUCATION: THE BACKDROP

In attempting to understand how inclusive education is construed in the Indian discourse and how it has shaped policies and practices, it is important to reflect on its genesis. In a paper written for the National Council for Educational Research and Training (NCERT), a national-level educational research and training institute, Jangira made the case for inclusive education in India by reflecting on the changing trends in special education.[29] He noted that the Warnock Report (considering the special education needs in the United Kingdom, published in 1978) had broadened the notion of special education by introducing the concept of special educational needs instead of continued categorization and labeling, and argued that this had further "evolved into a broader and natural concept of inclusive schooling in recent years."[30] Jangira argued that, for developing systems such as India, inclusive schooling is not an alternative but is inevitable. It is interesting to note in this claim the simple and uncritical manner in which a report published in the United Kingdom was transferred into Indian thinking. The very notion of inclusive education as put forth by Jangira has strong foundations in the field of special education and is regarded as having been adopted from the North.

Not surprisingly, this uncritical transfer of educational ideas across contexts is not unique to India. Such efforts have been facilitated by the close connections between educational training and research in India with work conducted in the United Kingdom and United States in particular. In addition, since 1986, India has turned to external funding to help pay for its programs to achieve UEE.[31] Before the economic reforms of the 1990s, foreign aid was accepted only for foreign-exchange and capital-intensive sectors or where foreign expertise was wanted. But more aid resources from abroad flowed to India from the 1990s onward, and these became increasingly directed at elementary education. In 2002–03, external aid was at its maximum level—equivalent to only 1.5 percent of education expenditure and 3 percent of expenditure on elementary education.[32] The main donors have been the World Bank (especially to the largest program, the District Primary Education Program or DPEP, later *Sarva Shiskha Abhiyan* or SSA) the European Union, the UK Department for International Development (DFID), UNICEF, and the Netherlands. International investment is much more significant than its size suggests, because about 95 percent of the budget for primary education is spent on salaries alone, leaving the development budget at less than 5 percent. In the SSA, for example, 30 percent of funding was provided by foreign agencies, the central government provided 45 percent and the state governments 25percent. Thus the otherwise meager external funding, when seen as an addition to the developmental budget, acquires much greater significance.[33] Although the Indian government has in general been very directive in deciding on the terms and direction of the aid to education it is willing to accept, the underlying assumptions of where this aid should be directed is not always clearly evident. Thus Kalyanpur, in her exploration of inclusive practices in India, reflects that there is "a tendency to be 'politically correct' by taking on current trends in the West without a real or common understanding of their meaning, resulting in dilution of service quality."[34]

Thus, examining issues of equity in relation to the education of children with disabilities seems extremely significant in the Indian context. However, undertaking this task is equally challenging, as there is a significant lacuna of writing that draws on empirical data rather than merely relying on anecdotal experiences.[35] The lack of rigorous studies examining issues at the micro, meso and macro levels has been an important failing in the field. This chapter primarily draws on findings from two studies, which the lead author designed and led. The first explored the different meanings of inclusive education at various levels of the Indian education system.[36] It involved a critical engagement with government officials and policies and crucially undertook an in-depth analysis of eleven schools in New Delhi that were commonly perceived as being inclusive schools. Using ethnographic approaches, it captured the experiences and practices of head teachers and teachers working in these schools, while providing rich insights into the assumptions, values, and beliefs shaping the development of inclusive education in an Indian context. The second study, undertaken as part of the Research Consortium on Educational Outcomes and Poverty, focused on examining the social and human development outcomes of education for young people with disabilities living in economically deprived urban and rural communities.[37] Among other things, this study entailed in-depth interviews with young people with disabilities (fifteen to thirty years old) to focus on their educational journeys and experiences and the role of education in their current lives—ranging from employment to marriage to construction of self. Initial findings from this research highlight the nature of young people's schooling experiences and their perceptions of current educational practices.

In deconstructing the discourse around inclusive education in India, we will reflect on some of the key issues that have shaped developments in the field. We begin by identifying the target group and explore the assumptions underpinning the identification of children with special needs. We then examine the nature of educational provisions developed for these children and efforts aimed at increasing their participation.

Inclusive Education and Children with Special Needs: Constructing the Target Group

When referring to issues of inclusive education, Indian documents refer to the education of *children with special needs* (CWSN). This term is not defined; rather, it is seen as being synonymous for children with disabilities. A background paper presented at the Rehabilitation Council of India stated that "every disability gives rise to special educational needs."[38] Thus the assumption that all children with disabilities have some educational need, which must be catered for in an "appropriate" learning environment, is central to the government's focus. While learning in an appropriate environment seems like a laudable goal, there is lack of critical reflection on what this environment might look like, and more significantly, who makes decisions about where a child is appropriately placed.

A report from the Ministry of Human Resource Development (MHRD) provides a list of disabilities that can be integrated in the normal school system—in formal as well as in non-formal schools.[39] These include: children with locomotor handicaps; mildly and moderately hearing impaired; partially sighted children; mentally handicapped educable group

(IQ 50–70); children with multiple handicaps (blind and orthopedic; hearing impaired and orthopedic; educable mentally retarded and orthopedic, visual impaired, and mild hearing impaired.[40] The assumption is that those with other disabilities need to attend special schools.

The naturalness of this grouping of those identified as CWSN is further reinforced by the existence of an "ideology of expertism."[41] In India a high degree of faith is placed in the knowledge of experts and their ability to make decisions regarding a child's abilities and capabilities, and the best place for her/him to study. A handbook published by the Planning Commission states a "three-member assessment team comprising a psychologist, a doctor and a special educator will determine whether the child should be directly enrolled into a 'normal' school."[42] The absence of the voices of teachers, parents, and even the child is noteworthy. Such a belief in the expert who identifies CWSN is further supported by the existing structures of educational delivery and professional training. The assumption here thus holds that within-child factors, such as IQ, result in a student's legitimate exclusion from the mainstream.

Evidence of such thinking is also reflected in practice, where mainstream teachers hold strong opinions about who belongs or does not belong in their classroom. Singal noted that teachers working in so-called "inclusive schools" held clear views about the children who should not be included.[43] In some cases such children were referred to in abstract terms, for example, children who are really weak, those with "little brains and cannot learn at par with others." Others regarded the type and degree of disability as a determining factor, wherein children with severe disabilities are not deemed suitable. Teachers also exhibited a strong belief in the connection between academic ability and IQ levels. Even though they were unclear about what an IQ score really entailed, they placed high faith in its utility. These reflections resonate closely with the rigid and child-centric assumptions about ability that are highlighted in the MHRD list, which draw further support from the existing sociocultural constructions of disability.[44]

In India, understandings of disability are largely dominated by a medical perspective. In macro discourses, disability is regarded as inherent in the individual's mind and body, and a condition that must be diagnosed, cured, or catered for, so that the person can function like "others." This understanding draws further support from prevalent religious norms, where disability is regarded as retribution for past *karmas* (bad actions or deeds) and punishment for sins committed in a previous life. However, it is important to note that the dominance of a medical perspective is reinforced by the fact that a high proportion of disabling conditions are the result of poor nutrition, limited access to vaccination programs, poor hygiene, and bad sanitation, etc. Nonetheless, such medicalized thinking has resulted in a complete neglect of the social dimensions and a failure to respond effectively to the needs of people with disabilities. This resonates at the micro level, where teachers view the "problems" as being situated in the child with disabilities. The natural recourse in such a scenario is then to respond to the child's needs by "fixing" the problem through additional resources aimed at making him or her as normally functioning as others, or to exclude the child to a special (different) setting. Both these approaches are evident in the Indian context.

An important focus of the government's efforts has been on providing children with disabilities who have been certified, with educational aids and appliances, such as hearing aids, visual aids, and orthotic aids. Under DPEP, identification and providing children with these aids was a primary focus.[45] In some of the DPEP reports on inclusive education, the number of aids and appliances distributed in a particular state was the primary concern. At the level of the school, this gets translated into efforts toward inclusion that are solely defined by making buildings physically accessible (e.g., by building ramps). Thus such a limited focus on access has resulted in a neglect of issues of processes, such as pedagogical skills, curriculum, assessment, etc.

Adopting a Dual Approach to Educational Provision

The assumption that there are some children who cannot participate in mainstream education is very strong in the Indian discourse, and a dual approach to meeting the educational needs of children with disabilities has been operative in policy texts since 1944. Both the Sargent Report and the Kothari Commission observed that "many handicapped children find it psychologically disturbing to be placed in an ordinary school, and in such cases they should be sent to special schools."[46] This approach was reaffirmed in section IV of NPE, entitled *Education for Equality*, and more recently in the People with Disabilities (PWD) Act, which states that "it endeavors to promote the integration of students with disabilities in the normal schools" and also promotes the "establishment and availability of special schools across the nation."[47] The government actively supports special schools, but it is not directly involved in establishing or running them. The Ministry of Social Justice and Empowerment (MSJE), provides grants-in-aid to various non-governmental organizations (NGOs) that run these schools. The number of special schools in

India has seen a significant increase from only 118 schools in 1956 to 2,500 in 2000.[48] These are largely concentrated in urban areas, where according to NSSO data, around 11 percent of children with disabilities in the five-to-eighteen age group are enrolled in special schools, while this figure was less than 1 percent in rural areas.[49] Children, who, on being assessed as having a disability, are issued with a *disability certificate*, which allows them to access various government benefits, one of these being free aids and appliances.

This dual approach is internally conflicting and financially draining. On one hand, the Department of Education, which is under the MHRD, is allocating substantial funds through SSA to develop an inclusive system; on the other hand, in 2003, the MSJE, responsible for special schools, increased its budgetary allocations to 2.1 billion rupees, of which 700 million rupees were given to NGOs.[50] Under the SSA, the government has further expanded its multiplicity of provisions by implementing a "multi-option model of educating CWSN," with the objective of providing "appropriate need based skills, be it vocational, functional literacy or simply activities of daily living . . . in the most appropriate learning environment."[51] This has primarily meant the development of "home based education for children with severe–profound disabilities" with the objective of preparing them for schools or for life by imparting to them basic life skills.[52]

This tendency to invariably place the disabled in a separate category is alarming, especially when it is accompanied by a significant narrowing of their perceived purpose of education. For example, advocating inclusive education, Sharma notes: "Education of the handicapped children should be an inseparable part of the general education system so that it can prepare them for adjustment to a socio-cultural environment designed to meet the needs of the normal."[53]

Even though Sharma advocates this as a rights-based argument, the premise here is that children with disabilities must be helped to become as "normal" as they possibly can. The notion of normalization noted here resonates with the common misinterpretation of the principle of normalization put forth by Wolfensberger.[54] Rather, these normalizing policies are often seen in line with Young's notion of the "ideal of assimilation."[55] Here the focus is on elimination of difference, and children are required to fit into existing systems.

Thus the perception that people with disabilities are deficient and hence need to be provided only with the bare minimum assumes that they are not capable of becoming productive citizens. Moreover, there seems to be a complete lack of economic and social perceptiveness about the inequalities that special education can produce. Even though there has been a lack of systematic collection and analysis of data, anecdotal experience from the field suggests that the skills, especially vocational skills, taught in many special school classrooms have little or no relevance outside the classroom—this being the case without even accounting for the human rights argument. Another disturbing trend has been the government's willingness to absolve itself of the responsibility of running special schools and regarding this as a task suitable for NGOs. By allocating this responsibility to the NGO sector, the government has in effect marginalized CWSN further from the mainstream and led to a dilution of services. The government has been unable to establish mechanisms of accountability and monitoring.

Moreover, a majority of these NGOs are perceived as public acts of charity, and their focus tends to be limited to delivering life-skills activities rather than education for better life opportunities. Notably, many of these NGOs are also recipients of food, old clothes, and money from the wider society, gifts that are driven by a cultural expectation of doing one's religious duty toward the needy in the same spirit as one would give alms to beggars. Even though the NGO sector has played an important role in facilitating educational access for children with disabilities, there is a significant lack of research that examines their role, purpose, and the quality of what is provided.

Rigid Professional Boundaries

The rigid dichotomy between special and mainstream education is further reinforced through various policies, institutional programs, and practices that continue to draw professional boundaries between mainstream teachers and teachers for CWSN, those working in mainstream and special schools. Swarup, in her examination of teacher training programs, draws attention to the current paradox where, on one hand, the thrust is on mainstreaming children with disabilities but on the other, teacher preparation is categorized as either general education or special education.[56] The 10th Five-Year Plan encourages the "appointment of special teachers for mildly handicapped children" and provides "special in-service training to teachers in schools for . . . disabled children."[57] A review of the syllabus for preservice teacher training reveals that mainstream teachers are offered "inclusive education" as an optional class, in which the focus in on issues concerning diagnosis and identification of CWSN and on awareness building. This training of teachers for CWSN is also regulated by different departments, and the inadequacy of its quality has come under increased scrutiny.

Using teacher interviews and classroom observations, Singal noted that teachers and special educators held very rigid views about their roles and responsibilities, which shaped their perceptions of the appropriate place for some children to study.[58] Teachers argued that children who cannot cope with the rules and demands of the mainstream, where the focus is primarily on completion of syllabus and good examination results, must be taught in special schools. One of the teachers aptly summed up the existing perceptions toward the mainstream by observing that it is "more like the real world." Driven by pragmatic concerns about existing mainstream pressures, teachers and heads unanimously argued for the continuing role of special schools. Special educators were perceived as having more time and being under no pressure to complete the whole curriculum. The quality of education being imparted in special schools was thus not seen as being of the same level as in mainstream classrooms, where children had to do well in a highly competitive environment in order to succeed later in life. Thus special schools are seen as imparting a kind of watered-down schooling that allows for the special educator to be emotionally responsive to children's needs, a luxury not accorded in "real" schools.

Even when children with disabilities do attend mainstream classrooms, classroom-based research suggests that teachers do not regard them as their primary responsibility. The onus of participation is either laid on the child or others, such as a private tutor at home (especially in the case of families from middle-class urban homes) or the child's parents.[59] Similar experiences of being neglected by teachers in mainstream settings were recounted by young people with disabilities and their parents.[60] During interviews, parents of these young people noted the difficulties they faced in trying to educate a child with disabilities. They recounted incidents when teachers asked them to withdraw their children, because they were not sure how to teach them or because of the negative response of the peer group. Of the few young people in the research sample who had been schooled, many of them spoke favorably of their experiences in the special schools they had attended. For instance, Rajkumar, a visually impaired man who had completed fourteen years of schooling and had experienced both mainstream and special settings, described the difference between his experiences in these schools as follows: "the difference is that in the special school everyone was like us . . . everything was taught according to our levels . . . there was no problem of blackboards and so on . . . there everything used to be explained orally and practically. There were teachers who were in touch with us; they knew Braille also, and whatever we could not be understood through Braille, they used to touch and hold with their hands and explain. But in a normal school, what happens is that the teacher explains on the board."

However, what is remarkable in many of these accounts is that even though these young people tended to support special schools, on being probed further, they highlighted the need for more mainstream engagement and participation. Their support for special schools seemed to be based on their frustration with, and negative experiences in, mainstream settings. For example, Rajkumar felt that early years spent in special schools were beneficial because he was taught daily life skills, whereas mainstream schools were more useful for further studies. But what he felt most strongly about was the usefulness of mainstream settings in terms of opportunities to make friends (especially lifelong ones who lived close by) and the opportunities to carry on with further education and participate in the wider world. Of the thirty young people in our sample, with different years of schooling—who at times were more "schooled" than their siblings—only four were in steady paid employment.

EMERGING THEMES IN ADDRESSING ISSUES OF EQUITY IN INCLUSIVE EDUCATION

In this chapter we have used the term *inclusive education* in line with the government's focus on the education of children with disabilities. However, as noted earlier, children from certain groups, such as those belonging to SC/STs, are also disproportionately marginalized from the system, nonetheless, the term as used in government policies (and majority of the academic debate in India) does not address their needs. While one can argue that such a narrow construction of inclusive education is limiting, there are some commonalities in the way in which the government has responded to the needs of different marginalized groups. A critical examination of these is useful in reflecting on the challenges facing issues of educational equity—here we discuss two main themes, namely addressing unique needs or perpetuating inequalities and the need to move beyond redistribution to reorganization.

Addressing Unique Needs or Perpetuating Inequalities

A dominant trend in the Indian government's approach to addressing educational equality for various marginalized groups has been its tendency to adopt a differentiated approach by drawing rigid boundaries between groups that are not necessarily homogeneous. As highlighted earlier, it has adopted various different schemes and programs targeted specifically as children from SC/STs, the girl child, etc. Moreover, the government has distributed these responsibilities across different ministries and departments. For example, the education of children belonging to SC/ST groups is under the purview of the MSJE, the Department of Education (DoE) (which is under the MHRD), and the Ministry of Tribal Affairs. This approach, as noted earlier, has been extended to the education of children with disabilities, which involves both the MSJE and DoE. The former caters to the education of children with disabilities in special schools, and the latter focuses on those deemed suitable for the mainstream. Such a fragmented approach has been conflicting and unhelpful.

In addition to devolving responsibilities across departments, the government has focused on the needs of marginalized groups by developing alternative systems of education. The argument supporting the development of these systems is based on the premise that they provide flexible educational experiences that are suited for those learners who cannot access the mainstream. For example, the Non-Formal Education (NFE), now known as the Education Guarantee Scheme and Alternative and Innovative Education, introduced in 1978, was established to meet the requirements of children unable to attend formal schooling, primarily from the weaker sections (especially SC/STs). However, the NFE has been accused of diluting learning achievement, while its characteristics of flexibility, localization, and need-specific strategy have often been used as loopholes for avoiding the need to provide good-quality education. Nambissan and Drèze and Sen have criticized it as offering second-track, subquality education.[61] While such an arrangement was expected to be transitory in nature, the government continues to invest in its development. The development of special schools and home-based education for children with disabilities, it can be argued, also falls under this category of building alternative systems with little regard to the effectiveness of such provisions. However, the lack of research that compares the outcomes of education for people with disabilities who have navigated these different education systems—mainstream, special, and home schools—makes it difficult to make any powerful claims. This fragmented approach of responding to perceived unique needs raises an important dilemma. On one hand, highlighting these groups (girls, children belonging to specific castes/tribes, children with disabilities, and so on) as being in need of specific attention may ensure that their needs are being met. However, making them stand apart also exposes them to marginalization from mainstream developments, and there is a danger that they will not be accounted for within the framework of general education. Such a concern highlights the classic dilemma of difference discussed by Minow, where the stigma of difference may be re-created both by ignoring it and by focusing on it.[62] This problem is further complicated by how the very notion of difference is construed. Difference might be seen as celebration of diversity, but is more often construed as undesirable, thus leading to stigma, rejection, or denial. This is even more of a concern in relation to people with disabilities because of their unique historical, sociocultural, and economic marginalization from mainstream. The dominant medicalized understanding of disability further reinforces this difference, hence the institutional convenience of making distinctions between children who can access educational opportunities available to the majority and others who are perceived as being limited by their own restricted (disabled) capabilities and therefore must attend specials chools, with little regard paid to the lifetime of existence on the margins of society that may result. The remarkable inattention to the ways in which dis/ability, caste, class, and other markers of perceived difference interact at the macro, meso, and micro levels obscure deeper analysis of the ways in which inclusive education, as conceptualized within India, serves multiple sorting purposes that limit access to education for a significant portion of the population and, in doing so, may increase access for others.

Need to Move Beyond Redistribution to Reorganization

Another common approach shaping official efforts toward social and educational advancement for various marginalized groups has been the notion of distributive justice. In *Distributive Justice Under Indian Constitution*, Sharma points out that distributive justice has been a defining feature in the framing of the Constitution and government agendas.[63] Such efforts have translated into reservations of seats in educational institutions, government employment, and in legislative bodies, etc., for people from SC/STs. Dealing with the many complexities of such efforts, Sharma argues that these have not yielded the desired results.[64] However, the government has adopted the same approach when responding to the needs of children with disabilities. Efforts aimed at developing inclusive education have been largely framed by the distributive paradigm of social justice. Here the focus has been on providing children with disabilities equality in terms of resources and access. Although the allocation of funds to the disability sector has increased, schemes such as Integrated Education for Disabled Children have focused narrowly on the provision of free aids and appliances, free uniforms, books and stationery, transport, etc.[65] However, working with such a conception of justice is rather limiting and has two basic flaws. The distributive view, as originally proposed by Rawls, has been criticized as adopting an individualistic perspective.[66] Christensen and Dorn argue that working with such individualism implies that disability is inherent in the individual—the deficit that is the target of Rawlsian redistribution.[67] Secondly, adoption of a redistributive view results in attention being focused away from questioning how social structures and institutional contexts uphold patterns of injustice.

While on one hand, such a focus on redistribution of resources and access is desirable and important—because children with disabilities tend to belong to the lower economic strata, and without these special schemes are likely to remain deprived of basic essentials—it is not the whole of justice. Such a focus addresses only first-generation concerns of inclusive education, wherein access does not automatically deliver equality.

Evidence from efforts aimed at the education of girls suggests that while establishing basic conditions for ensuring girl's access to education, such as infrastructure, is essential, there is also a need to focus on transformations in the curriculum and pedagogy. More recent research in this field has begun to challenge the role of schooling in reinforcing gender inequalities of socialization and social control. This focus has been very useful in developing more nuanced debates around issues of quality of provision alongside concerns of addressing gender equity.

These second-generation concerns, focused on curriculum and pedagogy, need to become an integral part of debates on inclusive education in India. Lewis rightly challenges practitioners and policy makers to "remember the 'education' in inclusive education."[68] By working on an assumption that the education being offered to the majority is "OK," and the task is merely to offer it to more students, the official position is restrictive and self-defeating. The focus cannot be simply about building more special schools or shifting children from these to the mainstream; rather, we need to be concerned about what they are being offered in these schools and its relevance to the lives they would like to lead (rather than the kind of lives which we think are appropriate for them).

As noted earlier, the quality of education being offered in Indian schools has time and again come under scrutiny. Flagging teacher morale, pedagogical inadequacies, rigid and irrelevant curriculum, high dropout and repetition rates highlight a pressing need for a critical engagement and reexamination of a general education system that has failed to deliver its promise of greater equality. However, efforts toward addressing these issues cannot be seen in isolation from the sociocultural context of education. Any attempt to develop a truly inclusive system (which extends beyond the narrow conceptions of education of children with disabilities as currently envisaged) ultimately requires a careful consideration of every aspect of schooling and societal context. It entails a need to address issues at macro, micro, personal, and interpersonal levels. In this view, not only does society's conception of difference become important, but critical focus is also brought to bear on the responsibilities of schools, the role of teachers, and indeed the vision of education for a developing society. In this regard, academic debates and educational efforts must address the issue of equity in consonance with quality—an integral dimension in the concept of inclusion.

9

From Equity to Difference
Educational Legal Frames and Inclusive Practices in Argentina

Carlos Skliar and Inés Dussel

In this chapter, we analyze the dimensions in which equity issues are played out in Argentina's education system, and discuss how these deployments affect the foundations, practices, and realities of inclusive education in Argentina. We analyze first what we call the *legal frame*, taking as a reference point the National Law of Education and some city regulations.[1] We then move to the consideration of some quantitative and qualitative data from the UNESCO World Report, *The Right to Education of People with Disabilities*, which offers a portrait of the educational situation of children with disabilities.[2] Third, we bring in additional evidence provided by teachers' statements in focus groups that discussed the images circulating in educational settings about students who are *different*, about diversity and difference, and the value attributed to *living together* in schools.[3] Our main interest is to examine the kinds of perceptions that emerge from inclusive education programs and the experiences that aimed to transform highly unequal educational environments into more equitable settings in the last decade.

SETTING THE FRAME: LEGAL CONSTRUCTIONS AROUND INEQUITIES

The discourses and practices about integration and inclusion are relatively recent in Argentina and have been influenced by technical assistance and academic literature from northern countries, particularly Spain and most recently, the United Kingdom and the United States. By *technical assistance*, we mean the work done by consultants who were hired to produce documents and recommendations for local governments. Also, trips to Spain and other European countries were usual in the 1990s not only for government officers but also for particular groups of teachers, partly encouraged by a good currency exchange rate that made such opportunities accessible.

The 1990s, in addition, were signaled by the application of neoliberal policies. These policies expanded schooling, especially at the secondary level, while producing new exclusions. The reforms had some basic principles that are well known, as they spread as a "contagious discourse": decentralization, accountability, managerialism, professionalization, and national standards.[4] The reforms depicted an old-fashioned system caught between struggles of interests and conservative tendencies. These policies' rhetoric promised to put Argentina in the twenty-first century and in the First World, and imagery of computers, English, and highly dynamic teachers and principals networking collaboratively was offered to portray the "school of the future."[5]

What interests us particularly is the attention to diversity given in these 1990s' reforms, which was read in terms of social deficiency or deprivation. Leaving behind the idea that universal policies needed to be effected, many compensatory programs were developed during that time that received the name *attention to diversity*, understood to be mostly the education of low-income, disabled, and immigrant students. Interestingly, poverty was to be considered a sign of a diverse and pluralistic society, and not the effect of injustice or inequality. In contrast to policies enacted by other countries that targeted specific marginalized groups that had been systematically excluded from the university or school system (e.g., affirmative action or positive discrimination policies), the compensatory programs in Argentina did not challenge the institutional or social conditions that produced exclusion and did not go beyond a prepolitical charity or political clientelism.[6] The ways in which inequalities and diversity were thought of, furthermore, had long-lasting effects that still need to be revised.

In the 1990s, the discourse on inclusive education began to spread among educators. And even though there is a lack of rigorous studies on the influence that pedagogical innovation linked to inclusive education had in Argentina, it can be said that the texts produced by the World Conference on Education for All, the Convention on the Rights of the Child, and the Salamanca Statement provided the language and ideas for designing proposals for inclusive education.[7] The influence of this literature and technical assistance from northern countries are evident in a stream of materials and resources for teacher education and documents and informative meetings that resulted in the insistence on attention to the diversity of student populations, first from an *integrationist perspective* (focusing on various groups defined by particular traits to be integrated) and later from an *inclusivist perspective*, still current, that focuses on the transformations that need to be done in educational settings.

Change has been slow but steady. Government offices, such as the ministries of education at the national (federal) and provincial (state) levels, have begun to adhere to the international education trends to solve inequality problems, guarantee inclusive education, and design strategies for diversity and living together, among others. Consequentially, in 2006, a legal frame was established, organized around two key words: equity and inclusion. In fact, the new National Law of Education enacted in 2006 pronounced that the state, the provinces and the City of Buenos Aires have the principal and indeclinable responsibility to provide an integral, permanent, and quality education for all the inhabitants of the nation, guaranteeing equality, free education and equity in the exercise of this right, with the participation of social organizations and families.[8] It is worth underscoring that the law was the result of a long and heated debate among educational agents such as teachers, members of the parliament and the ministries, families, and unions, which took place all over the country for two years.

If this first formulation names the state as responsible for educational equality and equity, more details are provided throughout the succeeding articles. Article 11, for example, declares that the ends and objectives of education are to assure equal opportunities and possibilities in education, without regional or social imbalances. In this respect, it indicates that equity has to be translated into an equal distribution of resources. Article 48 adds gender equity and cultural diversity as part of the basic tenets for education. It is clear that, in the rhetoric of the new Law of National Education, the notion of equity/inequity is closely linked to that of equality/inequality, and that the state is held responsible for mitigating the historical and cultural effects of inequities.

What has happened to the concept of *inclusion* in the text of this new law? The concept is permanently referenced as the actions, universal and particular, that must taken to solve inequity problems, but the law does not yet clarify either the pedagogical processes involved in the achievement of inclusion nor the essential guidelines for teacher education programs. *Digital inclusion* is also mentioned as part of the new requirements for citizenship in the information society. On the other hand, even though the notion of equity is framed in global and unspecified terms, *inclusion* seems to address particular priority populations, such as disenfranchised groups, unschooled young people, homeless children, freedom-deprived persons, and people with disabilities.

Let us take a closer look to how disabilities are presented in this new law. Article 42 defines special education as

> the modality of the educational system that has to ensure the education rights of persons with disabilities, either temporary or permanent, at all levels and modalities of the educational system. Special Education is ruled by the principle of educational inclusion . . . Special Education provides educational attention to all those problems that cannot be approached through common education.[9]

Article 43 specifies that

> the Provinces and the Autonomous City of Buenos Aires, seeking to articulate both the management and function of its governing organs, will establish the appropriate procedures and resources for an early identification of educational needs derived from disabilities or developmental disorders, with the aim of providing an interdisciplinary attention that will help to achieve their inclusion from preschool education [onward].[10]

The legal frame at the national level is very clear: there is an initial situation of educational inequity, inclusion has to be a resounding and effective answer to this degraded context, and particular attention must be given to the unschooled population and to people with disabilities. A call for interdisciplinary care and the articulation of different systems of schooling is also remarkable. The National Law of Education thus pushes for the inclusion of marginalized groups and particularly for people with disabilities in common schools. Yet it does not alter schools' structure, and offers a solution based on fragmented teams in which participants come from completely different institutions and organizations and hold diverging perspectives and credentials.

In April 2009, the City of Buenos Aires issued new legislation in reference to educational inclusion that sanctions the integration of students with special educational needs in common schools through an interdisciplinary approach. This has to be done "at all levels and in all modalities," as long as it is possible.[11] The decree suggests that educational inclusion is a process that has to be managed through a network of agreements and interventions to the benefit of its addressees, and provides for a Central Cabinet that will make the ultimate decisions.

What conclusions can be drawn in relation to the concept of educational equity and inclusion as they emerge in the legal discourse? Equity emerges as a concept from an educational diagnosis of failure and is associated with a deep transformation of material structures, and with a gravitational pull toward the future—as there is inequity, the horizon must be, perforce, equity. Thus inclusion takes the form of a remedy, the configuration of a transition between inequity and equity.

There is no doubt about the seriousness and enthusiasm that have steered the work done in the last several years to reverse a situation that was historically marked by inequalities and absence of educational justice. What we called the legal frame has been the result of a long process of construction and mobilization accomplished by different agents. A great deal of effort has been devoted to the search for alternative teacher-training models, which are central to the practice of inclusive education in schools. On the other hand, the strong presence of NGOs that promote the right to education of children and of people with disabilities has been very influential, although their reach and impact has not been yet sufficiently studied.[12] We should also note that universities in Argentina have been increasingly interested in studying and developing theories about inclusive education, although these efforts have focused largely on secondary schooling and have been related to the displacement of the subject *special education* to more vaguely defined terms such as *attention to diversity*. The perspectives that have been adopted by special education research (updated, or not, in its epistemology and practices) have derived from some research studies on classroom practices, centered on individual cases, or been based on teachers' narratives about their experiences with inclusion.[13] There have been no studies to date that can generalize findings to address the whole population, or that can present clear guidance for a politics that seeks educational inclusion.

Taken together, the actions of the ministries and the creation of a legal framework, the presence of the NGOs, and the results of academic inquiry have not yet reversed a problematic situation that is still characterized by educational inequality and exclusion from schooling. However, there is an open debate about whether educational practices

are influenced by the legal frame, official policies, and academic research, or by other variables—such as teachers' working conditions, possibilities for collaborative action in schools, pedagogical training that is
sensitive to the transformations of students and knowledge (e.g., the im-
poverishment of the middle class, the transformation of power relations
between adults and young people, the dis- and reorganization of knowledge by new technologies), the conceptions of diversity that are held
in particular cultures, discourses on disabilities and difference in school
contexts, among other factors.

Despite these efforts and debates, inequity still holds sway in Argentinean
education. Educational inclusion, particularly as it relates to secondary
schools and people with disabilities, is still an unresolved matter as the
following sections demonstrates.

THE EDUCATIONAL SITUATION OF PEOPLE WITH DISABILITIES

From the UNESCO World Report on the right to education for children and young people with disabilities, we can conclude that the situation of inclusive education in Argentina is dramatically similar to other
Latin American countries (with the exceptions of Costa Rica and Cuba,
though for different reasons) and to most African countries as well.[14] In
Argentina, there is a scarcity of data concerning children and young people with disabilities in schools. This lacuna is evidence of the remarkable
apathy or even indolence on the part of public authorities about knowing with precision and detail the educational trajectories and needs of
children and young people with disabilities and of their families. Not
knowing what is happening with a particular population in the educational system is already diagnostic evidence about the situation we are
facing in Argentina.

According to statistical information from a 2009 survey, 100,439 students attend special education schools. Of these, 42 percent are women
and 81 percent attend public schools. Of these 100,439 students, over
60,000 attend primary schools, and almost 28,000 of these students go
to pre-K and kindergarten institutions, while only 10,000 students attend special education schools at the secondary level.[15] The education
of young people with disabilities has been a long-standing problem, not
only in their access to education but also in the kind of institutional categories that have been produced to include them.[16] There are, in addition,
workshops for special education students, which reach nearly 23,500 students, and workshops for integral education, which nearly 25,000 stu-

dents attend. The number of teachers—which is difficult to determine, since teachers' contracts are done per hour and not per person—is nearly 17,000. Most teachers graduate from teacher training institutions which offer programs on special education of three or four years.

There are 42,503 students with disabilities who attend regular schools, of whom 23,414 are identified as students with mental retardation and 6,884 are reported to have learning disabilities. Several studies show that there has been an overreporting of mental retardation and learning disabilities, especially in schools that cater to marginalized populations, and that these diagnoses work as a *way out* for teachers and school principals who do not know how to address social and behavioral characteristics of such students.[17]

We can also gain interesting insights about the situation of inclusive education in Argentina from an examination of the answers to the questionnaire used to prepare the World Report, particularly with regard to policy making.[18] We will refer specifically to the dimensions that deal with discussing teacher education reforms, change in the organizational structure of schools, and programs that seek to develop inclusive education and evaluate its achievements. We should state, as a cautionary note, that the questionnaire responses were provided months before the passing of the National Law of Education.

For instance, with regard to the item *availability* for inclusion, the authorities and the NGOs in Argentina reported that

> There is a lack of a national program for inclusive education that promotes educational policies for all levels of schooling. Parents should have a very active role, even with appeals to courts or judicial interventions. In some provinces, there are interdisciplinary itinerant teams, whose efficacy and continuity is dependent on the availability of resources for transportation, which were dramatically cut since the economic emergency of 2001.[19]

There is no information on the percentage of schools attended, the quantity of specialized schools, and the presence of educational alternatives for this population.

The item about *accessibility* was answered in a similar vein:

> Even today, 70 percent of school buildings do not have installations of any kind for people with motor disabilities, and the barriers are higher in secondary schools. The delivery of the certification of disability, which grants free access to public transportation, is very slow. There is a remarkable trend toward segregated education, and there is no research

done on the comparative dropout rate (between children with/without disabilities), and the comparative school success or failure (considering school regimes: special education and common schooling).[20]

The answers related to the item *acceptability* can be synthesized as follows:

The Priority Learning Core sanctions tolerance and respect for difference. There are evaluations on the performance of students in common schools, but not in special education contexts. Teacher education does not include this subject.[21]

Finally, regarding the item *adaptability*, the the response is:

The National Law of Education foresees the participation of parents in the design of educational policy guidelines, and the right of parents to participate in the support organizations of school management. The incorporation of children with disabilities in schools depends, to a great extent, on the local decisions taken by school principals and teachers.[22]

How can we interpret this evidence, considering we do not have a clear picture of the educational needs and conditions that affect these students and that the basis of the existing descriptions is a set of vague legal pronouncements? As one of us has already mentioned in previous work, there is a dissociation between the legal discourse and the ethical responsibility associated with inclusive education.[23] Although there have been changes made by legal regimes with regard to education for all and inclusive education, this legal and formal recognition does not necessarily translate into actual practices that ensure quality education for children and young people with disabilities. The main challenge of the current situation in Argentina, thus, is related to the invisibility of students with disabilities, including those who are being schooled in special settings, those who are in common schools, and most of all, those who are left out of any kind of school.

When legal and ethical languages are turned into irreconcilable poles, or when the legal language is the only way to express a policy of nondiscrimination, acceptance, and recognition of differences, inclusion may be seen as a nondesirable effort, which is either inappropriate or impossible for the common school system. The language of ethics thus cannot be subordinated easily into the legal language. There is first and foremost a universal responsibility toward the other—a *Law*, in capital letters, that applies to everybody, whether he or she is disabled or not.

With this discussion, we do not intend to deny that much progress has been made in the judicial recognition of inclusion and even in the very existence of a legal system that is adapted and just to people with disabilities. However, if we were to consider the four main questions posed by the World Report in Argentina (i.e., Is there an appropriate legal context? Is the financial support for public policies adequate to this context? What percentage of the people with disabilities is included? and, Are there follow-up programs?), we would have to answer as follows:

1. The legal system that guarantees the educational rights of people with disabilities has reached its best in legal terms.

2. There has been relatively adequate financial support, but it is likely that it does not correlate with the content and aims of the legal texts relevant to inclusion. It is clear that budget issues linked to educational policies have to be carefully scrutinized. However, it can be said that in most cases the support has been used almost exclusively to implement partial and insufficient mechanisms for teacher training, and there has been no funding for research or for promoting better life conditions for people with disabilities, or even to improve the working conditions of their teachers.

3. There is a low percentage (1 to 5 percent) of school-age people with disabilities who effectively attend schools, independently of whether they do it in special schools or common schools.

4. There are no follow-up or monitoring programs, at least from the information gathered by the report, that bring support to projects that promote the inclusion of persons with disabilities in the educational system.

In summary, the rights of students with disabilities are legally established. There is some kind of financial support, the percentage of inclusion of this population ranges from 1 percent to 5 percent, and there is no monitoring policy to evaluate not only the presence but, more fundamentally, the existence of students with disabilities in the educational system.[24]

CULTURAL CONSIDERATIONS ON INCLUSIVE EDUCATION: RECONSIDERING TEACHERS' NARRATIVES

To have a deeper understanding of the way in which equality is played out in educational systems that aspire to be inclusive, it is important to consider teachers' practices and beliefs. Between 2007 and 2009, one of us conducted a series of group conversations with thirty-six teachers in the City of Buenos Aires. The teachers work at three different types of institutions: special education schools, recuperating schools, and common schools. (Recuperating schools offer temporary options for children who need a different teaching pace or who suffer from temporary illnesses.) Regarding these institutions in the City of Buenos Aires, there have been important debates about where to educate students who have learning or behavioral problems or have language difficulties (such as recent immigrants). Interestingly, these schools are commonly the only locus of these debates, which are seen as problems of the *others*.[25] The conversations took place every two weeks over a period of two years. They were taped, and the videos of each conversation were brought to the next meeting to aid in continuing the conversation.

The aim of this research strategy has not been to describe with more precision the nature of teachers' discourse or narrative, or their social representations, but to understand the tone in which inclusion is spoken about and how diversity and the notion of living together appear in teachers' discourses. In other words, our concern is with how the notion of difference is alluded to in the conversation, and what is emphasized when what is at stake is feeling and thinking about the meaning of words and when different perspectives, coincidences, and dissent among colleagues arise in the conversation. In these conversations, it is less important to arrive at definitions of inclusion or diversity, and more significant to discuss what takes place in educational experience without stopping to consider whether the latest definitions of these terms are followed.

For promoting and understanding these conversations, we have followed the theoretical framework provided by Larrosa and Morey.[26] Both authors are concerned with the costumes with which people cloak their ideas and words, and seek the evasive affiliations between the *what*, the *who*, and the *how* in the conversation. Larrosa and Morey look deeply at the institutional masks that are used to regulate, administer, and thus destroy conversations, and express their discomfort with the simulacra of conversation that takes place daily in some academic languages. The authors remark that phrases such as "Because I say so" and "So what?" should be forbidden in any conversation if it is to be, in fact, a conversation at all. A true conversation necessitates giving up the idea that a conversation is nothing but a monologue with two selves, which are always in parallel lines and never touch—that is, they never get to be affected by each other.

Some of the initial questions covered in our research conversations included:

- Which paths, trajectories, or stories have led you to think about inclusive education and living with others?
- Which texts, references, and materials have specific relevance to these issues, and have they been available to you?
- How is educational change thought about, and with what words, in relation to reforms, traditions, paradigms, transformation of the self, transformation of others?
- Which decisions and responsibilities are at stake when talking about inclusive education?

These questions changed quickly and different ones emerged: Did inclusion come from the outside, from a disciplinary movement that pressed for its adoption as a novelty? Has educational inclusion and the idea of living with others emerged out of the very experience of cohabitation and proximity in schools? Isn't the current educational environment where encounters and disagreements, conflicts and passions, uncertainties, affection and indolence, care for the other as well as lack of care for the other are produced? Isn't it in this environment where singularity, alterity, difference, diversity and the multiplicity of learning, the need for a relation that is played *among us*, hospitality, and hostility—where something we call *knowledge* and *educational experience*—takes place? Thus, do we *need* to use "inclusion" as a separate and distinct educational practice? Do we *need* the words and the themes of inclusion and living with others? How do we *include* the (notion, idea, experience, definition, presentation, discussion, intention, materiality, policy, politics, practice) of inclusion in education?

What we intend to portray here is the transformations of the teachers' initial questions into something different. These transformations show the deployment of the notion of inclusion into four related themes: (1) the problem of the emergence of the idea of inclusion and *living together/ living with others*, considered as pure exteriority or as an immanent question; (2) the relational dimension of pedagogical processes; (3) the *staging* quality with which teachers look at their own pedagogical experiences; and, most of all,(4) the transformation of an initial question (i.e., What happens with inclusion?) into something altogether different: What happens *to us* with inclusion?

This shift in emphasis is, without any doubt, a change in the position held in the conversation, as it is not concerned with a given category, concept, or axiom; instead, it looks for and wants to know something about our relationship to all these issues. The question compels us to listen to intimacy and interiority, to know how it resonates (if it resonates), which echoes it finds (if it finds any), what it provokes in others (if it provokes anything at all).

In the conversations, these issues emerged as images of inclusion, diversity, and living together that were associated to different ways of conceiving *gates* or *doors*. These images can be also thought of as related to justice, or more precisely, to the law—to the ways in which law opens up or closes possibilities for living together. The image/metaphor of the gate is not new, and it shows something pretty obvious: a closed door implies the inaccessibility or the impossibility (or denial) of entrance; an open door suggests the opening toward those who are not here yet, who are outside our institutions. From the point of view of a particular understanding of ethics, the idea of opening has its relevance: it assumes an opening of the self toward the other, toward what comes from the other, and toward the very existence of the other.[27]

The three images of inclusion that emerged from these conversations are: inclusion as *open doors*; inclusion as *revolving doors*; inclusion as *doors with metal detectors*. They refer to three different experiences of inclusion. The first comes from those institutions that have their gates open, and who do not request or demand anything of the one who arrives (similar to the idea of unconditional hospitality advanced by Derrida).[28] In one of the conversations, a teacher from a common school said, "Besides being a wide door, it should also be open all the time, so that the idea of entry, of getting access, starts being translated into real practice." The second refers to the institutions that exclude some people by virtue of a lack of specific projects for their special needs. In that respect, a teacher from a recuperating school remarked: "They take the inclusion as a starting moment, but then they leave the student to his or her own devices." The third one relates to institutions that, before letting someone in, ask all kinds of questions to have a diagnosis of the recently arrived: Who are you? Which language do you speak? What is your name? How do you learn? What do you have? What do you want from us? Along this line, a special education teacher observed, "The child is considered not as an educational subject, but as subject of evaluation and permanent suspicion."

We mentioned above the idea of hospitality. In our conversations with teachers, the idea of inclusion shifted from a formula loaded with preconditions (generally linked to personal and family traits) to a notion linked to attention, availability, and receptivity—in brief, hospitality. This change in perception is transcendental, not only because it re-fers to individual and institutional ethics that should welcome *any* body, but also because it involves a major responsibility and not simply an ap-parently personal virtue or a legal formula.[29] In this respect, one of the teachers advanced a thought by Maurice Blanchot that phrases the prob-lem in this way: "Responsibility or obligation toward our fellows . . . does not come from the Law, but the Law would come from them in what it makes it irreducible to any form of legality through which it is sought to regularize (this responsibility or obligation), claiming it entirely as an ex-ception or as something extraordinary that is not expressed in any lan-guage yet formulated."[30]

Another topic that emerged from the conversations was the notion of cohabitation, or living together with others, something that has been a hot issue in educational debates in Argentina, due to a perceived increase in discipline problems and school violence, and a feeling of failure at es-tablishing new community orders for schools.[31] In the conversation with teachers, we organized a collective reading of UNESCO's *Learning to Live Together: Have We Failed?*[32]

At first sight, the title talks about a substantial issue. It is associated with a rhetorical question that can be answered only ambiguously be-cause it involves an *us* (*we* have failed) that is difficult to attribute to any particular subject. The central issue, i.e., learning to live together, is a direct reference to the Delors Report, which defines a "necessary uto-pia" for the twenty-first century, based on four pillars: learning to know, learning to do, learning to be, and learning to live together/to live with others.[33] This last pillar "means the development of an understanding of others in a spirit of tolerance, pluralism, respect for difference, and peace. Its main point is the awareness—thanks to activities such as com-mon projects or conflict management—of increasing interdependence (ecologic, economic, social) of persons, communities, and nations, in a world that is increasingly smaller, more fragile, and interconnected."[34]

How do teachers react to this paragraph in particular? For most, the text is well known because it has been tirelessly reproduced in other re-ports and in pretentious academic discourses: it is not about living to-gether, but about learning how to do it. It is true that living together is asserted, but the spotlight focuses on *the others*. It calls for tolerance and respecting differences. The main aspects of the substantial issues surrounding living together, thus, are vaporized in the us/them duality. They vanish precisely because even when it alludes to *others*, it is the *us* who are the only subjects able to name and describe the social world, who are conscious about our own discourse, or who are even capable of a discourse.

The introduction to the report contains yet another title that introduces other rhetorical statements: "Education for all to learn how to live together in the twenty-first century: need, hypocrisy, or utopia?."[35] In our collective reading, teachers' attention is called to the fact that, after the initial questioning that calls for commonsense answers, the rest of the text opens an ambivalent opposition between need, hypocrisy, or utopia. The teachers formulated some questions in the conversations that followed this reading: Has the need to live together failed? Is it no longer necessary that we live together? Has it failed because it is hypocritical to say that it is possible? Has utopia failed because, in the end, it is no more than a utopia? Has the school failed because *all* students will never be included? Or has education failed, because it did not create the need, it did not erase the hypocrisy, and it did not keep the utopia of living together alive? In response to these questions, the group decided to go deeper into the meanings implied in the notions of inclusion and living together.

With the aim of bringing different readings to the conversation that contribute to give other meanings to the idea of *being together*, we offered them texts by Jean-Luc Nancy, Jacques Derrida, and Nuria Pérez de Lara, and asked them to choose passages that were particularly relevant to the conversation. The text selected from Nancy states that, "being in common, or being together, and even more simply or directly, being among various people, is being in the affect: to be affected and effect . . . To be touched and to touch. The 'contact'—proximity, friction, encounter, collision—is the fundamental modality of affect."[36] The Derrida text selected by the teachers asks the following: "Can we teach how to live? Can we teach how to live and to live with? Can we learn how to live? Can it be taught? Can we learn, through discipline or instruction, through experience or experimentation, to accept, or better, to assert life?"[37] Finally, the text chosen by the teachers from Pérez de Lara suggests: "[T]his is or has been for me inclusion: the daily practice of mutual un-recognition of oneself and of the other; the mutual un-recognition between men and women, deaf and hearing, able and disabled, those from here and those from there . . . Can there be another way of including? Can we think of the inclusion of differences in a way that does not involve un-recognition?"[38]

The three quotes together provoked the following teachers' commentaries: "There is neither inclusion nor living together without affection, without affecting and letting oneself to be affected"; "Affection is not only empathy, harmony and lack of conflict, which are the images that are permanently associated with it. Inclusion and living together have to do, above all other things, with friction and conflict." "It is possible to teach how to live together, not in some sort of naïve formula or recipe; what is at stake is to assert the life of others, of any other." "Inclusion has nothing to do with knowing somebody beforehand by using technical or rational devices already established to formulate a diagnosis, but it is related to entering or opening into an educational relationship of mutual un-recognition." Our cultural narratives, then, were deeply transformed by the act of conversation that affected the way we thought of inclusion, the kind of questions that could be posed, and the ethical and political positions of educators.

CONCLUDING REMARKS

Our discussion about the situation of inclusive education in Argentina suggests there are many contradictions between legal documents and real practices. A long journey lies ahead before we can say there is an equitable and inclusive educational system in Argentina. There are many paths to be redirected in teacher training and in the sensitivities and thought of school agents that will probably take years of conversations. There is also an excessive confidence on the legal reasoning and the efficacy of the legal frame that sometimes prevents people from putting more energy into much-needed institutional and pedagogical transformations.

But there is also something else at stake, which one of us has called *differentialism*, that has to be brought to the analysis.[39] We have been alluding to this issue throughout the chapter, and now it is time to define it more precisely as a point that needs to be challenged. There are two questions that recurrently appear in pedagogical debates in Argentina: (1) Does educational inclusion deal with issues of equity, equality, *and* differences? Or does it deal with issues of equity, equality, *or* differences?

It is timely, and politically relevant, to describe and clarify a certain confusion that derives from the use of the term *differences* in relation to a similar term, namely *the different*. *The different* are subjects who are identified as such through a long process of construction and invention of their difference. We called this process *differentialism*—a form of categorization, separation, and reduction of some identity markers in relation to the vast and chaotic set of human differences. Differences, whatever they might be, can never be described as better or worse, superior or inferior, good or bad, normal or abnormal. The fact that some identities or identity markers are considered different is suggestive of the production of a certain type of differentialism. In other words, these markers are considered negative traits and are opposed to a predefined idea of what it means to be normal. Differentialism, besides being a political and historical process, is a cultural and educational trap that causes, for instance, women to be considered as the different in the gender dimension, black people as the different ones in the race dimension, children and older people as the different in terms of age, disabled as the different in terms of body normality, learning normality, etc.

It is worth insisting once again on the idea of difference as a value that can and should be challenged, because very often the term *different* is used as an indication of abnormality. There is another ethical position that we would like to posit: *among the differences, there are no different subjects.* And if we speak of body differences, all bodies form part of it; if we speak of learning differences, all ways of learning are included; if we speak of language differences, all the modes of producing speech and understanding are included. However, there has always been a subtle shift from *difference* to *the different*, as if we were not capable of mentioning difference by itself and needed abnormal subjects, objects of permanent correction.

In many educational settings in Argentina, inclusion has been set forth as the ideal. Yet, in many of these settings inclusion has been steered by a strong obsession with the different. The term *difference*, however, does not refer to intrinsic characteristics of subjects but exists only as a relational term—the relation between subjects. This is a paradigm shift that, from our point of view, has not yet been made—an ethical transformation that shifts our gaze from those pointed out as different to a search into ourselves, into everything pedagogical that happens between us—for example, in our unfinished quest for educational inclusion.

10

Challenges to Inclusive Education in Kenya
Postcolonial Perspectives and Family Narratives

Kagendo Mutua and Beth Blue Swadener

Children and youth with disabilities in Kenya experience limited access and participation in education at higher rates than other children who also bear identities of *alterity*, or otherness, such as children who are homeless, poor, and/or female. In this chapter, we utilize a postcolonial–disability studies perspective to explore how the marginality of children with disabilities that is scripted in social policy and cultural practices impacts their access and participation in education. We examine how inequities in access and participation in inclusive education are located at the intersection of postcolonialism, culture, and disability. To provide a context for our analysis, we begin with a critical discussion of historical and policy contexts of education in Kenya. This is followed by a brief review and critique of traditional explanations for the lack of access and participation in education experienced by children with disabilities. In the reminder of the chapter, we draw from postcolonial/disability studies perspectives to examine issues of equity in inclusive education for children with disabilities in Kenya. Finally, we examine the intersections of culture, *postcoloniality* (as distinct from postcolonialism), and impairments as the im/plausible possible site for reimagining educational equity for children with disabilities in Kenya.[1]

HISTORICAL AND POLICY CONTEXTS OF (INCLUSIVE) EDUCATION

Education policy in Kenya, as in most African nations, took various forms in its early postindependence days, beginning in 1963. By 2006, nearly 33 percent of Kenya's national budget was dedicated to education, which accounts for the largest portion of government expenditure. This is a significant improvement, considering that right after independence the education budget made up only 15 percent of Kenya's government expenditures.[2] Significant progress has been made in providing universal education to Kenyans, with the national enrollment rate in primary education nearly doubling since independence and the enactment of free primary education in 2003.

Kenya is a signatory to numerous international commitments on the provision of education for all, such as the Universal Declaration of Human Rights, adopted in 1948, World Declaration on Education for All (EFA) adopted in 1990, and the Dakar Conference of 2000. Despite these commitments, however, many inequities still exist in regard to access to quality education, retention, completion, and postsecondary outcomes. In the area of special education, inequities are even more pronounced. The attitudes of both policymakers and the general public toward special education continue to be impacted by a colonial legacy that perpetuates the meritocracy and the distribution of access to higher levels of education only to the brightest and the best, as determined by performance in high-stakes national graduation examinations. Within that colonial and postcolonial arrangement, the education of individuals with disabilities continues to be marginalized despite the progress that has been made in other education sectors through the adoption of more culturally relevant policies for all students. The term *all*, however, contains many slippages; it excludes children with disabilities and other identities of alterity, such as homeless and street children, from receiving adequate education in terms of both content and depth.

While Kenya has made commendable progress when compared with many peer nations in Africa by enacting the Children's Act (2001) and the Persons with Disabilities Act (2003), there has been virtually no movement toward articulating a national policy on the education of children with disabilities.[3] Only minor revisions were made to the 1968

Education Act in 1970 and 1980.[4] This still-current legislation does not explicitly guarantee its citizens with disabilities rights to public education and conflicts with a number of other policy initiatives that Kenya has undertaken recently to provide greater access to education for all. These later initiatives, including the 2003 free primary education and the 2008 free secondary education initiatives, as well as the recent passage of the Children's Act, represent steps to greater equity and access for all.[5] Specifically, the Children's Act provides every Kenyan child with a disability the right to be treated with dignity and to be accorded appropriate medical treatment, special care, education, and training free of charge or at a reduced cost. Collectively, these initiatives have strengthened the resolve of full inclusion advocates in Kenya. As a second-generation or emerging inclusive education nation, Kenya has enacted education policies influenced by discourses and initiatives borrowed from Western nations and associated with UNESCO and other international bodies.[6] However, while EFA mandates exist, the infrastructure, including buildings, teachers, texts and learning materials, and funding have lagged far behind national goals.

Four decades after Kenya's independence, there is an education bill that specifically addresses the need for special education. Although this marks a significant milestone toward fully including learners with disabilities, advocates of special education in Kenya have raised the following three main concerns about this legislation: (1) it does not explicitly mention that special education would be provided free of charge, (2) it does not address the need for specialized teacher training, and (3) it does not specifically allocate the finances necessary for implementing its mandates. Advocates fear that without funding allocated to special education programs, familiar practices in education that are anchored in meritocracy will persist and children with disabilities will be the fallout. Critics argue that Western-educated ruling elites who often lead neocolonial educational institutions are themselves so entangled in the status quo that they lack the insight and vision to challenge it, much less change it.[7] Thus, inclusive education remains a desirable ideal but is not adequately supported by current practices. Deeply anchored in themes of meritocracy, competition, and survival of those with the financial ability to privately fund their own education, colonial education persists, evidenced by exclusionary practices within schools that reinscribe citizens with disabilities to an immaterial status.

Citizens of Kenya, including those with disabilities, are guaranteed protection against discrimination in article 82 of the 1969 amendments to the Constitution of Kenya.[8] The definition of nondiscrimination encompasses the right and access to health services, education, and employment. While this constitutional protection has existed for close to half a century, it is only recently that the discourse of appropriate public education for citizens with disabilities has entered the lexicon of education policy in Kenya—even though it has been a well-known fact that 60–75 percent of the world's population of individuals with disabilities live in developing countries like Kenya.[9] This exclusion of a disability discourse is further evidenced in the dearth of empirical studies on disability conducted in Kenya.[10]

Access to appropriate public education continues to be a critical index of equity for persons with disabilities. A decade ago, scholars noted the reliance of many developing countries on external sources to finance educational expenditures and the influence wielded by donor agencies and foreign governments' aid.[11] The value of education in many developing countries has continued to be measured in rates of return and social opportunity costs of capital.[12] In Kenya, studies have shown that, as in many other developing nations, access to education is most typically determined by identifying those who are most likely to produce positive (i.e., quantifiable) outcomes for the family, thereby justifying the investment in their education.[13] In a context of limited resources, families are forced to make the difficult choice of who among their children will likely yield a higher return rate for the family's investment in education. The children who stay home are those perceived as being the least able to benefit from education.[14] Indeed, in Kenya, like in many parts of the developing world, children with disabilities account for one third of all out-of-school children.[15] According to Ngigi and Macharia, the population of people with special education needs in Kenya is estimated at 10 percent of the total population; about 25 percent of these are children of school age.[16] Enrollment in special education is low, given that out of the estimated total population of 750,000 children with special needs who have reached school age, only an estimated 90,000 have been assessed to identify their special needs.[17] Of this number, about 26,885 are enrolled in educational programs.[18] This suggests that over 90 percent of children with special needs (i.e., children with disabilities) are at home. On average, these children go to school when they are eight years old or older. Consequently, they become adults before they complete their educational programs. At the tertiary level, the enrollment of people with disabilities is very low.

Additionally, as in many postcolonial nations, access to education in Kenya is largely based on performance on national tests and by an economic-based competition for access to secondary education (and beyond) and better schools. This competition begins in standard 1 (first grade) and sometimes in preschool, as children are prepared for their standard 1 interview (screening assessment). Furthermore, cultural beliefs, challenging life circumstances, an educational system that is resistant to change, and disparities in service delivery that exist between urban and rural areas pose significant challenges for equity and inclusivity.[19] Together, these factors converge to limit access to inclusive education not only for children and youth with disabilities, but for girls and many individuals from pastoralist communities, refugees, and other marginalized ethnic groups. However, for the purposes of this chapter, we will focus primarily on issues of educational equity for individuals with disabilities.

TRADITIONAL EXPLANATIONS OF LACK OF ACCESS AND PARTICIPATION IN EDUCATION: A BRIEF REVIEW

This section reviews theories that have traditionally been used to explain educational participation and access by children in developing countries. Specifically, Shultz's human capital theory is reviewed and critiqued.[20] Similarly, a review and critique of cultural understandings of disabilities is also provided, specifically examining ways in which disability was culturally scripted and how messages about a person's value, ability, and humanness were embedded both in language and other cultural expressions. A final section explores how these explanations omit critical aspects of access and participation for children with disabilities in Kenya.

Human Capital Theories

Attempts at explaining inequities in access to education in Kenya have tended to focus on the macro and microlevel of analysis. Used extensively in macrolevel of analysis, *development theory*, based on the work of the economist Paul Baran (in particular, his book *The Political Economy of Growth*), argues that the emergence of one region is associated with the underdevelopment of another.[21] In other words, development and underdevelopment are inversely related. On the other hand, *human capital theory* (HCT) has informed most analyses at the micro level. Human capital theorists maintain that variations in educational access result from differences in household- and individual-level factors, including family income, division of labor within the household, and perceptions of the rate of economic return on education. One group of human capital theorists, *microstructural theorists*, focuses on how individuals or households make rational decisions and engage in strategies that optimize wealth.[22]

Macrostructural theorists argue that variation in access to education results from societal-level differences. These theorists maintain that industrialization, urbanization, the state's provision of education, and the structure of the labor force are the critical determinants of access to education.[23] Within classical HCT, human beings are viewed not merely as consumers of goods and services but as capital that can be developed; education is seen not only as a form of direct investment in output, but also a consumer good that enables people to experience higher quality of life. In HCT, education produces quantifiable economic returns. Schultz, for instance, postulated that the value of education can be measured in quantifiable terms—in other words, benefits reaped from education are evident in the individual's economic successes and achievement.[24]

Though flawed in its logic and rejected as a theoretical framework for understanding educational access and participation in western countries, HCT has continued to be used in the analysis of educational participation in many parts of the developing world, including Kenya.[25] HCT falls significantly short in its ability to account for the education of children with disabilities, whose rates of return on education are not self-evident in economic terms and who have been historically marked as uneducable, dreaded, and immaterial.[26] Furthermore, HCT decouples economy from society, denying the role of individuals' agency as well as the impact that society has on individuals' actions. For instance, a family's decision to invest in a child's education is impacted by more than economic rates of return on the investment. HCT, therefore, fails to acknowledge the intricate interconnections between cultural and political factors and the realities of people's daily lives.

In addition, HCT fails to acknowledge the fact that people can be irrational and that not every action they undertake is necessarily geared toward maximizing quantifiable material gains. Even if the basic premise of HCT were correct (i.e., that individuals act rationally and their actions are for the explicit purpose of maximizing wealth), the underlying argument would still be faulty because it fails to recognize that the pursuit of economic self-interest is itself a cultural creation. As such, it is governed by deeply held and quite often unexamined collective beliefs. Therefore, in view of these inadequacies of HCT to fully account for the educational participation of children with disabilities in Kenya, we turn to cultural constructions of disability as reflected in local languages in Kenya to understand how those constructions might play into decisions of access and participation in education by children with disabilities.

Culturalist Explanations

The term *culturalist* implies that culture is static, neatly bounded, and knowable. In this section, we problematize and critique this idea by highlighting the dialectic relationship between culture, space, and time. In order to understand how disability has been constructed and understood from a culturalist standpoint, we examine the repositories of indigenous knowledge forms, including oral texts such as legends, folktales, proverbs, songs, and the indigenous lexicon associated with disability. Elsewhere, we have argued that those repositories of indigenous epistemologies worked to illuminate how disability was culturally constructed.[27] In this section, we focus exclusively on the way disability is constituted in the lexicon of Swahili, Kenya's national language, and how it permeates and mediates everyday meaning-making about dis/ability. Following the lead of other disability activist scholars, we use the referent *disabled people* rather than *people with disabilities* to foreground the politics of disablement that are evidenced in the terminology used to describe disabilities.[28]

The meaning of disability, while seemingly fixed in the lexicon of many Kenyan languages, is not absolute. For instance, the Swahili word *kilema* (an overarching term that means *disabled*) is often applied broadly to several formulations of disability, including handicapped, crippled, disablement, deformity, faulty, or with blemish.[29] Several other terms, also belonging to the *Ki-Vi* noun class in Swahili grammar, are used for specific types of disabilities, including *kipofu* (blind), *kiziwi* (deaf), *kengeza* (cross-eyed), and *chongo* (blind). Words within this noun class begin with *ki* (singular) and *vi* (plural), with a few exceptions that begin with *ch* (in both their singular and plural formulations). Within this class also are words that refer to inanimate objects like *kiatu-viatu* (shoe-shoes), *kikombe-vikombe* (cup-cups), *kiti-viti* (chair-chairs), *kitu-vitu* (thing-things), etc. On the other hand, the *M-Wa* and *M-Mi* noun classes constitute humans, animals, and living things, respectively. In the latter class, are found nouns like *mtu-watu* (person-persons), *mtoto-watoto* (child-children), *mdudu-wadudu* (insect-insects), *mnyama-wanyama* (animal-animals), etc. Living things include nouns like *mti-miti* (tree-trees), *mlima-milima* (mountain-mountains), *mto-mito* (river-rivers). These two classes stand in stark contrast to Ki-Vi class to which the terms for disabilities belong.

The objectification of disability terms is not an exception to the rule. Collectively, these terms contrast the outer boundaries of deviance with what is culturally considered human normalcy. For instance, by placing these terms in the broader Swahili linguistic context, one is struck by how starkly they demarcate the marginalization and indeed, the erasure of disabled persons' humanity. These terms also connote a sense of permanence that suggests that disability is an unalterable, inescapable condition. Additionally, these terms are used in an all-encompassing way that reduces people with disabilities to only their dis/abled condition.

The terms also strategically degenderize people with disabilities and confer a static permanence. For instance, *kilema* is neither male nor female, man nor woman, boy nor girl. Degendering disabled people is not a new phenomenon, as seen in English language terms such as person, people, or individual with disability. Elsewhere, Erevelles and Mutua have argued that this strategic erasure of disabled persons' gender forecloses any discourses that involve changing identities involving gender, maturation, manhood or womanhood, sex, sexuality, and marriage or significant partnerships between adults.[30] *Kilema* is also neither young nor old. *Kilema* is just *kilema*, inscribing the permanence and static nature of the condition.

However, we argue that by focusing exclusively on the terms (i.e., *what* is read), the analysis misses the more critical message carried in their *textuality* (i.e., *how* the term is read and the interpretations that are associated with it or its meaning structures). Cultural inscriptions that mediate the banalities of everyday existence for disabled Kenyans are understood in the textuality of the Swahili lexicon. The cultural messages about everyday relations with persons who bear the disability assignation are seen as ordinary. Thus, prejudices are seen as natural and therefore unquestioned, telling disabled persons whether they can attend school or not, be included, or marry. Simultaneously, those markers enforce normalcy and accord privilege and humanness to *able-bodiedness*.[31]

Another important note about this Swahili disability lexicon is that textually transfixes the *un-humanity* of persons with disabilities with a static permanence as *things*, not humans. What makes this problematic is that "impairments that render someone 'disabled' are almost never absolute or static; they are dynamic, contingent conditions affected by many external factors and usually fluctuating over time."[32] While the indigenous encryptions of disability are negative and devalue the worth and lives of disabled people in Kenya, a complete critique of the position of disabled people must go beyond spatiality—for instance, the national boundaries of Kenya—and take into account temporality, as in global-ized twenty-first-century postcolonial Kenya. The interaction of spatial-temporal dimensions of disability creates dynamic responses to the ways in which disability is constructed and how it is understood (or wishes to be understood).

This push to rethink disability emerged from disability rights ad-vocacy. Recognizing the oppression that is directed toward disabled Kenyans, disability advocacy movements at the local and national lev-els have banded together to create more powerful collective actions (e.g., the National Council for People with Disabilities [NCPWD]). NCPWD has been instrumental in lobbying the government for the welfare and political inclusion of Kenyan citizens with disabilities. Disability advo-cates reject the pathologizing of disability; they reject the cultural view of disabled individuals as nonpersons. In many of the forty-two Kenyan ethnic groups/cultures (particularly those of the Bantu group, of which Swahili is one), the disabled person has always been seen as a nonper-son (as illustrated in the textual analysis presented in the previous sec-tion). Deficiency is viewed as within individuals, not as a byproduct of environment or external conditions that might exacerbate disability by making particular impairments matter. For instance, if individuals with physical disabilities have trouble with ambulation on uneven and un-paved terrains, the problem is viewed as the individual's innate defi-ciency rather than the inaccessible structural environment that many persons with disabilities in Kenya live in and navigate. This viewpoint that locates disability as a deficiency within the individual aligns with the medical model of disability that has been rejected by disability advo-cates who blame their oppression on the synergistic interplay between exclusionary infrastructures that include environmental inaccessibility, lack of policy frameworks, negative cultural attitudes, and other barriers to access and participation.

Emerging Dialectics

The re-encrypting of disability extends to the language of disability. Disability advocates have rejected identities as nonpersons embedded in indigenous lexicons, and embrace the term *wasiojiweza*. Within the past decade, the term, which aligns with international language of disabili-ties, has become increasingly popular in Kenya. This newly transliterated Swahili referent for person with disabilities—*Asiojiweza* (singular)/*wasio-jiweza* (plural)—literally means *the un-abled/disabled*. This word is both a reflection of the influence of global disability advocacy movements and a temporal response to international disability issues. Further, the new terminology has powerfully and effectively relocated the disabled individual into the *M-Wa* noun class that denotes humans in the Swahili and other Bantu languages. *Asiojiweza* is the shortened referent to *mtuasiojiweza* (meaning a *person* who is un-abled/disabled).The adoption of this terminology is a commendable first step toward a more inclusive Kenya. This step, however, does not dismantle established linguistic and semiotic representations of disability that are embedded in all the other terms for disabilities that still flood the daily Swahili lexicon. Kenya must examine and question the postcolonial heritage that still embraces and celebrates meritocracy. An educational stance that advances a one-size-fits-all system ensures that a significant cross-section of its populace is left behind. A more complete and accurate reading of disability in Kenya is one that views the disabled body as bearing etchings of both the cultural (spatial) and postcolonial history (temporal), which jointly coinscribe the worth of an individual along a capitalist axis that connects human value to economic productivity. Today, disability in Kenya is constructed from both traditional-spatial and postcolonial-temporal discourses.

TOWARD A POSTCOLONIAL–DISABILITY STUDIES PERSPECTIVE ON INCLUSIVE EDUCATION IN KENYA

We reimagine access and participation of children with disabilities during this postcolonial/global moment with an acknowledgement that "the global experience of disabled people is too complex to be rendered in one unitary model or set of ideas, considering the range of impairments under the disability umbrella, considering the different ways in which they impact on individuals and groups over their lifetime, considering the intersection of disability and other axes of inequality, and considering the challenge which impairment issues to notions of embodiment."[33]

Indeed, the simple claim to utilizing a disability studies perspective itself is not without complications. Disability studies do not represent a unitary voice. However, disability studies scholars ground their analyses in a social model that defines disability as a social/relational rather than biologically determined phenomenon that is manifested in the active and purposive social exclusions and disadvantaging of people with impairments.[34] Despite their differences in theoretical orientations, the different camps that constitute disability studies are united in their collective challenge to the hegemony of *normativism* and their opposition to a medical model of disability that locates the deficits that cause disability within the individual person. Critics of the social model argue that by focusing exclusively on the social construction of disability, the social modelists produce totalizing meta-narratives of disability that ignore the embodiment of disability. Specifically, some of the criticism stems from the distinctions between impairment and disability, which creates a forced binary. Authors of this criticism advocate the embodiment of disability in order to recognize the reality of impairment effects.[35] *Impairment effects* are the material cartography that demarcates the functional differences between disabled bodies from those bodies that a society constructs as normal. Therefore, those critics argue that impairment effects are the medium along which society responds to disability by enacting social exclusionary and discriminatory practices.

In this chapter, we argue that disability is a social relational rather than a biologically determined phenomenon that acknowledges the centrality of disability embodiment (as described above). Within this position, we can account for the exclusionary practices that oppress children with disabilities in Kenya, such as their limited access to and participation in education. Additionally, a postcolonial perspective broadens our theoretical frameworks to problematize the colonial underpinnings and assumptions that undergird inequities in educational participation and access in Kenya—particularly those inequities that stem from children's embodiment of disability. Indeed, we argue that the more self-evident children's disabilities are, the more impairment effects children's experiences and, therefore, the more excluded those children are likely to be. We revisit this point later when we discuss colonial education. Jointly, these perspectives allow us to explore and to reimagine spaces of inclusion of children with disabilities.

Disabled people in Kenya, particularly disabled children, are located at the sociopolitical and ideological intersection of culture, coloniality, and impairment. By this we mean that the identities of this subpopulation of Kenyans is enmeshed, mired in, and produced by discourses of culture, coloniality, and the functional limitations stemming from one's impairment (i.e., disability). The relationship between these discourses that produce disabled identities is not linear but rather dialectic. Thus, to get a more complete understanding of disability, one must understand how each discourse contributes to the construction of disability without being reductionist in the process. In the previous section, we have attempted to map the cultural construction of disability and therefore answer the question of what disability has meant and who has been considered disabled within specific cultural contexts in Kenya.

Within a culturalist construction of disability, functional deficits are located within the individual. *Coloniality*, the process of imposing political ideologies, invasion, and occupation and exploiting lands inhabited by local populations, uses policies that promote group disharmony among colonized peoples. Writing about postcoloniality, Loomba argues that *postcolonialism* is not a term that signifies the end of colonialism, but rather signifies new forms of contesting colonial domination and its legacies.[36] In this sense, *postcoloniality* is understood as examining the processes of domination between and within nations, races, or cultures and recognizing the historical roots of such practices within colonialism. Applying this logic to disability, we see merit in the arguments of some social modelists within disability studies scholarship who locate the roots of disability in the capitalist social relations of production.[37] Those theorists argue that economics is the ideological superstructure that defines who is constructed as disabled within specific cultures. However, this social modelist thinking downplays the centrality and importance of cultural processes and discourses (such as those described in the Swahili lexicon) that produce, generate, and constitute disability and dis/ableism and reinforces categories of difference.[38] By using imperialist policies to favor one group over others, distributing resources unequally, and systematically denying certain populations their social, political, human, and economic rights, coloniality has exacerbated the oppression of groups of people who were already culturally scripted as marginal, such as disabled people.

This intersection of culture, coloniality, and impairment is visible through the enactment of education policy in Kenya. Colonial government policies remained silent on the education of persons with disabilities. Where education was provided, it was done in separate institutions that provided custodial care, promoting segregation and exclusion. Indeed, colonial education policies did not address the need to invest in education for people with disabilities. Rather, education and other social services for disabled people were seen as acts of kindness that were relegated to charitable and philanthropic acts. Even today in postcolonial Kenya, the majority of existing disability services, including education, are provided by charitable and philanthropic organizations, although there are a number of community-based rehabilitation programs that are provided by the government or receive government subsidies. However, in many instances, the investment made by the government is at best nominal. Like many other public services in postcolonial Kenya that are only partly funded by the government, those publicly supported disability programs require significant cost-sharing—a practice enforced since the 1990s in response to the structural adjustment policies (SAPs) imposed by the World Bank. Through cost-sharing, such government funding mechanisms only function to transfer the burden of footing the cost of running those programs to communities that quite often are already financially strapped.

Writing about similar conditions in India, Erevelles argued that "the additional costs of these services continue to be absorbed by both the paid and the unpaid labor of women."[39] Under these conditions and in such contexts, the idea of inclusion becomes exploitative, in that community-based rehabilitation programs that are ostensibly aimed at assuring that individuals with disabilities utilize and receive services within the locales of their homes only serve to transfer the cost of the services to communities that can ill-afford to pay for them. Kalyanpur argued that such community-based programs that are ostensibly intended to foster and promote inclusion of persons with disabilities into their local communities "mobilize people's resources for government programs."[40] This postcolonial practice illustrates the limits of western intervention where western ideals and practices are imported and implemented without critique to local communities with adverse consequences for those communities. For instance, a western definition of inclusion requires that it is implemented in the same way that it is done in the West without taking into account conditions in local communities. Additionally, it illustrates how colonial practices devalued and erased indigenous inclusive practices that did not necessarily mimic western conceptions of inclusion. In this section, we reimagine several of those spaces where inclusive programming is occurring in Kenya that do not mimic western conceptions of inclusion.

We have examined how macro level factors, including national policies, exclude disabled citizens, particularly in the area of formal education, even when the policies are scripted as a right for all children. In the remainder of this section, we examine how the intersections of coloniality, culture, and impairment mediate a child's experience of inclusion or exclusion at the micro level of the family/community. Drawing on narratives and participant observations of families and community members in selected communities in Kenya, we utilize postcolonial and disability studies lenses to make meaning of how families and community members responded about access and participation in education for their children with disabilities. The data used for our analyses is part of a larger mixed-methods study of social and cultural constructions of disability, including views on access to education and services for children and youth with disabilities in Kenya.[41] We discuss in particular three overarching themes that emerged from the narratives and were related to issues of access and participation in education for children with disabilities in selected communities in Kenya.

Disability as Variable Normalcy

Narratives and observations of family participants chronicled their responses to childhood disability, which ranged from viewing children as deficient to treating them as different but not disabled. In general, children whose families described them as deficient were children who possessed visible markers of disability predicated on physical or sensory appearance or who were unable to assume culturally ascribed roles typical of their specific age group. Disability studies scholars have advocated for disability embodiment, which advances the view that impairment affects the script for social relations that are always negative or oppressive toward the people with disabilities.[42] In Kenya, however, the impairment did not always result in an adverse effect on family relations. For instance, some children with physical disabilities who had visible markers of impairments were not considered disabled if their impairments did not interfere with their ability to carry out age-appropriate chores and tasks such as herding livestock, picking tea, taking care of younger siblings, etc. Acceptance of children with varying degrees of *normalcy* was more apparent in rural contexts, where familial and community relations were more closely bound, than in Nairobi, where there was a diminished sense of community, even among neighbors. Talle drew similar conclusions in a study of rural disabled Maasai children.[43] These dynamic boundaries of disability, which were evident in families' response to their children's disability, negated culturalist understandings of disability as a fixed category. Social modelist Thomson asserts that disability is not a static category, but a dynamic one that changes in response to contingent conditions and is affected by changing spatial and temporal factors.[44]

That the parents of children with disabilities saw spaces for meaningful inclusion of their disabled children in culturally valuable activities opens a space for our reimagining a rescripting of inclusiveness and what that might mean. Viewed through a postcolonial lens, we see children as included in ways that resisted colonial views of disabled persons and their ability to contribute in meaningful ways. Children, despite their disabilities, contributed meaningfully to their communities. The post-colonial perspective allows for the resistance to the colonial impulse to minimize and devalue the inclusive activities of rural communities in Kenya. Indeed, a major achievement of postcoloniality has been its insistence on noticing how imperialism deploys cultural tools of coloniality to discredit and/or dismantle indigenous ways of being that fail to reify the centrality of imperialism.

Parents' narratives showed that they did not base the value they saw in their disabled children on quantifiable economic measures. Rather, the outcomes that seemed the most critical to the families, particularly in rural areas, were the children's abilities to integrate into community life. Because rural parents did not conceptualize their children's worth as predicated on their ability to compete in a westernized educational system, their children were included in age-appropriate culturally normative activities. The contributions those children made to their families and communities' well-being were valued. Likewise, children with mild to moderate forms of intellectual disabilities who were able to contribute to the daily cultural practices of their families were not considered disabled. This familial/community response to disability offers a space for reimagining inclusivity and blurring the disability-normalcy binary.

Top-down legislative approaches to education or international commitments like EFA are colonial interventions that fail to capitalize on conceptions of inclusiveness that are already embedded in the daily practices of rural communities. We argue, therefore, that radical changes can take root from the unlegislated resources already present in indigenous communities. Critics of social modelists reject the binary between body and mind, cultural and economic, biological and social, and so forth.[45] They argue that disability and impairment, like other social phenomena, are braided from cultural ideas and the discursive practices that produce and reconstitute social and embodied constructs of disability. Some disability studies scholars argue that "there is no 'reality' independent of the ideas concerning it."[46] Similarly, inclusivity is a cultural product that has unique and specific configurations depending on its spatial and temporal contexts.

As the narratives of families and community members revealed, a wide variability exists in the construction of normalcy. For instance, terms like *learning disabilities* were foregrounded only among professionals whose life's work was focused within the field of disability. There were no indigenous linguistic designations for specific disabilities because they were produced in the spatial context of school—that is, woven out of western/postcolonial educational ideas. Individuals whose differences were mild were accommodated and included in their communities in ways that their differences did not matter. Such inclusivity supports the disabilities studies' perspective that understands disability as relational rather than a biologically determined phenomenon.

Autism as the Invisible Limits of Physical Appearance

Autism did not appear to be located along the construction of disability as variable normalcy, but rather as a separate phenomenon. It was perhaps the disability that many parents found to be the most perplexing because of a number of factors. First, autism did not bear exterior markers of difference. Children with autism did not look any different from their nondisabled peers. Yet, their functional ability was far different from children with other disabilities. Second, to most parents, there was no cultural or biomedical explanation that provided a sufficiently sound explanation that answered their lingering questions about autism's etiology. Therefore, parents found themselves teetering between biomedical and cultural explanations in understanding autism. For instance, a mother in Nairobi stated, "This child, the doctors told me he is autistic, but I see that his head is not well. I look at him and his cousins. If I sent him to the *kiosk*, he would be lost. He would not know how to count money or if he got the correct change. But, you know, that is autism."

In this interview, it became apparent that the mother's faith in the medical notion of disability was absolute. The mother did not question the finality of the diagnosis because it came from a medical doctor— an authority in medical matters. This unquestioning faith speaks to a broader issue of not only of the medicalization of disability in professional discourse in Kenya but also of the cultural imperialism inherent in postcolonial arrangements that imbue and raise "expert" knowledge above indigenous knowledge. Because disability was scripted within the medical model that located the problem as residing in the child, it led the child's mother to accept the son's disability as natural and inevitable. Her son's autism was seen as something that could not be helped, since the deficits were inside of him and had nothing to do with what was culturally or educationally available to him.

Arguably, there were more spaces in rural communities for children to be included in families' everyday activities. Parents identify disabilities in relation to the functional abilities of children to execute roles and perform chores in the community. For instance, a group of parents in Meru, a rural community, responding to questions concerning the education of children with disabilities, expressed that children with autism were "children with bad heads"and viewed them as uneducable. "Children with bad heads," a transliteration of the Kimeru phrase *aana bathukibiongo*, was a general phrase used to describe children with cognitive disabilities, such as intellectual disabilities. When the referent was applied to children with autism, parents would provide an example of such a child. In this particular community, this group of parents gave the example of Muriungi, a child with autism whom the researcher knew. Muriungi had savant abilities to connect familial relations in the community, e.g., knowing who was married to whom, who their children and their in-laws were, etc. Therefore, in Muriungi's case, the community was very accommodating. Although he was not able to assume socially normative roles or carry out social conversations, the community included and welcomed him to social events in the community, especially weddings. At those events, people would ask him to help them recall names of people and to whom they were related. Muriungi could easily be considered the unofficial community genealogist.

The discussion with this Meru group included the question of whether there were children who are actually too disabled to learn. "Learning" in this case was equated with schooling. Parents linked their perceptions of limited life prospects of their disabled children with their limited access to and participation in school. These families accepted that the colonial and indeed postcolonial narrative could improve their lives. Such meta-narratives devalued indigenous knowledge that could produce a counternarrative of inclusivity and the community value of people with disabilities.[47]

Childhood Disability as Liminal

During a focus interview with a group of parents from Kitui district, several attributed the cause of children's intellectual disabilities to the mother's handling of/practicing witchcraft, or to an evil spell cast on the mother while she was pregnant. Kitui had more participants than other districts who expressed beliefs in witchcraft and supernatural powers. John Mbiti, a prominent expert in African religions and beliefs, explains that magicians, sorcerers, and witches were viewed with great fear, dread, and trepidation.[48] Therefore, when an event occurred that could not be explained from the standpoint of anything that was within the repertoire of the known, the causation of such an event was likely to be explained from the standpoint of the supernatural. Among those Kitui families, some forms of childhood disability could be explained with *known* facts while some disabilities could not. In the latter case, the disability was attributed to supernatural causes. The data from our interviews suggested that placing the cause of certain disabling conditions above mortal ken earned the parents the right to deny their responsibility for the care of the disabled child and thereby justified their relative neglect of the child's needs. Devlieger stated that children constructed as owing their lives to something supernatural occupied the liminal space that lay between good and evil.[49] Among the Kitui families interviewed, their explanations for the cause of the disability included, "evil spells cast upon the child,""divine gift," or a "test of God." These explanations created the disabled/normal binary. Davis argues that, by definition, normalcy relies on the disabled or not normal to achieve its meaning.[50] Thus, to understand people who are disabled, their disability is anatomized through engaging in an obsessive examination of the deficiencies that culturally constitute their lack of normalcy/disability. Following Davis's argument, this sociocultural dissection process of disability allowed community members to conveniently sidestep the issue of how best to care for the disabled persons in their communities. The problem of Davis' argument, however, is its restrictive focus on language and signs of disability. Consequently, other key dimensions of the people with disabilities' experiences, including social relations, exclusions from the banalities of everyday life, and the modes and technologies of production become invisible. On this note, parental engagement with their children's life (e.g., parental engagement with the question of school access and participation) comes to be seen as an engagement with the domain of language and signs rather than as a political act in which parents have agency. Indeed, the representation of disability is critical to understanding how it is reproduced in daily life. We argue, however, that to fully understand why groups that are grounded in communal responsibility for caring for their own (in particular the elderly and the young) neglect children with disabilities, one must go beyond semiotic representations of disability to examine the political capitalist structures that mediate human relations and models of technologies of production in postcolonial Kenya. These parents understood the futility of pursing the redemptive and enlightenment project known as postcolonial education that would only further marginalize their children and rescript their erasure.

In *African Religions and Philosophy*, Mbiti argues that among traditional African peoples, a child who was born with a significant disability was typically not expected to live for very long.[51] So those children who lived beyond what was expected, despite facing life-threatening conditions, were accorded deity-type status. Such were the children that these parents spoke about. Given the severity of the children's disability, parents understood that in its current condition, education would be of little benefit to their children, and they therefore chose not to invest in it. One can easily (and simplistically) argue that those parents were applying HCT thinking in that decision; that is, they saw no possible returns to their investment in the education of those children and therefore they did not send them to school. We think, however, that such a critique oversimplifies the knowledge and insight that parents brought to bear in decisions about the education of their children. Moreover, to assume that HCT steered all parental decisions about their disabled children would mean to deny the role of agency.[52] Parents' agency in such decisions has often been excluded from colonial research. As stated repeatedly in this chapter, postcolonial education bore the etchings and trimmings of its colonial legacy where it was hatched to be a redemptive, enlightenment project intended to *civilize* the natives. Indeed, many of those families spoke of the uselessness of formal education even for their able-bodied children who did not make passing grades in high-stakes exams. They understood that education was not the answer for their children. On this note, one is forced to reevaluate inclusivity: inclusion in postcolonial education for what? Parents did not find it desirable to have their children with disabilities excluded because they recognized that their children would be unable to compete in an inequitable system. Tensions, therefore, are emerging between how families make educational decisions and the ways in which conceptions of education are impacted by postcolonial capitalism and the individualism that it fosters. A context in which resources are deemed exhaustible and competitiveness becomes a precondition for *success* serves to commodify education itself.

While cultural beliefs infuse parents' discussions about the causes of a disability, parents were also quite savvy in deconstructing postcolonial education in terms of its benefits for their children. Some parents saw education as a waste of time for their children not only because it could not undo the witchcraft, but because it often failed to make quality-of-life differences even for many of their ablebodied children. For example, a mother from Kitui made the following observation: "Some children are bewitched and there is nothing that can be done . . . Education cannot help them." When families spoke of education, the referent was formal, westernized schooling, which in postcolonial Kenya is competitive and exclusionary. Students must have both the financial and intellectual resources to compete. Many children with disabilities meet neither precondition, since the education system devalues the resources that children with disabilities bring to schooling. Parents who understand what education values also understand that their children with disabilities have little chance for succeeding.

CONCLUSIONS AND FUTURE DIRECTIONS

In this chapter, we have attempted to place the conceptions of disability in Kenya within broader contexts of education, social policy, politics, and culture. The chapter highlights the limitations of defining disability as merely structural impairments that cause functional limitations in individuals or a medical model that views disability as a biomedical phenomenon. Drawing on a disability studies perspective, we demonstrated ways in which disability is a social-relational condition that scripts dis/ability onto people's bodies. To understand issues of equity related to access and participation in inclusive education, the chapter both theorized disability and provided examples based on narratives and community observations of particular locales in Kenya. Inclusivity happens in some of these rural communities, though this kind of inclusivity does not fit western conceptions of inclusive education.

Community conceptions of disabilities do not always align with western formulations of disability or inclusiveness. Pursuing equity in access and participation in the future may require starting with a sound understanding of ways in which local communities understand and make available inclusive spaces for all, including persons with disabilities. Additionally, it may require abandoning western conceptions of disability in order to learn from local communities' understandings of this concept. Letting the meanings of disability emerge from the community rather than superimposing them on families or communities may yield a more complete understanding of how disability and inclusivity emerge in local dialectics.

For Kenya's continued pursuit of local and national inclusivity, it must answer the question, *Education for what?* While inclusivity is a noble ideal worth pursuing and working to achieve, everyday practices do not yet provide the foundation. Signing on to EFA does not make it so. Using the means that have previously been employed to achieve equity for all in education will not work. Years of failed top-down approaches to social policy are testimonies to its futility. Perhaps it is time to think about ways to harness and support the efforts that are already taking place within local communities to bring about change (e.g., supporting more self-advocacy of disabled persons, organizing and supporting disability advocacy movements that are emerging as a reckonable force in Kenya's policy activism, and supporting family and community activism). To achieve this, however, requires thoughtful consideration in the articulation of policy that is robust enough to imagine what inclusiveness might look like in local communities.

CONCLUSION

Global Norming

Ray McDermott, Brian Edgar, and Beth Scarloss

Statistical laws can be employed in the science and art of politics only so long as the great masses of the population remain (or at least are reputed to remain) essentially passive in relation to the questions which interest historians and politicians.

—Antonio Gramsci, *Prison Notebooks* [1]

The twentieth-century nation-state has had its say on how we must educate, measure, and explain children and schooling. For better and for worse, the twentieth-century state made promises of progress, development, democracy, education, and, for every new generation, enough equality to justify a story about a level playing field for schoolchildren. Almost all countries make these promises and keep track of just how much they have delivered. To take a seat among the great nations of the world, every country has had to make an accounting of itself: of its populations, its economies, its inequalities, and its possibilities. Every state has had to produce data and reports on its markets, its systems of health care and education, and its laws and promises of justice.

All this has seemed quite right. The promises have pointed to a better world, and the data reports have offered guidance for evaluating and planning. Rationality has been the rallying call. States should plan for and develop constructive environments for their citizens, and individual decision makers should pick and choose their way, if not to great personal success, then to a reasonable place somewhere along the way. Rational planning and reasonable outcomes have been the stuff of dreams and of promises.

At the same time, all this has seemed sometimes wrong, not so much in what has been stated, but as has been played out and played upon. For better and for worse, for richer and for poorer, the promises have delivered much more to some than to others, on a scale that has made rational planning look either inept or in the service of only the few. The economic and political context for the promises of progress, development, democracy, education, and level playing fields has been capitalism, and at the heart of capitalism—for so much better, and not a little worse—has been competition for resources across states, ethnic and racial groups, and social classes. Is it possible to build access to equality in education when it is not possible to do so in other institutions? Yes, we can—of course, well, at least a little. Certainly enough that we should try, right? Yes, again—but how? Plans, measures, explanations, and reforms follow rapidly, one upon the other, enough to invite a couple kinds of cynicism and blame: deprived kids, depraved parents, untrained teachers, and selfish unions head the most wanted list, and for every target there is a data bank—now an international data bank—on differential achievement. Global norming leads the way, and because minority, poor, and disabled children fill the bottom percentiles of test data around the world, color and class racism and the reign of TABs (the *temporarily able-bodied*, a term of nonendearment in the disabilities community for the upright thoughtless) are never far below the surface.

The volume in hand brings matters up to date on what has been accomplished. For the past forty years, children all around the world have been tested relentlessly, on the surface for purposes of planning, but always as well for the purposes of political rhetoric around competition across groups both within and across nation-states.[2] There is no shortage of data for measuring one group in relation to some other group, however defined, and the analyses presented in these chapters give an overview of how eight countries (and one city—Chicago) organize schooling for children traditionally excluded from access to success. Together the chapters offer a set of things to worry about, explain, plan for, and overcome. They invite us to examine a half-century of test data for diagnoses of who needs what and why. What do they tell us?

There is good news. Every nation-state's education laws have been informed by guidelines from UNESCO. The benefits seem obvious. The intent is to correct long-standing and historical exclusions based on racial, economic, linguistic, and other differences. Laws and policies attempt to increase access and decrease the amount of segregation. The current measurement of inclusive education shows progress: more kinds of children are gaining access to school systems, and in some countries, Sweden especially, children bearing various labels are doing quite well.

There is bad news as well. Current measurements also show setbacks: more kinds of children, measured and labeled this way and that—by race, native language, citizenship, and physical and cognitive disabilities—are getting gathered near the bottom of many school systems for all to see, theorize about, and diagnose. The papers in this volume ask us to worry more about the hidden politics of inclusion, by which we mean not just how nations create laws and plans for making their education system more inclusive, not just their dreams and wishes, but how the ways we measure and plan for more inclusion—the very means to our end—if not carefully scrutinized, can be used to make things worse. The important chapter 2, on the United States, notes that "although inclusive education was defined as a project for advancing a transformative agenda that focused on examining the processes and legacies that marginalized students because of race, class, gender, religion, language, and ability, inclusive education primarily focused on the construction of difference particularly as it related to within-child deficits." It is rarely good to get caught with a "within-child deficit"—especially if you do not have one. It is everywhere a short road from getting named to getting explained, blamed, and gamed. And so the excellent chapter 3, on England, reveals that those interested in enhancing inclusive education have had to engage in "a continuing interrogation of established understandings of and responses to learner differences to uncover the ways in which they devalue or otherwise discriminate against particular groups." Difficult situations seem able to outrun good intentions.

It is not unusual for solutions to social problems, or even proposed solutions, to make things worse: military invasions, jails, and mental institutions come to mind; hospitals and surgeons should not yet be off our list (Florence Nightingale said that); and we should not forget learning disabilities and psychotropic medicines for children as a way to hide the problems of schooling. Once identified, social problems tend to grow to fill any social space available, once institutions are built to house them (complete with administrators, budget, and experts), and once people become invested in having them, they can expand to the shape of a cultural assumption and expectation—an always already there.[3] This is not the whole story, of course, but even if only a small part of the story, we must attend to whether and how our own desires for our children might be tied to doing damage, if not to our children directly, then, perhaps worst of all, to other people's children. For every step forward, there is a corresponding step back.

In this commentary, we engage the chapters by identifying two major dilemmas facing studies of and policies for inclusive education: first, the dangers of labeling and, second, the difficulties of moving from labels, even appropriate labels, to building institutions that can make proper use of them. With two warnings in tow, we can then celebrate suggestions in this volume for how we might rethink inclusive education without further constraining the lives of children in school. In particular, we appreciate the attempts in these papers to root people and their problems in historically constructed and geographically maintained circumstances.

THE DANGERS OF A LABEL

The first problem is that most labels for kinds of people are messy. The labels we produce to talk about each other are more about what we have to get done with (and done to) each other than they are about actually describing each other. Data-collection agents of the modern state prefer simple categories: easy to codify, measure, interpret, summarize, and report. That's what they have to get done. These simplifications make the process of categorizing students quick and efficient. Test results make an easy target for further plans, whether appropriate or not, and they are perfect for reporting to the media. Politicians can push them any way they like, to make just about any case that needs to be made. Bad science makes great political fodder.

The point is that every "thing" in the social world is on the move. Every category is subject to the interpretations of people in interaction with other people, and in this way the world is filled with "things" that are hard to make still and unchanging.[4] Without repression or violence, one's status, family, sex, race, intelligence, even desires, all seem to shift about by situation, circumstance, design, mood, and the alignments of the moment among loved ones or passers-by. Let's consider just a few wobbly words that accompany global norming. *Race* seems easy to describe, and so it in a racist society, but the term leaks so much that biologists have given up on it as a category for the description of populations. *Ethnicity* is so difficult to discern and/or easy to fabricate that it can be put on sale and moved about to fit the demands of international markets.[5] *Social class* is slippery enough that one group can argue that it is central to everything and another group that it is trivial in the organization of people's lives, and this can be done with both groups working from the same data. *Learning disabilities* are notoriously difficult to diagnose and can mean something quite different depending on the tests used or the purposes for which the diagnosis is sought.[6] For the tests used, consider only Hill and Larson's powerful analysis of how linguistically misleading the questions on reading tests can be.[7] For divergent purposes, consider only the differences between newly immigrant children getting locked out of classes because of their learning disabilities and upper-middle-class children using the seemingly same diagnosis to get more time on tests and to do better in school as a result. Leaky categories make some lives easier and some lives harder; they offer a certain mayhem that can be politically manipulated.

On the plus side, the pressure for more inclusive education has brought about a gradual shift in the kinds of labels that can be used to describe children. Even mayhem can be given direction, and most countries can now report that they are trying to offer access to everyone and that they consistently use an increasingly more polite, or less degrading, language for describing the problems of children who have been traditionally locked out of their educational system. If the early-twentieth-century problem child was called a *feeble-minded idiot, imbecile,* or *lazy dullard,* by midcentury, the same child might have been called *intellectually disabled, educably retarded, culturally deprived,* or, at the start of what would become the most productive/predictive category of all, *learning disabled.* Today, the same child, and now in many nations, might be given a more neutral sounding medical label like *attention deficit disorder, bipolar disorder, Asperger's syndrome,* or *autism.*[8]

Progress in the direction of politeness does not solve the problems of degradation, and may in fact make things worse. While the same account could come from any other country, chapter 8, on India, expresses it directly: "Such medicalized thinking has resulted in a complete neglect of the social dimensions and a failure to respond effectively to the needs of people with disabilities. This resonates at the micro level where teachers view the 'problems' as being situated in the child with disabilities. The natural recourse in such a scenario is then is to respond to their needs by 'fixing' the problem through additional resources aimed at making them as normally functioning as others, or to exclude the child to a special (different) setting." A medical language insists on the "within-child deficit" model that isolates the problem inside the individual.

Different countries toy with the isolating consequences of a disability in wonderfully nuanced and dangerous ways. Chapter 10, from Kenya, offers a rich story that illustrates both the arbitrariness and the specificity of terms for learning disabilities. The Swahili language divides the material world into animate and inanimate objects. Living things, including people, animals, plants and insects, belong to the *m-wa* and *m-mi* noun classes. Inanimate objects belong to the *ki-vi* noun classes. Many of the terms for disabilities, such as blind, deaf, or cross-eyed, and the general word for disabled itself (*kilema*), belong to the class of words that also describe shoes, cups, chairs, and other *things*. This linguistic distinction assigns people to fixed categories that have a sense of permanence and inevitability about them. The terms deny agency and growth, and the question of whether children who have been branded with such immutable disabilities are worthy of an education is a nonstarter. In human capital terms, the education of such a child will not yield financial returns on any public or private investments. Disability advocates in Kenya had to work hard to rebrand problem children with more lively labels better aligned with international sensitivities around the issue of "disability."

Foundational work on what can be subliminal and unknowing contributions to a labeling issue highlight a problem that too easily crosses national boundaries. The quantification of anything brings some things into sharp focus, while obscuring other aspects of a reality. The danger is that local and/or more humane ways of coping with inequality, disability, or difference simply get trodden over, delegitimized, and obliterated by international regimes, in particular because they carry the force of science, the language of objectivity, and the medicalization of disability.

At their best, labels provide a shorthand that allows a specific insight and efficiency; they can do the work of guiding attention and observation and help one to a new approach. By the same logic, they can obscure, hide, and inhibit. This second trend is most pernicious with generic terms such as *at risk* and *learning disabled,* which signify everything and don't mean much. Seeing beyond, or through, the labels is what locals can do better than regional officials or temporarily visiting testers.

Have you ever wondered what exactly *at risk* means? For many, the answer is obvious. It is another term for Black or brown or poor. Or it could mean that the kids can't stand the standardized reading tests that dominate class every day, and rightly so. It could mean simply that the kids have not turned in their homework. Almost always, it means that the child's parents are having trouble paying the rent. The point is that the term doesn't tell us much about what is actually happening and nothing about how to how to help. The label, like all other labels, keeps us all at risk.

USES AND MISUSES

The second problem is that even labels or test results we like can be used in ways that are dangerous. We make the point twice, first by pointing to the misuse of labels in school contexts and second by pointing to a more systemic problem that comes with trying to promise equality, or even conceiving of equality, in societies that have already organized massive inequalities.

Whether or not labels are in some sense adequate—by the minimum requirement that they at least refer to problematic behavior that can be seen—the bigger problem is how they are applied and acted upon in schools. When labels provide the hammer of the category, every child becomes a nail. They harm more frequently than they help. Our quandary is not that some kids don't have real problems; our quandary is that, in our desire to help, we often overlook the actual problems in favor of categorizing the student based on our label. Practitioners often have no idea that the labels they use have been often hastily assembled, messily constructed with tape and glue, and do not adequately or accurately inform practitioners about how to help a child. Instead, the labels often become a way to shift a child to another class or school with a readymade explanation of why he or she is uneducable, deficient, or otherwise incapable.

Teaching plans based on labels often backfire precisely because they start with abstractions rather than the realities of the classroom situation. This should not surprise us: most large-scale efforts at standardization fail because they do not consider local conditions, pressures, constraints, and the ingenuity of the adaptations made by people on the spot.[9] Students are not met where they are, nor are they offered a curriculum connected to what they know or take to be important. Instead, they are met by their teachers who have already labeled them as deficient, inadequate, and subpar. Ironically, the labels hurt more than just the students. They do not do teachers any favors either; the label *at risk* creates a crisis, which makes the teacher the sole person who can "solve" or remedy the problem. Instead of serving the needs of children, we can, by labeling, create the problem child and alienate the teacher.

The second challenge exists on a different level. There is a difference, argued Louis Dumont, between being at the bottom of a caste society and being at the bottom of a modern democracy in which everyone has been told that "all men are created equal"—and so too women, and African Americans, at least now if not in 1776.[10] In a caste society, everyone is where they belong according to the traditional theory. There is no recourse, no other course, no way up. By contrast, in a democracy, everyone has the opportunity of moving up. Now comes the hard part. What to say when some do not move up? The logic seems to go in three steps: everyone is born equal and is free to move up, but not everyone moves up, so those who do not move up must have something really wrong with them. In school, the same three steps deliver a similar magic: all children can learn, but many do not, so those who do not learn must have something really wrong with them.

Oh dear! The more equality a person is promised, the more degrading the punishments for not attaining it. The more learning everyone is promised, the more need for theories of personal disabilities and "within-child deficits." The labels will not go away, for they are needed. They make social structural sense. The alternative is to recognize that the people running the nation-state have no interest in everyone being equal, no interest in every child learning as much as the successful children. Every modern nation-state seems to be well organized and hell-bent on turning every difference, every glance to the side, every move in the direction of communal excellence into an occasion for defining more people as being inherently less, unable, broken, and problematic for those who have already, as they say, made it. By the principles espoused in this book, every disability is best understood as a situation rather than a personal trait. One cannot be disabled alone; it takes a village, it takes a state, it takes a capitalist democracy in which every person being less means that someone else is being more. And so the labeled are treated.

So it is that in Germany (chapter 4), "language problems are often redefined into learning difficulties." So it is that in Austria (chapter 1), "second-generation youths who have lived in Austria all their lives frequently are referred to as foreigners. Their constructed otherness is regarded as hindering integration into society . . . The existence of separate and marginal communities is then taken as evidence of failure to integrate, and this in turn is perceived as a threat to the host society." So it is in India (chapter 8) that teachers working on inclusion choices can perpetuate exclusion by referring to IQ or disability labels in combination with caste and tribal status. So it is that chapter 5 on Sweden—even Sweden—has to warn that the medicalization of disability poses a real threat to the enormous gains won by reforms aimed at making education more inclusive. And so it is that in Argentina (chapter 9), reformers have had to focus their energies on moving beyond differences between students to a more general language of "attention, availability, receptivity—in brief, hospitality"; that is, to a more ethical position we might all embrace, to a more ethical position by which "if we speak of body differences, all bodies form a part of it; if we speak of learning differences, all ways of learning are included; if we speak of language differences, all modes of producing speech and understanding are there." In such a world, people with disabilities are not inherently different as much as they are in different situations relative to all the people who set up the sometimes false ties between problems and solutions, between differences and similarities, between outcasts and invitees, between those who help and those who harm, between those with grace and those who withhold it.

THE INGENUITY OF LIVES IN ACTION

If global norming is dangerous because it too quickly answers questions about what is wrong with people who do not do well on tests, how can we focus on what might be right about them? One way is to look at them more carefully, to look at what they do based on a description of the environments with which they interact.

A few of the papers, especially chapter 2, on Chicago, but so too those on England (chapter 3), Germany (chapter 4), and Kenya (chapter 10), suggest the importance of geography for understanding patterns in school performance. This is most obvious for rural and urban differences in countries like Kenya and India, but chapter 2 presents evidence that geography plays a determinative role in Chicago as well, that neighborhoods—location culturally defined—affect the ways "teachers and students alike identify intellectual and cultural capital in the classroom" and orchestrate access to opportunities.

It is as if individual children do not take a test as much as a whole neighborhood takes a test and, by the same phrasing, drops its children into their place among the rest of the children in Chicago. We must be careful how we talk about test performance. Certainly individual children can outperform their neighborhood—the three of us did, and so too probably most of the authors in this book. So we do not want to lose sight of individual variation and achievement. That is on the one hand, but on the other hand, there is an important analytic point to be made. Neighborhoods tell an important story. Neighborhoods are about connections, about who can be called on, for what, under what circumstances, and for what price. Neighborhoods organize ways of walking and talking, ways of knowing, ways of showing. Teenagers in one neighborhood might be connected to the people who administer or even make up the tests. That is one kind of cultural capital. Teenagers in another neighborhood may have no connections with the testing and besting mode of production and deduction, but may be better connected to the responsibilities of child care and contributing to family finances one minimum wage hour after another. Both situations offer a kind of cultural capital, and both have their place in the overall structure of constraints and opportunities that organize neighborhoods in relation to each other. No one is without either culture or capital relative to the connections available to different people playing their roles and paying their tolls in the larger system.

It is in this sense that, when differential test performances follow neighborhood contours, we can say that the neighborhood, and not the individual student, takes the test. Is it really accurate to say that the children in the first neighborhood "know more," or are "smarter," than those in the next neighborhood? Or would it be more accurate to say that the children from various neighborhoods have different connections with the world, different connections to school ways of speaking or to the type of texts used on tests. The individual makes a good unit of concern, but the neighborhood might be a better unit of analysis.[11]

Two of us (McDermott and Scarloss, with the help of dozens of students) mapped school performance and correlating factors for a number of large American cities. We plotted the location of, for example, Starbucks for coffee, Curves for exercise, check-cashing stores for people without bank accounts, tutoring services for those already doing well, but wanting to do better, car thefts, murders, and bookstores, as well as pawn and porn shops.[12]

It was amazing how quickly the major borders of each city became apparent, and of course, everything correlated with school performance. But why?[13] What are the cognitive consequences of having parents who go to Starbucks or Curves? In Dallas, the best predictor of outstanding school success was the proximity of horses to a child's home (horses are a high-ticket item in Dallas). Looking at a variety of cities, we were able to find clear local identifiers that predicted academic performance based on proximity to things (for example, bus stops, libraries), hobbies (horseback riding, boating), dress (hats, sundresses), and high-style speech registers. If we had limited ourselves to studying just people's vocal cords, we could have come up with the champion predictor of school performance along the East Coast: the intermedial *r*! It is the difference between *god* and *guard*, which, like *pawn* and *porn*, only the upper echelons can include in their talk without special effort. Having a intermedial *r* can get you a leg up on school tests from Boston to Atlanta, and not having it will help you navigate working class neighborhoods. It is a nonfactor in (mostly) *r*-less languages (Hebrew, Japanese), and we guarantee that wherever you are, no matter what it correlates with, it will do nothing special for your intellectual capacities. Intermedial *r* neighborhoods rule when it comes to tests.

With data like these in hand, anecdotal, yes, but somehow (make that *sumhow*; they add up) significant, how are we to understand other correlations between native language or skin color with school performance? They might be equally spurious, or not, but either way, they cannot be allowed to speak for themselves. The deeper question concerns what we can do with the information. Buy every child in Dallas a horse? Of course not. It is not really a school performance growth factor, no more than an intermedial *r* is a sign of intelligence. Poor and working-class children wouldn't be able to feed or house a horse any more than they could afford professional tutors.[14] The problems are in the details, and so too the solutions. The test data brought to us by global norming do not explain what is going on. Rather, the test data, the categories that they foster and the interpretations they invite, also need to be explained—or better, they need to be confronted for their biases and consequences.

AND WHAT CAN WE DO?

Let's return to twentieth-century promises of progress, development, democracy, education, and equal playing fields. Yes, of course everyone believes the story. It is our only hope. And there is evidence that it is true. For the United States anyway, for most of Western Europe, and for Japan perhaps most of all, the argument can be made that modern schooling has done more for social mobility that any other institution in the history of the world! This is a strong foundation to build on, and there is no reason to stop trying to bring the promises of the twentieth-century state into reality in the twenty-first century. So it is that Americans, all Americans, both richer and poorer, no matter how cut off from any obvious progress, mobility, economic development, and the excitement of a level playing field, continue to believe: that schooling is the road to success; that psychometric tests are accurate, predictive, and good for holding children and their teachers accountable; and that the labels attached to children as kinds of learners are both accurate and a helpful source of special attention and caring.

Why should we be nervous that the nations of the world are testing children and reporting on their progress? Why should we be nervous that kids almost everywhere are getting categorized and labeled and then worried about and planned for by well-intentioned, caring people working at well-funded schools?

Here is the problem: precisely because the story is so easy, we can be lulled into not looking at how it works on the ground, on the shop floor, in the classroom. The story has a hidden underbelly that keeps us working against ourselves. As attractive as the promises are, they are filled with danger when aligned with the sorting demands of the population and the sorting powers of their institutions. So what can go wrong? What has already gone wrong, that's what! Global norming will continue to get the divided societies we already have.

Adam Smith warned us in 1776. The father of free market ideologies—of markets working on their own for everyone's benefit—specified three conditions under which a sovereign must intervene: first, when there are monopolies that restrict participation and competition in the market; second, when there are too many poor people locked out of the market; and, third, when the people need education to be informed enough to participate—rationally and reasonably—in the market (the last point was developed near the back of the full treatise and not available in most downsized editions). The sovereign, said Smith, has to restrict monopolies, find ways to employ the poor, and educate all the people so they can participate in the intelligence of the marketplace.[15]

To achieve all this, one would need to know about the ins and outs of corporate financing, the situation of the poor and their numbers, and the best curriculum for educating the most people in the best way for the economy to develop a nation's wealth. It is in this sense that the promises of the twentieth-century state—the promises of progress, education, development, democracy, and equality, if only at the starting point—make such good sense. So gather the data and write the reports. Get thee a plan. Make sure everyone gets educated, that everyone is included: your tired, your young, and your poor, most certainly, and so too your minority and underrepresented, your learning disabled and your slow, your abused and confused. A functioning democracy, like a functioning capitalist market of the type Smith imagined, needs input from every hand, from every heart and mind.

Smith's warning also suggests why education hasn't fulfilled its promise. At present, corporate monopolies are running the world, and the poor remain an "unmanageable problem." Income disparities in the United States, and in other countries according to machinations of their own history, are worse than at any time in the past century. With the bottom 80 percent of the people controlling only 2 percent of the resources, can we really think that equal education can outrun unequal resource distribution, that inclusion can outrun exclusion, that charters announcing that all children can and should learn can be backed up by institutional conditions delivering a level playing field?

These are the big issues we must discuss while considering the fate of children in schools around the world, and in particular while planning for the best care of various kinds of children—by ability, disability, language, aptitude, race, social class, and citizenship status—in different societies.

The tests themselves, the commodification of knowledge, and the very idea of a measured accountability for something like teaching and learning are instruments for legitimizing those with access (the 20 percent who control 98 percent of the resources) ahead of those without access. They rarely get challenged. Building on the promises of the twentieth-century state in twenty-first-century educational settings calls on us to reevaluate the elements we know can affect not just education, but the lives of people in families and neighborhoods in a way that advances those promises. Knowing is not enough. Knowing has taught us that recognizing and even naming barriers to educational achievement does not remove them. What all of the papers in this volume echo is not the cry to measure our differences, but to celebrate our similarities. Across cultures, geographic distance, educational systems, and learning outcomes, the unifying characteristic of the future seems to be our likenesses—and how lessons learned well in one area can benefit people, not unconnected, in another.

NOTES

INTRODUCTION

Authors' note: The first and second authors acknowledge the support of the Spencer and Motorola Foundations and the Equity Alliance at ASU under OESE's Grant S004D080027. We also acknowledge the support and hospitality of Stanford University's Center for Advanced Study in the Behavioral Sciences and Leibniz University (Hannover, Germany). The third author is grateful for the support of an Office of Special Education Programs Leadership Grant H325D050017. Endorsement by these organizations of the ideas expressed in this manuscript should not be inferred.

1. E. Said, *Culture and imperialism* (New York: Vintage Books, 1994), 319.
2. R. Slee, "The inclusion paradox: The cultural politics of difference," in *The Routledge international handbook of critical education*, eds. M. W. Apple, W. Au, and L. A. Gandin (New York: Routledge, 2009), 177–189.
3. A. J. Artiles, E. B. Kozleski, and T. Gonzalez, "Para além da sedução da educação inclusiva nos Estados Unidos: Confrontando o poder, construindo uma agenda histórico-cultural," *Revista Teias* 12, no. 24 (2011): 285–308.
4. G. Berhanu, "Ethnic minority pupils in Swedish schools: Some trends in overrepresentation of minority pupils in special educational programs," *International Journal of Special Education* 23, no. 3 (2008): 17–29.
5. A. J. Artiles and E. B. Kozleski, "Beyond convictions: Interrogating culture, history, and power in inclusive education," *Journal of Language Arts* 84, no. 4 (2007): 351–358.
6. A. J. Artiles et al., "Learning in inclusive education research: Re-mediating theory and methods with a transformative agenda," *Review of Research in Education* 30, no. 1 (2006): 65–108.
7. Ibid.
8. Dyson, "Inclusion and inclusions," in *World yearbook of education 1999*, ed. H. Daniels and P. Garner (London: Kogan Page, 1999), 36–53.
9. See, for example, K. Magiera and N. Zigmond, "Co-teaching in middle school classrooms under routine conditions: Does the instructional experience differ for students with disabilities in co-taught and solo-taught classes?," *Learning Disabilities Research & Practice* 20 (2005): 79–85; J. Bulgren and J. Schumaker, "Teacher practices that optimize curriculum access," in *Teaching adolescents with disabilities: Accessing the general education curriculum*, ed. D. Deshler and J. Schumaker

(Thousand Oaks, CA: Corwin Press, 2006), 79–156; D. L. Ferguson, E. B. Kozleski, and A. Smith, "Transformed, inclusive schools: A framework to guide fundamental change in urban schools," *Effective Education for Learners with Exceptionalities* 15 (2003): 43–74.

10. D. Braswell, "Special education in Western Europe," in *Encyclopedia of special education*, ed. C. R. Reynolds and E. Fletcher-Janzen (New York: Wiley, 1999), 1906–1909; A. Sander and A. Hausotter, "Special education in Germany," in *Encyclopedia of special education*, 431–432; B. Woll, "Special education in the United Kingdom," in *Encyclopedia of special education*, 1861–1864.

11. Y. Abe, "Special education reform in Japan," *European Journal of Special Needs Education* 13, no. 1 (1998): 86–97; M. T. Eglér Mantoan and J. A. Valente, "Special education reform in Brazil: An historical analysis of educational policies," *European Journal of Special Needs Education* 13, no. 1 (1998): 10–28; L. Shipitsina and R. Wallenberg, "Special education in Russia," in *Encyclopedia of special education*, 1575–1579.

12. G. Arredondo and K. Ryan-Addedondo, "Special education in Mexico," in *Encyclopedia of special education*, 1182–1184; M. Deng, K. F. Poon-McBrayer, and E. B. Farnsworth, "The development of special education in China: A sociocultural review," *Remedial and Special Education* 22 (2001): 288–298.

13. UNESCO, *The Salamanca statement and framework for action on special needs education* (Paris: UNESCO: 1994).

14. N. Gwalla-Ogisi, Z. P. Nkabinde, and L. Rodriguez, "The social context of the special education debate in South Africa," *European Journal of Special Needs Education* 13, no. 1 (1998): 72–85.

15. UNESCO, *Rate of primary school age children out of school* (Paris: UNESCO, 2010).

16. Artiles, Kozleski, and Gonzalez, "Para além da sedução da educação inclusiva nos Estados Unidos."

17. Artiles et al., "Learning in inclusive education research."

18. T. Fletcher and A. J. Artiles, "Inclusive education and equity in Latin America," in *Contextualising Inclusive Education*, ed. D. Mitchell (London: Routledge, 2005), 202–229.

19. A. J. Artiles, "Special education's changing identity: Paradoxes and dilemmas in views of culture and space," *Harvard Educational Review* 73 (2003): 164–202.

20. Artiles and Kozleski, "Beyond convictions"; Artiles, Kozleski, and Gonzalez, "Para além da sedução da educação inclusiva nos Estados Unidos"; Slee, "The inclusion paradox."

21. We note this point to explain that the work included in this volume was not always grounded in the Vigotskyan perspective that is typically associated with the term *cultural historical model*.

22. A. J. Artiles and A. Dyson, "Inclusive education in the globalization age: The promise of comparative cultural-historical analysis," in *Contextualising inclusive education*, 24–36.

CHAPTER 1

1. United Nations, *Human development index*, http://hdr.undp.org/en/statistics/.

2. Statistics Austria, "1,353 Mio. Menschen in Österreich mit Migrationshintergrund," www.statistik.at/web_de/presse/027382.

3. Statistics Austria,"Bevölkerung am 1.1.2002 nach detaillierter Staatsangehörigkeit und Bundesland," (Vienna: Statistics Austria, 2002), www.statistik.at/web_de/static/bevoelkerung_am_1.1.2002_nach_detaillierter_staatsangehoerigkeit_und_bunde_023445.pdf.

4. OECD, *Children of immigrants in the labor markets of EU and OECD countries: An overview* (Paris: OECD, 2009).

5. G. Baumgartner and B. Perchinig, "Minderheitenpolitik in Österreich—die Politik der österreichischen Minderheiten," in *6 x Österreich: Geschichte und aktuelle Situation der Volksgruppen*, ed. G. Baumgartner (Vienna: Initiative Minderheiten 1995).

6. Statistics Austria, "Volkszählung 2001," www.statistik-austria.at/web_de/statistiken/bevoelkerung/ percent20volkszaehlungen/ percent20bevoelkerung_percent20nach_demographischen_merkmalen/index.html.

7. H. Pechar, M. Unger, and M. Bönisch, *Equity in education: An inventory of the situation in Austria* (Vienna: Ministry of Education, Science, and Culture, 2005); P. Simon, "Equity and education—Country note: Austria," in *Equity and Education: Country notes of a Central-European project* , ed. P. Simon et al. (Budapest: Tempus Public Foundation, 2009), 7–36.

8. OECD, *Access, participation and equity* (Paris: OECD, 1993), cited in another OECD document, www.oecd.org/dataoecd/27/30/26527517.pdf; M. Demeuse, M. Crahay, and C. Monseur, "Efficiency and equity," in *Pursuit of equity in education: Using international indicators to compare equity policies*, ed. W. Hutmacher, D. Cochrane, and N. Bottani (Dordrecht, Netherlands/Boston/London: Kluwer Academic Publishers, 2001), 65–92.

9. A. J. Artiles and E. B. Kozleski, "Beyond convictions: Interrogating culture, history, and power in inclusive education," *Journal of Language Arts* 84, no. 4 (2007): 351–358; UNESCO, *Guidelines for inclusion: Ensuring access to education for all* (Paris: UNESCO, 2005), 13.

10. UNESCO, *Guidelines for inclusion*, 16.

11. J. Corbett and B. Norwich, "Common or specialized pedagogy," in *Curriculum and pedagogy in inclusive education: Values into practice*, ed. M Nind et al. (London: Routledge/Falmer, 2005), 34–47.

12. UNESCO, *The Salamanca statement and framework for action on special needs education* (Paris: UNESCO: 1994), 12.

13. Richard Thompkins and Pat Deloney, "Inclusion: The pros and cons," *Issues . . . About Change* 4, no. 3 (1995), SEDL Online, www.sedl.org/change/issues/issues43/definition_inclusion.html.

14. Corbett and Norwich, "Common or specialized pedagogy."

15. Ibid., 17.

16. K. Black-Hawkins, L. Florian, and M Rouse, *Achievement and inclusion in schools* (London: Routledge, 2007)

17. Ibid., 25.

18. Ibid., 22.

19. Cited in J. Kiesner et al., "Risk factors for ethnic prejudice during early adolescence," *Social Development* 12, no. 2 (2003): 288–308.

20. R. Berne and L. Stiefel, *The measurement of equity in school finance: Conceptual, methodological, and empirical dimensions* (Baltimore: The Johns Hopkins University

Press, 1984); UNESCO, *Educational equity and public policy: Comparing results from 16 countries* (Paris: UNESCO, 2007).

21. A. J. Artiles, N. Harris-Murri, and D. Rostenberg, "Inclusion as social justice: Critical notes on discourses, assumptions, and the road ahead," *Theory into Practice* 45, no. 3 (2006): 260–268.

22. Ibid.

23. M. Ainscow, T. Booth, and A. Dyson, *Improving schools, developing inclusion* (London: Routledge, 2006), 3.

24. Statistics Austria, "Bildung in Zahlen, Tabellenband, 2007/ 08," www.statistik.at/web_de/statistiken/bildung_und_kultur/index.html.

25. European Agency for Development in Special Needs Education, *Initial identification of special educational needs—Austria*, www.european-agency.org/agency-projects/assessment-in-inclusive-settings/assessment-database-of-key-topics/austria/initial-identification-of-special-educational-needs.

26. M. Luciak, "Behinderung oder Benachteiligung? SchülerInnen mit Migrationshintergrund und ethnische Minderheiten mit sonderpädagogischem Förderbedarf in Österreich," *SWS Rundschau* 49, no. 3 (2009): 369–390.

27. E. Feyerer, "Qualität in der Sonderpädagogik: Rahmenbedingungen für eine verbesserte Erziehung, Bildung und Unterrichtung von Schüler/inne/n mit sonderpädagogischem Förderbedarf " in *Nationaler Bildungsbericht Österreich 2009*, ed. W. Specht (Graz, Austria: Leykam, 2009), 73–97.

28. R. Seebauer, *Frauen, die Schule machten* [Women who set a precedent] (Vienna and Berlin: LIT, 2007).

29. S. Ellger-Rüttgardt, *Geschichte der Sonderpädagogik* [History of special education] (Munich: Reinhardt (UTB), 2008); H. Engelbrecht, *Geschichte des österreichischen Bildungswesens: Erziehung und Unterricht auf dem Boden Österreichs* [History of the Austrian education system], vol. 3 (Vienna: ÖBV, 1984).

30. F. Selbmann, *Jan Daniel Georgens: Leben und Werk* (Gießen, Germany: University of Gießen, 1982).

31. G. Biewer, *Grundlagen der Heilpädagogik und Inklusiven Pädagogik* (Bad Heilbrunn, Germany: Klinkhardt (UTB), 2009).

32. "Wien: Metropole durch Migration," *Forschungsnewsletter*, January 2006, http://forschungsnewsletter.univie.ac.at/newsletters/jaenner-2006/viewpage/article/wien-metropole-durch-migration/?tx_ttnews percent5BbackPid percent5D=9364&cHash=e1aa816e39f7aef083acc22ccada989c.

33. M. Glettler, *Die Wiener Tschechen um 1900: Strukturanalyse einer nationalen Minderheit in der Großstadt* [The Viennese Czechs in 1900: A structural analysis of a national minority in a metropolis] (Munich and Vienna: R. Oldenbourg Verlag, 1972).

34. Seebauer, *Frauen, die Schule machten*.

35. Engelbrecht, *Geschichte des österreichischen Bildungswesens*, 3.

36. H. Friedlander, "Von der 'Euthanasie' zur 'Endlösung,'" in *Tödliche Medizin im Nationalsozialismus: Von der Rassenhygiene zum Massenmord*, ed. K. D. Henke (Köln, Germany: Böhlau, 2008), 185–202.

37. M. Luciak, "Education of ethnic minorities and migrants in Austria," in *The education of diverse populations: A global perspective*, ed. G. Wan (Dordrecht [Netherlands] and London: Springer, 2008), 45–64.

38. W. Brezinka, "Heilpädagogik an der Medizinischen Fakultät der Universität Wien: Ihre Geschichte von 1911–1985," *Zeitschrift für Pädagogik* 43 (1997): 395–420.

39. H. Asperger, *Heilpädagogik: Einführung in die Psychopathologie des kindes für ärzte, lehrer, psychologen, richter und fürsorgerinnen* [Remedial education: an introduction to the psychopathology of children for doctors, teachers, psychologists, judges, and welfare workers], 5th ed. (Vienna: Springer, 1968).

40. O. Anlanger, *Behinderten Integration. Geschichte eines Erfolges* [Integration of people with disabilities: A history of success] (Vienna: Dachs-Verlag, 1993).

41. Luciak, "Behinderung oder Benachteiligung?"

42. OECD, *Children of immigrants in the labor markets of EU and OECD countries.*

43. Ibid., 36.

44. *Zahlenspiegel 2007: Statistiken im bereich schule und erwachsenenbildung in Österreich* (Vienna: Ministry for Education, Arts, and Culture, 2008); H. Weiss and A Unterwurzacher, "Soziale Mobilität durch Bildung? Bildungsbeteiligung von MigrantInnen," in *Österreichischer Migrations- und Integrationsbericht. 2001–2006*, ed. H. Fassmann (Klagenfurt, Austria: Drava, 2007), 227–241.

45. J. Bacher, "Bildungsungleichheit und Bildungsbenachteiligung im weiterführenden Schulsystem Österreichs: Eine Sekundäranalyse der PISA 2000-Erhebung," *SWS-Rundschau* 45 (2005): 37–63.

46. Weiss and Unterwurzacher, "Soziale Mobilität durch Bildung?."

47. OECD, *Children of immigrants in the labor markets of EU and OECD countries.*

48. Feyerer, "Qualität in der Sonderpädagogik."

49. Austrian Parliament, *Anfragebeantwortung*, Bundesministerium für Unterricht, Kunst und Kultur (4767/AB XXIII,2008), www.parlament.gv.at/PG/DE/XXIII/AB/AB_04767/fnameorig_141249.html.

50. Feyerer, "Qualität in der Sonderpädagogik."

51. Ibid.

52. Ibid.

53. Luciak, "Behinderung oder Benachteiligung?"

54. Ibid.

55. E. Begemann, "Sozio-kulturelle Benachteiligung pädagogisch verstehen," *Die Neue Sonderschule* 3, no. (2002): 191–216.

56. Luciak, "Behinderung oder Benachteiligung?"

57. Ibid.

58. M. Luciak and B. Liegl, "INSETRom project summative report," in *Teacher inservice training for Roma inclusion: A resource book*, ed. Y. Karagiorgi, L. Symeou, and G. Crozier (Nicosia, Cyprus: Comenius Project Report to the European Commission, 2008), 1–35.

59. *Gesetzliche Grundlagen schulischer Maßnahmen für SchülerInnen mit einer anderen Erstsprache als Deutsch: Gesetze und Verordnungen* (Vienna: Ministry of Education, Science, and Culture, 2006).

60. OECD, *Children of immigrants in the labor markets of EU and OECD countries*, 41.

61. Ibid., 43.

62. M. Luciak and G. Khan-Svik, "Intercultural education and intercultural learning in Austria: Critical reflections on theory and practice," *Intercultural Education* 19, no. 6 (2008): 493–504.

63. Luciak and Liegl, "INSETRom project summative report."
64. W. Specht et al., *Quality in special needs education: A project of research and development* (Graz, Austria: Center for School Development, 2006), 24.
65. Ibid., 34.
66. Ibid.
67. B. Herzog-Punzenberger, "Die 2. Generation an zweiter Stelle? Soziale Mobilität und ethnische Segmentation in Österreich: Eine Bestandsaufnahme," (2003), www.interface-wien.at/system/attaches/10/original/Studie_2Generation.pdf?1246968285.; B. Herzog-Punzenberger and A. Unterwurzacher, "Migration—Interkulturalität Mehrsprachigkeit: Erste Befunde für das österreichische Bildungswesen" in *Nationaler Bildungsbericht Österreich 2009*, ed. W. Specht (Graz, Austria: Leykam, 2009), 161–182; H. Weiss, ed., *Leben in zwei Welten: Zur sozialen Integration ausländischer Jugendlicher der zweiten Generation* (Wiesbaden, Germany: VS Verlag für Sozialwissenschaften, 2007); Weiss and Unterwurzacher, "Soziale Mobilität durch Bildung?"; B. Suchan et al., eds., *TIMSS 2007 Mathematik & Naturwissenschaft in der Grundschule: Erste Ergebnisse TIMSS 2007* (Vienna: Bundes Institut, 2008); Projektzentrum für Vergleichende Bildungsforschung (ZVB), "Presseinformation zu PIRLS 2006," www.bmukk.gv.at/medienpool/15723/pirls_2006_pressetextzvb.pdf.
68. OECD, *Where immigrant students succeed: A comparative review of performance and engagement in PISA 2003* (Paris: OECD, 2006).
69. OECD, *Children of immigrants in the labor markets of EU and OECD countries.*
70. Weiss, *Leben in zwei Welten.*
71. Unterwurzacher, "'Ohne Schule bist du niemand!': Bildungsbiographien von Jugendlichen mit Migrationshintergrund," in *Leben in zwei Welten*, 71–96.
72. *Bildungsbericht Schweiz 2006*, 2nd ed. (Aarau: Schweizerische Koordinationsstelle für Bildungsforschung, 2007).
73. Feyerer, "Qualität in der Sonderpädagogik."
74. E. Feyerer, *Behindern Behinderte? Auswirkungen integrativen Unterrichts auf nichtbehinderte Kinder in der Sekundarstufe I* (Linz, Austria: J. K. Universität Linz, 1997).
75. B. Herzog-Punzenberger, "Schule und Arbeitsmarkt ethnisch segmentiert? Einige Bemerkungen zur 'zweiten Generation' im österreichischen Bildungssystem," in *Heraus Forderung Migration*, ed. S. Binder, M. Six-Hohenbalken, and G Rasuly-Paleczek (Vienna: Institut für Geographie und Regionalforschung der Universität Wien, 2005), 191–211.
76. M. Crul and H. Vermeulen, "The second generation in Europe: Introduction to the special issue," *International Migration Review* 37, no. 4 (2003): 965–986.
77. OECD, *Children of immigrants in the labor markets of EU and OECD countries.*
78. D. Strohmeier and C. Spiel, "Gewalt in der Schule: Vorkommen, Prävention, Intervention," in *Nationaler Bildungsbericht Österreich 2009*, ed. W Specht (Graz and Vienna: Leykam, 2009).
79. Feyerer, "Qualität in der Sonderpädagogik"; C. Klicpera, *Elternerfahrungen mit Sonderschulen und Integrationsklassen: Eine qualitative Interviewstudie zur Schulwahlentscheidung und zur schulischen Betreuung in drei österreichischen Bundesländern* [Parents' experiences with special schools and integrative settings: a qualitative study on school choice and school support in three Austrian provinces] (Vienna: Lit, 2005); C. Klicpera and B. Gasteiger-Klicpera, "Soziale Erfahrungen

von Grundschülern mit sonderpädagogischem Förderbedarf in Integrationsklassen betrachtet im Kontext der Maßnahmen zur Förderung der sozialen Integration," *Heilpädagogische Forschung* 29, no. 2 (2003): 61–71.

80. OECD, *Children of immigrants in the labor markets of EU and OECD countries*.
81. Wroblewski and B Herzog-Punzenberger, *OECD Thematic review of migrant education: Country background report for Austria* (Vienna: Ministry of Education, Arts, and Culture website, 2009), 10.
82. M. Böse, R Haberfellner, and A Koldas, *Mapping minorities and their media: The national context—Austria* (Vienna: Center for Social Innovation 2001), 4.
83. S. Castles, "World population movements, diversity, and education," in *The Routledge International Companion to Multicultural Education*, ed. J. A. Banks (New York/London: Routledge, 2009), 49–61, 56–57.
84. Ibid.
85. Ibid., 59.
86. H. Weiss, "Die Identifikation mit dem Einwanderungsland: das Ende des Integrationsweges? in *Leben in zwei Welten*, 189–215.
87. R. Kaloianov, *Affirmative action für MigrantInnen? Am Beispiel Österreich* [Affirmative action for migrants? The example of Austria] (Vienna: Braumüller, 2008).
88. P. Ulram, *Integration in Österreich: Einstellungen, Orientierungen, und Erfahrungen von Migrantinnen und Angehörigen der Mehrheitsbevölkerung*, www.bmi.gv.at/cms/BMI_Service/Integrationsstudie.pdf.
89. H. Fasching, "Problemlagen Jugendlicher mit Behinderungen in Bezug auf die berufliche Integration," in *Integrations- und Sonderpädagogik in Europa: Professionelle und disziplinäre Perspektiven*, ed. A. Sasse, M. Vitková, and N Störmer (Bad Heilbrunn, Germany: Klinkhardt, 2004), 359–72.
90. *Development of education in Austria 2004–2007* (Vienna: Ministry of Education, Arts, and Culture, 2008), 3, www.bmukk.gv.at/medienpool/17147/bildungsentwicklung_07_e.pdf.
91. Ibid., 29–92.
92. Luciak, "Education of ethnic minorities and migrants in Austria"; and "Behinderung oder Benachteiligung?"
93. Wroblewski and Herzog-Punzenberger, *OECD Thematic review of migrant education: country background report for Austria*.
94. K. Crenshaw, "Demarginalizing the intersection of race and sex: A black feminist critique of antidiscrimination doctrine, feminist theory and antiracist politics," in *Foundations of feminist legal theory*, ed. D. K. Weisberg (Philadelphia: Temple University Press, 1989), 383–395.
95. Herzog-Punzenberger and Unterwurzacher, "Migration—Interkulturalität—Mehrsprachigkeit: Erste Befunde für das österreichische Bildungswesen,"
96. OECD, *Children of immigrants in the labor markets of EU and OECD countries*.

CHAPTER 2

Authors' note: The first and second authors acknowledge the support of the Equity Alliance at ASU under OESE's Grant S004D080027. The first author is grateful to the Center for Advanced Study in the Behavioral Sciences at Stanford University for the Residential Fellowship that allowed him to do the research for the theoretical model outlined in this manuscript. The third author is grateful for the support of an Office of Special Education Programs' Leadership Grant H325D050017. Endorsement by these organizations of the ideas expressed in this manuscript should not be inferred.

CHAPTER 3

1. UNESCO, *Policy guidelines on inclusion in education* (Paris: UNESCO, 2009), 9.
2. The four parts of the United Kingdom—England, Northern Ireland, Scotland, and Wales—have many economic, social, and educational similarities. Social and economic data in particular are often reported at the UK level. However, each part of the country has its own, separately governed, education system; these pursue similar but nonetheless distinct policies. This chapter focuses on the system in England, but where necessary refers to scholarly work and to social and economic data from across the United Kingdom.
3. B. Davies, *Social needs and resources in local services* (London: Michael, 1968); J. Rawls and E. Kelly, *Justice as fairness: A restatement* (Cambridge, MA: The Belknap Press of the Harvard University Press, 2001).
4. See L. Barton and S. Tomlinson, eds., *Special education: Policy, practices and social issues* (London: Harper and Row, 1981); L. Barton and S. Tomlinson, eds., *Special education and social interests* (London: Croom Helm, 1984); S. Tomlinson, *A sociology of special education* (London: Routledge & Kegan Paul, 1982); S. Tomlinson, "The expansion of special education," *Oxford Review of Education* 11, no. 2 (1985): 157–65.
5. CSIE, *The inclusion charter: ending segregation in education for all students with*
6. *disabilities or learning difficulties*, Centre for Studies in Inclusive Education www.csie.org.uk/publications/charter-05.pdf.
7. *Evaluating Educational Inclusion* (London: Ofsted, 2000), 4.
8. T. Booth, "Keeping the future alive: putting inclusive values into action," *Forum* 47, no. 2–3 (2005): 151–158.
9. Ibid., 153.
10. Department for Education and Employment, *Special educational needs in England, January 2010: Statistical first release (SFR) 19/2010* (London: The Stationery Office, 2010).
11. Ibid; B. Lamb (chair), *Lamb inquiry: Special educational needs and parental confidence* (Nottingham: DCSF Publications, 2009); Department for Education and Skills, *Every child matters*, Cm. 5860 (London: The Stationery Office, 2003).
12. P Clough, "Routes to inclusion," in *Theories of Inclusive Education*, eds. P. Clough and J. Corbett (London: Sage, 2000), 1–32.
13. Dyson and F. Gallannaugh, "National policy and the development of inclusive school practices: a case study," *Cambridge Journal of Education* 37, no. 4 (2007): 473–488.
14. J. Corbett and R. Slee, "An international conversation on inclusive education," in *Inclusive education: Policy contexts and comparative perspectives*, eds. F. Armstrong, D. Armstrong, and L. Barton (London: David Fulton, 2000), 133–146.
15. T. Booth and M. Ainscow, *Index for inclusion: Developing learning and participation in schools*, 2nd. ed. (Bristol: Centre for Studies on Inclusive Education, 2002).

16. N. Fraser, *Scales of justice: Reimagining political space in a globalizing world* (Cambridge, UK: Polity Press, 2008).

17. F. Almeida Diniz, "'Race' and the discourse on 'inclusion'," in *Inclusion, participation and democracy: What is the purpose?* ed. J. Allan (London: Kluwer Academic Publisher, 2003), 195–206.

18. Ibid.

19. Fraser, *Scales of justice.*

20. OECD, *Growing unequal? Income distribution and poverty in OECD countries—Country note: United Kingdom* (Paris: OECD, 2008.

21. Equality and Human Rights Commission, *How fair is Britain? Equality, human rights and good relations in 2010. the first triennial review* (London: Equality and Human Rights Commission, 2010), 7.

22. Sir William Beveridge, *Social insurance and allied services* (London: Her Majesty's Stationery Office, 1942).

23. R. Cassen and G. Kingdon, *Tackling low educational achievement* (York: Joseph Rowntree Foundation, 2007); Department for Education and Skills, "Ethnicity and education: The evidence on minority ethnic pupils," Research Topic Paper RTP01-05 (London: DfES, 2005); Fabian Society (Great Britain), Commission on Life Chances and Child Poverty, *Narrowing the gap: The final report of the Fabian Commission on Life Chances and Child Poverty,* (London: The Fabian Society, 2006); D. Gillborn and H. S. Mirza, *Educational inequality: Mapping race, class and gender: A synthesis of research evidence for the office for standards in education* (London: Ofsted, 2000); S. Machin and S. McNally, *Education and child poverty: A literature review* (York: Joseph Rowntree Foundation, 2006).

24. K. Duckworth, *The influence of context on attainment in primary school: Interactions between children, family and school contexts* (London: Centre for Research on the Wider Benefits of Learning, Institute of Education, 2008).

25. Cassen and Kingdon, *Tackling Low Educational Achievement*; Duckworth, *The influence of context on attainment in primary school*; C. Raffo et al., *Education and poverty: A critical review of theory, policy and practice* (York: Joseph Rowntree Foundation, 2007); S. Strand, *Minority ethnic pupils in the longitudinal study of young people in England: Extension report on performance in public examinations at age 16,* DCSF-RR029 (London: Department for Children Schools and Families, 2008).

26. See HM Government, PSA Delivery Agreement 10, *Raise the educational achievement of all children and young people*; and PSA Delivery Agreement 11, *Narrow the gap in educational achievement between children from low income and disadvantaged backgrounds and their peers,* (London: The Stationery Office, 2008).

27. Schools Analysis and Research Division, Department for Children Schools and Families, *Deprivation and education: the evidence on pupils in England, foundation stage to key stage 4* (London: Department for Children Schools and Families, 2009)

28. D. Dorling et al., *Poverty, wealth and place in Britain, 1968 to 2005* (Bristol: The Policy Press for the Joseph Rowntree Foundation, 2007).

29. T. MacInnes, P. Kenway, and A. Parekh, *Monitoring poverty and social exclusion 2009* (York: Joseph Rowntree Foundation, 2009).

30. T. Hunt, *Building Jerusalem: The rise and fall of the Victorian city* (London: Phoenix, 2004); Dorling et al., *Poverty, wealth and place in Britain, 1968 to 2005.*

31. R. Lupton, *Places apart? The initial report of CASE's areas study* (London: Centre for the Analysis of Social Exclusion, London School of Economics, 2001), 2.

32. K. Kintrea and R. Atkinson, *Neighbourhoods and social exclusion: The research and policy implications of neighbourhood effects* (Glasgow: Urban Change and Policy Research Group, University of Glasgow, 2001); R. Lupton, "'Neighbourhood effects': Can we measure them and does it matter?" Case Paper 73 (London: Centre for Analysis of Social Exclusion, 2003).

33. DfES, *The characteristics of low attaining pupils* (London: The Stationery Office, 2005); Ofsted, "London Challenge," (London: Ofsted, 2010).

34. R. Lupton, *How does place affect education?* (London: IPPR, 2006).

35. S. Power et al., *Education in deprived areas: Outcomes, inputs and processes* (London: Institute of Education, 2002).

36. Ofsted, *Evaluating educational inclusion*.

37. Harris and C. Chapman, "Improving schools in difficult contexts: Towards a differentiated approach," *British Journal of Educational Studies* 52, no. 4 (2004): 417–431.

38. R. Lupton, *Schools in disadvantaged areas: recognising context and raising quality. Case paper 76.* (London: London School of Economics and Political Science, 2004); M.Thrupp and R. Lupton, "Taking school contexts more seriously: The social justice challenge," *British Journal of Educational Studies* 54, no. 3 (2006): 308–328.

39. Davies, *Social needs and resources in local services*.

40. Social Exclusion Unit, *A new commitment to neighbourhood renewal: National strategy action plan* (London: Social Exclusion Unit, 2001), 5.

41. J. Griggs et al., *Person- or place-based policies to tackle disadvantage? Not knowing what works* (York: Joseph Rowntree Foundatioon, 2008); G. R. Smith, *Area-based initiatives: The rationale and options for area targeting*, CASE paper 25 (London: Centre for Analysis of Social Exclusion, London School of Economics, 1999).

42. A. Dyson et al., "What is to be done? Implications for policy makers," in *Education and poverty in affluent countries*, ed. C. Raffo, et al. (London: Routledge, 2010).

43. Central Advisory Council for Education (England), *Children and their primary schools*, vol. 1 (London: HMSO, 1967).

44. H. Halsey, ed. *Educational priority: EPA problems and practices*, vol. 1 (London: HMSO, 1972); G. Smith, "Whatever happened to Educational Priority Areas?" *Oxford Review of Education* 13, no. 1 (1987): 23–38.

45. D. Blunkett, *Excellence for the many, not just the few: Raising standards and extending opportunities in our schools* (London: DfEE, 1999).

46. D. Blunkett, *Social exclusion and the politics of opportunity: A mid-term progress check* (London: DfEE, 1999).

47. Social Exclusion Unit, *Tackling social exclusion: Taking stock and looking to the future: Emerging findings* (London: ODPM Publications, 2004).

48. DfEE, *Meet the challenge: Education Action Zones* (London: DfEE, 1999); DfES, *City Challenge for world class education*, ed. DfES (London 2007).

49. G. Rees, S. Power, and C. Taylor, "The governance of educational inequalities: the limits of area-based initiatives," *Journal of Comparative Policy Analysis* 9, no. 3 (2007): 261–274.

50. DfES, *"City challenge for world class education"*; Ofsted, *London Challenge.*
51. DCSF Schools Analysis and Research Division, *Deprivation and education*, 20; Ofsted, *Improvements in London schools 2000–06* (London: Ofsted, 2006).
52. L. Kendall et al., *Excellence in Cities: The national evaluation of a policy to raise standards in urban schools 2000–2003*, Research Report RR675A (London: DfES, 2006).
53. R. Bénabou, F. Kramarz, and C. Prost, *The French Zones d'Education Prioritaire: Much ado about nothing?* CEPR Discussion Paper No. 5085, Centre for Economic Policy Research, www.cepr.org/pubs/dps/DP5085.asp.
54. Griggs et al., *Person- or place-based policies to tackle disadvantage?*
55. Plewis, "Inequalities, targets and zones," *New Economy* 5, no. 2 (1998): 104–108; S. Power, G.Rees, and C. Taylor, "New Labour and educational disadvantage: the limits of area-based initiatives," *London Review of Education* 3, no. 2 (2005): 101–116; Rees, Power, and Taylor, "The governance of educational inequalities: the limits of area-based initiatives."
56. Smith, "Whatever happened to Educational Priority Areas?"; NFER, *National evaluation of Excellence in Cities, 2002–2006*, Research Report DCSF-RR017 (London: DCSF, 2007).
57. Plewis, "Inequalities, targets and zones."
58. DfES, *City Challenge for world class education*, 3.
59. T. Chamberlain, S. Rutt, and F. Fletcher-Campbell, *Admissions: Who goes where? Messages from the statistics* (Slough: NFER, 2006).
60. DfEE, *The importance of teaching*, Cm 7980 (London: The Stationery Office, 2010).
61. Rees, Power, and Taylor, "The governance of educational inequalities," 271.
62. S. Power and S. Gewirtz, "Reading Education Action Zones," *Journal of Education Policy* 16, no. 1 (2001): 39–51; Power, Rees, and Taylor, "New Labour and educational disadvantage"; Rees, Power, and Taylor, "The governance of educational inequalities."
63. Power, Rees, and Taylor, "New Labour and educational disadvantage."
64. R. Lupton, "Area-based initiatives in English education: what place for place and space?," in *Education and poverty in affluent countries*, ed. Carlo Raffo et al. (London: Routledge, 2010), 111–134.
65. Ibid.
66. Ibid.
67. P. Hubbard, R. Kitchin, and G. Valentine, "Editors' introduction," in *Key thinkers on space and place*, ed. Phil Hubbard, Rob Kitchin, and Gill Valentine (London: Sage, 2004), 1–15, 4-5.
68. R. Webber and T. Butler, "Classifying pupils by where they live: how well does this predict variations in their GCSE results?," *Urban Studies* 44, no. 7 (2007): 1229–1253.
69. *White British* is an ethnicity category in the United Kingdom.
70. Ibid.
71. E. Green and R. J. White, *Attachment to place: social networks, mobility and prospects of young people* (York: Joseph Rowntree Foundation, 2007).
72. Ibid., 8.
73. Kintrea et al., *Young people and territoriality in British cities* (York: Joseph Rowntree Foundation, 2008).

74. Ibid., 5.

75. Taylor, "Towards a geography of education," *Oxford Review of Education* 35, no. 5 (2009): 651–669.

76. Lupton, "Area-based initiatives in English education."

77. M. Ainscow et al., *Equity in education: Responding to context* (Manchester: Centre for Equity in Education, University of Manchester, 2008).

78. H. Rowley and A. Dyson, "Academies in the public interest: A contradiction in terms?" in *The state and education policy: The academies programme*, ed. Helen M. Gunter (London: Continuum, 2011), 79–91.

79. Cummings, A. Dyson, and L. Todd, *Beyond the school gates: Can full service and extended schools overcome disadvantage?* (London: Routledge, 2011); DfES, *Extended schools: Access to opportunities and services for all: A prospectus* (London: DfES, 2005).

80. Barnsley Metropolitan Borough Council, *Remaking learning: Leading change for success* (Barnsley, UK: Barnsley MBC, 2005); Knowsley Council, *Future schooling in Knowsley: A strategy for change 2008–2010* (Knowsley, UK: Knowsley Council, 2008); H. Carpenter et al., *Extended services evaluation: end of year one report*, Research report DFE-RR016 (London: Department for Education, 2010); C. Cummings and A. Dyson, "The role of schools in area regeneration," *Research Papers in Education* 22, no. 1 (2007): 1–22.

81. DfES, *Every child matters*; National Strategy for Neighbourhood Renewal, http://webarchive.nationalarchives.gov.uk/+/www.communities.gov.uk/documents/localgovernment/pdf/135457; Sir Michael Lyons, "National prosperity, local choice and civic engagement: A new partnership between central and local government for the 21st century," ed. Lyons Inquiry into Local Government (London: Her Majesty's Stationery Office, 2006); DfES, *Report of the special schools working group* (London: DfES, 2003).

82. Prescott, "Maisntreaming social justice for the 21st century," speech delivered to the Fabian Society/New Policy Institute conference 'Building Partnerships for Social Inclusion," Congress House, Great Russell Street, 2002 http://archive.cabinetoffice.gov.uk/ministers/ministers/2002/dpm/fabian%2015%2001%2002v2.htm.

83. HM Government, "PSA Delivery Agreement 10: *Raise the educational achievement of all children and young people*; PSA Delivery Agreement 11: *Narrow the gap in educational achievement between children from low income and disadvantaged backgrounds and their peers.*

84. Power, Rees, and Taylor, "New Labour and educational disadvantage: the limits of area-based initiatives."

85. Dyson et al., "What is to be done? Implications for policy makers."

86. Diniz, "'Race' and the discourse on 'inclusion'."

87. Oliver, "Intellectual masturbation: A rejoinder to Soder and Booth," *European Journal of Special Needs Education* 7, no. 1 (1992): 20–28.

88. Ibid., 21.

89. Ibid., 22.

90. Hubbard, Kitchin, and Valentine, "Editors' introduction."

91. Cummings and Dyson, "The role of schools in area regeneration"; C. Cummings et al., "Evaluation of extended services: thematic review: Reaching disadvantaged

groups and individuals," (London: DCSF, 2010); C. Cummings et al., *Evaluation of the full service extended schools initiative: Final report*, Research report RR852 (London: DfES, 2007).

92. Oliver, "Intellectual masturbation."

CHAPTER 4

1. R. Werning, J. M. Löser, and M. Urban, "Cultural and social diversity: An analysis of minority groups in German schools," *Journal of Special Education* 42 (2008): 47–54; R. Werning and B. Lütje-Klose, *Einführung in die pädagogik bei lernbeeinträchtigungen* [Introduction to education of students with learning difficulties] (Munich: Reinhardt, 2006).

2. A. Hinz, "Inklusive pädagogik in der schule:Veränderter orientierungsrahmen für die schulische sonderpädagogik?" *Zeitschrift für Heilpädagogik* 5 (2009): 171–179.

3. We use the term *immigrant students* to refer to students who themselves or whose parents have immigrated to Germany. At times we use the term *foreign students* interchangeably with immigrant students because the German government's data use citizenship as an indicator for immigrant status. Foreign students do not have German citizenship, but attend German schools. Because immigrant students comprise cultural and ethnically diverse students with and without German citizenship, we prefer to use the term *immigrant* rather than *foreign* to describe this population.

4. I. Gogolin, *Der monolinguale habitus der multilingualen schule* [The monolingual habitus of the multilingual school] (Münster, Germany: Waxmann, 1994).

5. Ibid.; I. Gogolin and M. Krüger-Potratz, *Einführung in die interkulturelle pädagogik* [Introduction to multicultural education] (Opladen, Germany: Budrich, 2006); J. M. Löser, *Der Umgang mit kultureller und sprachlicher Vielfalt an Schulen. Ein Vergleich zwischen Kanada, Schweden und Deutschland* [Cultural and lingustical diversity in schools. A comparison of Canada, Sweden and Germany] (Frankfurt am Main, Germany: Brandes & Apsel, 2010).

6. Gogolin and Krüger-Potratz, *Einführung in die interkulturelle Pädagogik*.

7. K. Crenshaw, "The intersection of race and gender," in *Critical race theory*, ed. K Crenshaw et al. (New York: The New Press, 1995), 357–383.

8. R. Werning and H. Reiser, "Sonderpädagogische Förderung," in *Das Bildungswesen in der Bundesrepublik Deutschland:Strukturen und Entwicklungen im Ueberblick*, ed. K. S. Cortina et al. (Reinbek bei Hamburg, Germany: Rowohlt, 2008), 505–539.

9. Kultusministerkonferenz, "Basic structure of the education system in the Federal Republic of Germany," 2005, www.kmk.org/fileadmin/doc/Dokumentation/Bildungswesen_en_pdfs/en-2009.pdf.

10. R. Werning, "Integration zwischen Ueberforderung und Innovation: Eine systemisch-konstruktivistische Perspektive" in *Lernen und Lernprobleme im systemischen Diskurs*, ed. R. Balgo and R. Werning (Dortmund, Germany: Verlag Modernes Lernen, 2003), 115–129; Werning and Lütje-Klose, *Einführung in die Pädagogik bei Lernbeeinträchtigungen*.

11. Konsortium Bildungsberichterstattung, *Bildung in Deutschland:Ein indikatorengestützter Bericht mit einer Analyse zu Bildung und Migration* [Education in Germany: An indicator proved report with an analysis of education and immigration] (Bielefeld, Germany: Bertelsmann, 2006).

12. Kultusministerkonferenz, "Basic structure of the education system in the Federal Republic of Germany."

13. G. Bellenberg, G. Hovestadt, and K. Klemm, *Selektivität und Durchlässigkeit im allgemein bildenden Schulsystem: Rechtliche Regelungen und Daten unter besonderer Berücksichtigung der Gleichwertigkeit von Abschlüssen* [Selectivity and transparency in the basic educational system: Legal regulations and data regarding the equality of school leaving certificates] (Essen, Germany: bfp, 2004).

14. Werning and Reiser, "Sonderpädagogische Förderung."

15. Kultusministerkonferenz, "Sonderpädagogische Förderung in Schulen 1994 bis 2003," Bonn, Germany, 2005, www.kmk.org/statist/Dokumentation177.pdf).

16. Werning and Lütje-Klose, *Einführung in die Pädagogik bei Lernbeeinträchtigungen.*

17. J. J. Powell, "To segregate or to separate? Special education expansion and divergence in the United States and Germany," *Comparative Education Review* 53, no. 2 (2009): 161–187, 175.

18. United Nations, *Convention on the Rights of Persons with Disabilities*, www.un.org/disabilities/convention/conventionfull.shtml.

19. Ibid.

20. J. Aab et al., *Sonderschule zwischen Ideologie und Wirklichkeit: Für eine revision der Sonderpädagogik* [Special schools between ideology and reality: Toward a revision of special education] (Munich, Germany: Juventa, 1974); A. Hildeschmidt and A. Sander, "Zur Effizienz der Beschulung sogenannter Lernbehinderter in Sonderschulen," in *Handbuch Lernen und Lern-Behinderungen*, ed. H. Eberwein (Weinheim, Germany: Beltz, 1996), 115–134.

21. Werning and Reiser, "Sonderpädagogische Förderung."

22. Kultusministerkonferenz, "Sonderpädagogische förderung in schulen 1997 bis 2006," Bonn, 2008.

23. Hildeschmidt and Sander, "Zur Effizienz der Beschulung sogenannter Lernbehinderter in Sonderschulen."

24. M. Ainscow, T. Booth, and A. Dyson, *Improving schools, developing inclusion* (London: Routledge, 2006); G. Bunch and N. Persaud, *Not enough: Canadian research into inclusive education* (Toronto: Roeher Institute, 2003); G. Bunch et al., *Finding a way through the maze: Crucial terms used in education provision for Canadians with disabilities* (Toronto: The Marsha Forest Centre, 2005); E. Feyerer and W Prammer, *Gemeinsamer Unterricht in der Sekundarstufe I* [Inclusive instruction in grades 5–10] (Berlin: Beltz, 2003); A. Hinz, "Von der Integration zur Inklusion: Terminologisches Spiel oder konzeptionelle Weiterentwicklung?" *Zeitschrift für Heilpädagogik* 53 (2002): 3554–3361; Werning and Lütje-Klose, *Einführung in die Pädagogik bei Lernbeeinträchtigungen.*

25. Hinz, "Von der Integration zur Inklusion."

26. Ibid.

27. H. Reiser, "Vom Begriff Integration zum begriff Inklusion:Was kann mit dem Begriffswechsel angestoßen werden?" *Sonderpädagogische Förderung* 48, no. 4 (2003).

28. A. J. Artiles et al., "Learning in inclusive education research: Re-mediating theory and methods with a transformative agenda," *Review of Research in Education* 30, no. 1 (2006): 65–108.

29. A. Hinz, *Heterogenität in der Schule:Integration—Interkulturelle Erziehung—Koeduka-tion* [Heterogeneity in schools: Integration—intercultural education—coeduca-

tion] (Hamburg: Curio, 1993); A. Prengel, *Pädagogik der Vielfalt:Verschiedenheit und Gleichberechtigung in interkultureller, feministischer und integrativer Pädagogik* [Education of diversity: Diversity and equality in intercultural, feminist and integrative education] (Opladen, Germany: Leske & Budrich, 1993); Crenshaw, "The Intersection of Race and Gender."

30. Crenshaw, "The intersection of race and gender"; H. Lutz and N. Wenning, "Differenzen über differenz: Einführung in die debatten," in *Unterschiedlich verschieden:Differenz in der Erziehungswissenschaft* ed. H. Lutz and N. Wenning (Opladen, Germany: Leske & Budrich, 2001), 11–24; A Prengel, "Intersektionalität und Sonderpädagogik: Ein Beitrag zur Debatte um prekäre Bildungssituationen von Jungen,"" in *Professionelle Kooperation bei gefühls- und verhaltensstörungen: Pädagogische Hilfen an den Grenzen der Erziehung*, ed. H. Reiser, A. Dlugosch, and M. Willmann (Hamburg: Kovac, 2008), 105–116.

31. N. S. Nasir and V. M Hand, "Exploring sociocultural perspective on race, culture, and learning," *Review of Educational Research* 76, no. 4 (2006): 449–475.

32. R. McDermott, J. D. Raley, and D. Seyer-Ochi, "Race and class in a culture of risk," *Review of Research in Education* 33, no. 1 (2009): 101–116.

33. Crenshaw, "The intersection of race and gender."

34. H. Diefenbach, "Bildungschancen und Bildungs(miss)erfolg von ausländischen Schülern oder Schülern aus Migrantenfamilien im System schulischer Bildung," in *Bildung als privileg? Erklärungen und Befunde zu den Ursachen der Bildungsungleichheit*, ed. R. Becker and W. Lauterbach (Wiesbaden, Germany: Verlag für Sozialwissenschaften, 2004), 217–241.

35. Statistisches Bundesamt, *Bildung und Kultur* [Education and culture] (Wiesbaden, Germany: Statistisches Bundesamt, 2008).

36. Ibid.

37. J. Baumert and G. Schümer, "Familiäre Lebensverhältnisse, Bildungsbeteiligung und Kompetenzerwerb," in *PISA 2000: Basiskompetenzen von Schülerinnen und Schülern im internationalen Vergleich*, ed. Deutsches PISA-Konsortium (Opladen, Germany: Leske & Budrich, 2001), 159–202.

38. Diefenbach, "Bildungschancen und Bildungs(miss)erfolg von ausländischen Schülern oder schülern aus Migrantenfamilien im system schulischer Bildung."

39. H. Diefenbach, *Kinder und Jugendliche aus Migrantenfamilien im deutschen Bildungssystem: Erklärung und empirische Befunde* [Children and adolescents from families with immigration backgrounds in the German education system: Explanations and empirical findings] (Wiesbaden, Germany: VS Verlag für Sozialwissenschaften, 2010).

40. G. Klein, "Sozialer Hintergrund und Schullaufbahn von Lernbehinderten/ Förderschülern 1969 und 1997," *Zeitschrift für Heilpädagogik* 52 (2001): 51–61; Werning and Reiser, "Sonderpädagogische Förderung."

41. Deutsches PISA-Konsortium, *PISA 2006: Die Ergebnisse der dritten internationalen Vergleichsstudie: Zusammenfassung*, ed. Manfred Prenzel, Cordula Artelt, Jürgen Baumert, Werner Blum, Marcus Hammann, Eckhard Klieme, und Reinhard Pekrun, 2007, www.ipn.uni-kiel.de/pisa/zusammenfassung_PISA2006.pdf

42. See also R. D. Alba, J. Handl, and W. Müller, "Ethnische Ungleichheiten im deutschen Bildungssystem," *Kölner Zeitschrift für Soziologie und Sozialpsychologie* 46 (1994): 209–237; U. Hunger and D. Thränhardt, "Vom katholischen

Arbeitermädchen vom Lande zum italienischen Gastarbeiterjungen aus dem bayrischen Wald: Zu den neuen Disparitäten im deutschen Bildungssystem," in *Integration und Illegalität in Deutschland*, ed. K. J. Bade (BadIburg, Germany: IMIS, 2001), 51–61; A. G. Müller and P. Stanat, "Schulischer Erfolg von Schülerinnen und Schülern mit Migrationshintergrund: Analysen zur Situation von Zuwanderern aus der ehemaligen Sowjetunion und aus der Türkei," in *Herkunftsbedingte Disparitäten im Bildungswesen: Differenzielle Bildungsprozesse und Probleme der Verteilungsgerechtigkeit; vertiefende Analysen im Rahmen von PISA 2000*, ed. J. Baumert, P. Stanat, and R. Watermann (Wiesbaden, Germany: VS Verlag für Sozialwissenschaften, 2006), 221–255.

43. Hunger and Thränhardt, "Vom katholischen Arbeitermädchen vom Lande zum italienischen Gastarbeiterjungen aus dem bayrischen Wald"; C. Kristen, "Ethnische Diskriminierung in der Grundschule? Die Vergabe von Noten und Bildungsempfehlungen," *Zeitschrift für Soziologie und Sozialpsychologie* 58 (2006): 79–97.

44. Hunger and Thränhardt, "Vom katholischen Arbeitermädchen vom Lande zum italienischen Gastarbeiterjungen aus dem bayrischen Wald."

45. Diefenbach, *Kinder und Jugendliche aus Migrantenfamilien im deutschen Bildungssystem*; R. Kornmann, P. Burgard, and H. M. Eichling, "Zur Überrepräsentation von ausländischen Kindern und Jugendlichen in Schulen für Lernbehinderte," *Zeitschrift für Heilpädagogik* 50 (1999): 106–109.

46. Gogolin, *Der monolinguale Habitus der multilingualen Schule*; Werning and Reiser, "Sonderpädagogische Förderung."

47. Diefenbach, *Kinder undJjugendliche aus Migrantenfamilien im deutschen Bildungssystem.*

48. Ibid; M. Gomolla and O. Radtke, *Institutionelle Diskriminierung* [Institutional discrimination] (Opladen, Germany: Leske und Budrich, 2002).

49. McDermott, Raley, and Seyer-Ochi, "Race and class in a culture of risk."

50. S. Wagner and J. J. Powell, "Ethnisch-kulturelle Ungleichheit im deutschen Bildungssystem: Zur Überrepräsentanz von Migrantenjugendlichen an Sonderschulen " in *Wie man behindert wird*, ed. G Cloerkes (Heidelberg, Germany: Winter, 2003), 183–208.

51. A. J. Artiles, S. C. Trent, and J. Palmer, "Culturally diverse students in special education: Legacies and prospects," in *Handbook of research on multicultural education*, ed. J. A Banks and C. M Banks (San Francisco: Jossey Bass, 2004), 716–735; H. Varenne and R. McDermott, *Successful failure: The school America builds* (Boulder, CO: Westview Press, 1998).

52. McDermott, Raley, and Seyer-Ochi, "Race and class in a culture of risk."

53. Artiles, Trent, and Palmer, "Culturally diverse students in special education."

54. Hunger and Thränhardt, "Vom katholischen Arbeitermädchen vom Lande zum italienischen Gastarbeiterjungen aus dem bayrischen Wald"; Kronig, "Das Konstrukt des leistungsschwachen Immigrantenkindes," *Zeitschrift für Erziehungswissenschaft* 6, no. 1 (2003): 126–141.

55. Hunger and Thränhardt, "Vom katholischen Arbeitermädchen vom Lande zum italienischen Gastarbeiterjungen aus dem bayrischen Wald."

56. Ibid.

57. Gomolla and Radtke, *Institutionelle Diskriminierung*; Deutsches PISA-Konsortium, *PISA 2000: Basiskompetenzen von schülerinnen und schülern im internationalen vergleich* (Opladen, Germany: Leske und Budrich, 2001).

58.   McDermott, Raley, and Seyer-Ochi, "Race and class in a culture of risk."
59.   Gogolin, *Der monolinguale Habitus der multilingualen Schule.*
60.   I. Diehm and O. Radtke, *Erziehung und Migration* [Education and migration] (Stuttgart, Germany: Kohlhammer, 1999); Gogolin, *Der monolinguale Habitus der multilingualen Schule*; M Krüger-Potratz, *Interkulturelle Bildung: Eine Einführung* [Intercultural education: An introduction] (Münster, Germany: Waxmann, 2005).
61.   Löser, *Der umgang SET mit kultureller und sprachlicher vielfalt SETan schulen.*
62.   Gogolin, *Der monolinguale Habitus der multilingualen Schule.*
63.   Gomolla and Radtke, *Institutionelle Diskriminierung.*
64.   Lutz and Wenning, "Differenzen über Differenz."
65.   A. J. Artiles and A. Dyson, "Inclusive education in the globalization age: The promise of comparative cultural-historical analysis," in *Contextualising inclusive education,* ed. D Mitchell (London: Routledge, 2005), 24–36, 49.
66.   Diehm and Radtke, *Erziehung und migration*; Krüger-Potratz, *Interkulturelle Bildung.*
67.   Gomolla and Radtke, *Institutionelle Diskriminierung*; Löser, *Der umgang SET mit kultureller und sprachlicher v SETielfalt an sSETchulen*; Werning and Lütje-Klose, *Einführung in die Pädagogik bei Lernbeeinträchtigungen.*
68.   Kronig, "Das Konstrukt des leistungsschwachen Immigrantenkindes."

CHAPTER 5

1.   C. Clark, A. Dyson, and A. Millward, eds., *Theorising special education* (London: Routledge, 1998); A. Dyson and A. Millward, *Schools and special needs: Issues of innovation and inclusion* (London: Sage, 2000).
2.   M. Billig et al., *Ideological dilemmas* (London: Sage Publications, 1988), 163.
3.   B. Norwich, "Dilemmas of difference, inclusion and disability: International perspectives on placement," *European Journal of Special Needs Education* 23, no. 4 (2008): 287–304.
4.   C. Nilholm, *Including av elever 'I behov av särskilt stöd': Vad betyder det och vad vet vi?* (Malmö, Sweden: Malmö University 2006).
5.   E. Hjörne, *Excluding for inclusion? Negotiating school careers and identities in pupil welfare settings in the Swedish school* (Göteborg: Acta Universitatis Gothoburgensis, 2004); H. Mehan, "Beneath the skin and between the ears: a case study in the politics of representation," in *Understanding practice: Perspectives on activity and context,* ed. S. Chaiklin and J. Lave (Cambridge: Cambridge University Press, 1993), 241–268; Skolverket, *Handikapp i skolan: Det offentliga skolväsendets möte med funktionshinder från folkskolan till nutid* (Stockholm: Skolverket, 2005).
6.   Arnesen and L. Lundahl, "Still social and democratic? Inclusive education policies in the Nordic welfare states," *Scandinavian Journal of Educational Research* 50, no. 3 (2006): 285–300.
7.   OECD, *Equity in education thematic review: Sweden, country note* (Paris: OECD, 2005).
8.   Ibid.
9.   Arnesen and Lundahl, "Still social and democratic?"; OECD, *Education at a glance: OECD indicators* (Paris: OECD, 2010); OECD, *Special needs education:Statistics and indicators* (Paris: OECD, 2000); OECD, *Equity in education thematic review: Sweden, country note*; A. Wildt-Persson and P. G. Rosengren, "Equity and Equivalence in the Swedish School System," in *In pursuit of equity in education: Using international*

indicators to compare equity policies, ed. W. Hutmacher (Hingham, MA: Kluwer Academic Publishers, 2001), 288–321.

10. Nirje, *The normalization principle papers* (Uppsala: Uppsala University Center for Handicap Research, 1992); W. Wolfensberger, *The principle of normalization in human services* (Toronto: NIMR, 1972).

11. *Läroplan för grundskolan* (Stockolm: Skolverket och Fritzes AB, 1962); see also *Läroplan för det obligatoriska skolva¨sendet, förskoleklassen och fritidshemmet* [LPO] (Stockholm: Skolverket och Fritzes AB, 1994), 6.

12. Emanuelsson, P. Haug, and B. Persson, "Inclusive education in some western european countries: Different policy rhetoric and school realities," in *Contextualizing Inclusive Education: Evaluating Old and New International Perspectives*, ed. D. Mitchell (London: Routledge/Falmer, 2005), 114–138.

13. K. Göransson, C. Nilholm, and K. Karlsson, "Inclusive ducation in Sweden? A critical analysis," *International Journal of Inclusive Education* (2010), www.informaworld.com/10.1080/13603110903165141.

14. United Nations, *Convention on the Rights of the Child*, http://www2.ohchr.org/english/law/crc.htm; United Nations, *The standard rules on the equalization of opportunities for persons with disabilities adopted by the united nations general assembly* (Paris: United Nations, 1993); UNESCO, *The Salamanca statement and framework for action on special needs education* (Paris: UNESCO: 1994).

15. Emanuelsson, Haug, and Persson, "Inclusive education in some Western European countries."

16. *Läroplan för grundskolan*, 120.

17. Skolverket, *Handikapp i skolan.*

18. Emanuelsson, "Reactive Versus Proactive Support Coordinator Roles: An International Comparison," *European Journal of Special Needs Education* 16, no. 2 (2001): 133–142; Emanuelsson, Haug, and Persson, "Inclusive education in some Western European countries."

19. Mitchell, "Introduction: Sixteen propositions on the contexts of inclusive education," in *Contextualizing Inclusive Education: Evaluating Old and New International Perspectives*, ed. D. Mitchell (London: Routledge/Falmer, 2005), 1–21.

20. Emanuelsson, "Reactive versus proactive support coordinator roles."

21. Ibid., 131.

22. Heimdahl Mattsson, *Mot en inkluderande Skola* [Toward inclusive schools] (Stockholm: HLS Förlag, 2006).

23. Ibid.

24. Arnesen and Lundahl, "Still social and democratic?"; T Englund, "The discourse on equivalence in Swedish education policy," *Journal of Education Policy* 20, no. 1 (2005): 39–57; OECD, *Equity in education thematic review: Sweden, country note*; Wildt-Persson and Rosengren, "Equity and equivalence in the Swedish school system."

25. Z. Bauman, *Intimations of postmodernity* (London: Routledge, 1992).

26. B. Persson, "Exclusive and inclusive discourses in special education research and policy in Sweden," *International Journal of Inclusive Education* 7, no. 3 (2003): 271–280.

27. L. Asp-Onsjö, ed., *Åtgärdsprogram-dokument eller verktyg: En fallstudie i en kommun* (Göteborg: Acta Universitatis Gothoburgiensis, 2006).

28. Skolverket, *Barnomsorg, skola och vuxenutbildning i siffror 2002 del 2* (Stockholm: Skolverket, 2002); J. Rosenqvist, *Specialpedagogik i mångfaldens sverige: Om elever med annan etnisk bakgrund än svensk i särskolan* [Special education in multicultural Sweden: Ethnic minorty pupils in education for intellectually disabled] (Härnösand, Sweden: Specialpedagogiska Institutet, 2007), 67.

29. See, for example, Nilholm, *Including av elever "I behov av särskilt stöd."*

30. J. Corbett and R. Slee, "An International Conversation on Inclusive Education," in *Inclusive education: Policy, Contexts and comparative perspectives*, ed. F. Armstrong, D. Armstrong, and L. Barton (London: David Fulton, 2000), 133–146.

31. Bernstein, as cited in Nilholm, *Inkludering av elever "I behov av särskilt stöd."*

32. Persson, "Exclusive and Inclusive Discourses in Special Education Research and Policy in Sweden"; L. Vislie, "From Integration to Inclusion: Focusing Global Trends and Changes in the Western European Societies," *European Journal of Special Needs Education* 18, no. 1 (2003): 17–35.

33. Heimdahl Mattsson, *Mot en inkluderande skola* ; Nilholm, *Inkludering av elever "I behov av särskilt stöd."*

34. *Läroplan för det obligatoriska skolva¨sendet, fo¨rskoleklassen och fritidshemmet.*

35. Rosenqvist, *Specialpedagogik i mångfaldens Sverige*; G. Berhanu, "Ethnic minority pupils in Swedish schools: some trends in overrepresentation of minority pupils in special educational programs," *International Journal of Special Education* 23, no. 3 (2008): 17–29.

36. J. E. Gustafsson, *Barns utbildningssituation: Bidrag till ett kommunalt barnindex* [Children's educational situation: Contribution to a local child index] (Stockholm: Rädda Barnen, 2006).

37. OECD, *Equity in education thematic review.*

38. Bel Habib, *Elever med invandrarbakgrund i särskolan: Specialpedagogik eller disciplinär makt* [Pupils with immigrant background in education for intellectually disabled] (Kristianstad, Sweden: Högskolan i Kristianstad. Enheten för Kompetensutveckling, 2001); K. Hahne Lundström, *Intagningskriterier till gymnasiesärskolan i Göteborg* [Admission criteria to upper highschool for educationally disabled in Gothenburg] (Stockholm: Arbetslivsinstitutets Företagsläkarutbildning, 2001); Skolverket, *Hur särskild får man vara? En analys av elevökningen i särskolan* (Stockholm: Skolverket, 2000); SOU, "För den jag är. Om utbildning och utvecklingsstörning" (Stockolm: Swedish goverment, 2003).

39. Rosenqvist, *Specialpedagogik i mångfaldens sverige.*

40. Arnesen and Lundahl, "Still social and democratic?" 294.

41. Skolverket, *Handikapp i skolan.*

42. See, for example, G. Berhanu, "Framgångsfaktorer för delaktighet och jämlikhet," (Gothenburg, SwedenI Specialpedagogiska institutet, 2006); L. Eriksson, *Participation and Disability: A Study of Participation in School for Children and Youth with Disabilities* (Stockholm: Universitetsservice AB, 2006); K. Göransson, *Man vill ju vara som alla andra* (Stockholm: Specialpedagogiska Skolmyndigheten 2008); Heimdahl Mattsson, *Mot en inkluderande skola*; U. Janson, *Funktionell olikhet och kamratsamspel i förskola och skola* [Functional differences and peer interaction in preschool and school] (Härnösand, Sweden: Specialpedagogiska Institutet, 2006); L Palla, *Den inkluderande skolan* [The inclusive school] (Härnösand, Sweden: Specialpedagogiska Institutet, 2006).

43. Eriksson, *Participation and disabilitys*.
44. See Arnesen and Lundahl, "Still social and democratic?"
45. Wildt-Persson and Rosengren, "Equity and equivalence in the Swedish school system," 307.
46. Education Act of 1985 (Stockolm: Ministry of Education and Science in Sweden, 1985), 1100.
47. *Läroplan för det obligatoriska skolva¨sendet, förskoleklassen och fritidshemmet.*
48. Wildt-Persson and Rosengren, "Equity and equivalence in the Swedish school system," 301.
49. Skolverket, *Handikapp i kolan*; Vislie, "From integration to inclusion"; Wildt-Persson and Rosengren, "Equity and equivalence in the Swedish school system."
50. OECD, *Special needs education: Statistics and indicators*; OECD, *Education at a Glance.*
51. J. O. Jonsson, "Persisting inequalities in Sweden," in *Persistent inequality: Changing educational attainment in thirteen countries*, ed. Y Shavit and H. P Blossfeld (Boulder, CO: Westview Press, 1993), 101–132; Wildt-Persson and Rosengren, "Equity and equivalence in the Swedish school system."
52. Englund, "The discourse on equivalence in Swedish education policy," 42.
53. Wildt-Persson and Rosengren, "Equity and equivalence in the Swedish school system," 308.
54. As cited in ibid.
55. *Läroplan för det obligatoriska skolva¨sendet, förskoleklassen och fritidshemmet*, 1994, 4.
56. Wildt-Persson and Rosengren, "Equity and equivalence in the Swedish school system."
57. *Läroplan för det obligatoriska skolva¨sendet, förskoleklassen och fritidshemmet*, 1994,303.
58. OECD, *Equity in education thematic review.*
59. Berhanu, "Ethnic minority pupils in Swedish schools"; Skolverket, *Handikapp i skolan.*
60. As cited in C. Nilholm, "Special education, inclusion and democracy," *European Journal of Special Needs Education* 21, no. 4 (2006): 431–445.
61. J. Artiles, N. Harris-Murri, and D. Rostenberg, "Inclusion as social justice: Critical notes on discourses, assumptions, and the road ahead," *Theory into Practice* 45, no. 3 (2006): 260–268.
62. J. Artiles et al., "Learning in Inclusive education research: Re-mediating theory and methods with a transformative agenda," *Review of Research in Education* 30, no. 1 (2006): 65–108.
63. OECD, *Equity in education thematic review: Sweden, country note* 47.
64. Ibid., 48–49.

CHAPTER 6

1. The term *students of color* in this paper specifically refers to Black and Latino students, though in a broader framework it can be used be to describe all students who, by being racialized, are not ascribed the label *White*. While we recognize that language of labels is imbued with hegemonic structures that can serve to devalue individuals and groups, this term is meant to connote a particular

emphasis on racialization and racism in the US context, as well as the common experiencing being "othered."

2. H. Mehan, A. Hetweck, and J. L. Meihls, *Handicapping the handicapped: Decision making in students' careers* (Stanford, CA: Stanford University Press, 1986), 165.

3. E. G. Fierros and J. W. Conroy, "Double jeopardy: An exploration of restrictiveness and race in special education," in *Racial inequity in special education*, ed. D. J. Losen and G. Orfield (Cambridge, MA: Harvard Education Press, 2002).

4. D. J. Losen, "Minority overrepresentation and underservicing in special education," *Principal* 81, no. 3 (2002):45–46.

5. The terms "Black" and "Black" as well as "Hispanic" and "Latino" are often used interchangeably for the purpose of style and consitancacy. Except in the cases of direct quotes, we have chosen to use the term "Black" with the intent of being conscious of the greater variety of people who may be ascribed or self-identify as Black beyond those who are Blacks. At the same time, we are sensitive to the fact that these phrases have different meanings and implications.

6. C. O'Connor and S. D. Fernandez, "Race, class, and disproportionality: Reevaluating the relationship between poverty and special education placement," *Educational Researcher* 35, no. 6 (2006): 6–11.

7. See, for example P. C. Gorski, "Peddling poverty for profit: Elements of oppression in Ruby Payne's framework," *Equity & Excellence in Education* 41, no. 1 (2008): 130–148.

8. See M. Fine, *Framing dropouts: Notes on the politics of an urban public high school* (Albany, NY: State University of New York, 1991); P. Lipman, *Race, class, and power in school restructuring* (Albany, NY: State University of New York Press, 1998).

9. B. Harry and J. K. Klingner, *Why are so many minorities in special education? Understanding race and disability in schools* (New York: Teachers College Press, 2006).

10. See, for example, R. J. Skiba et al., "The context of minority disproportionality: Practitioner perspectives on special education referral," *Teachers College Record* 108 (2006): 1424–1459.

11. Ibid.

12. B. Harry, J. K. Klingner, and J. Hart, "Black families under fire: Ethnographic views of family strengths," *Remedial and Special Education* 26, no. 2 (2005): 101–112.

13. A. Lewis, *Race in the schoolyard: Negotiating color line in classrooms and communities* (New Brunswick, NJ: Rutgers University Press, 2009); A. J. Artiles, J. K. Klingner, and W. F. Tate, "Representation of minority students in special education: Complicating traditional explanations (Introduction to special issue)," *Educational Researcher* 35, no. 6 (2006): 3–5. M. Pollock, *Colormute* (Princeton, NJ: Princeton University Press., 2004).

14. B. A. Ferri and D. J. Connor, "Tools of exclusion: race, disability, and (re)segregated education," *Teachers College Record* 107, no. 3 (2005): 453–474; D. K. Reid and M. G. Knight, "Disability justifies exclusion of minority students: A critical history grounded in disability studies," *Educational Researcher* 35, no. 6 (2006): 18–23.

15. "Branch" is a pseudonym for a neighboring school district.

16. Harry and Klingner, *Why are so many minorities in special education?*

17. S. Lawrence-Lightfoot, *The essential conversation: What parents and children can learn from each other* (New York: Random House, 2003), 3.

18. A. Lareau and E. M. Horvat, "Moments of social inclusion and exclusion: Race, class, and cultural capital in family-school relationships," *Sociology of Education*, no. 72 (1999): 37–53.

19. Harry and Klingner, *Why are so many minorities in special education?* 178.

20. W. J. Blanchett, "Disproportionate representation of Black Students in special education: Acknowledging the role of white privilege and racism," *Educational Researcher* 35, no. 6 (2006): 24–28.

21. K. M. Anderson-Levitt, "Teacher interpretation of student behavior: Cognitive and social processes," *Elementary School Journal* 84 (1984): 315–337; H. Mehan, "The competent student," *Anthropology & Education Quarterly* 11, no. 32 (1980); 131–152; R. Rist, "Student social class and teacher expectations: The self-fulfilling prophecy in ghetto education," *Harvard Educational Review* 40, no. 5 (1970): 411–451; R. Rist, "HER Classic: Student social class and teacher expectations: The self-fulfilling prophecy in ghetto education," *Harvard Educational Review* 70, no. 3 (2000): 257–301.

22. Mehan, "The Competent Student."

23. P. M. Cooper, "Effective White teachers of Black children: Teaching within a community," *Journal of Teacher Education* 54, no. 5 (2003): 413–427; D. L. Ferguson, E. B. Kozleski, and A. Smith, "Transformed, inclusive schools: A framework to guide fundamental change in urban schools," *Effective Education for Learners with Exceptionalities* 15 (2003); G. Ladson-Billings, "Preparing teachers for diverse student populations: A critical race theory perspective," *Review of Research in Education*, no. 24 (1999): 211–247.

24. See L. Delpit, *Other people's children: Cultural conflict in the classroom* (New York: New Press, 1996); J. J. Irvine, *Black students and school failure: Policies, practices, and prescriptions* (Westport, CT: Greenwood Press, 1990); L. C Moll, "Literacy research in community and classrooms: A sociocultural approach," in *Multidisciplinary perspectives in literacy research*, ed. R. Beach, et al. (New York: Hampton Press, 1992); A. Valenzuela, *Subtractive Schooling: U.S.-Mexican youth and the politics of caring* (Albany, NY: State University of New York Press, 1999).

25. T. J. Andrews, J. J. Wisniewski, and J. A Mulick, "Variables influencing teachers' decisions to refer children for school psychological assessment services," *Psychology in the Schools* 34, no. 3 (1997): 239–244; L. I. Neal et al., "The effects of Black movement styles on teachers' perceptions and reactions," *Journal of Special Education* 37, no. 1 (2003): 49–97.

26. Rist, "Student social class and teacher expectations"; and "HER classic: Student social class and teacher expectations."

27. Irvine, *Black students and school failure*.

28. S. H. Zucker and A. G. Prieto, "Ethnicity and teacher bias in educational decisions," *Instructional Psychology* 4, no. 3 (1977): 2–5; S Tobias et al., "Teacher-student ethnicity and recommendations for special education referrals," *Journal of Educational Psychology* 74, no. 1 (1982): 72–76.

29. See F. R. Waitoller, A. J. Artiles, and D. Cheney, "The miner's canary: A review of overrepresentation research and explanations," *Journal of Special Education* 44, no. 1 (2010): 29–49. Those considering the research on teacher's racial bias should

pay particular attention should to the context in which the study was conducted and the subjects involved. From a context perspective, special attention should be paid to the extent to which students of color experience disparate outcomes—in situations where there are no significant disproportionate outcomes, an observer should not expect to find bias. From the subject perspective, particular attention should be paid to the extent to which the subjects are responsible for the large number of recommendations for referral to special education in studying teachers who do not regularly recommend students for special education, the extent of bias may not impact disproportionate outcomes.

30. Harry and Klingner, *Why are so many minorities in special education?*; B. Harry et al., "Of rocks and soft places: Using qualitative methods to inverstigate disproportionality," in *Racial inequity in special education*, ed. D. J. Losen and G. Orfield (Cambridge, MA: Harvard Education Press, 2002).

31. J. L. Hosp and D. J. Reschly, "Referral rates for intervention or assessment: A meta-analysis of racial differences," *Journal of Special Education* 37 (2003): 67–80; M. Rock and N. Zigmond, "Intervention assistance: Is it substance or symbolism?" *Preventing School Failure* 45, no. 4 (2001): 163–161; J. E Ysseldyke, M. L. Vanderwood, and J. Shriner, "Changes over the past decade in special education referral to placement probability: An incredibly reliable practice," *Assessment for Effective Intervention* 23, no. 1 (1997): 193–201.

32. D. N. Figlio and L. S. Getzler, "Accountability, ability and disability: Gaming the system," in *Advances in applied microeconomics*, ed. T. J. Gronberg and W. J. Dennis (Bingley, UK: Emerald Group Publishing Limited, 2002).

33. T. A. Gravois and S. A Rosenfield, "Impact of instructional consultation teams on the disproportionate referral and placement of minority students in special education," *Remedial & Special Education* 27, no. 1 (2006): 42–52; J. F. Kovaleski, "Best practices in operating pre-referral intervention teams," in *Best Practices in School Psychology*, ed. A. Thomas and J. Grimes (Bethesda, MD: National Association of School Psychologists, 2002).

34. Mehan, Hetweck, and Meihls, *Handicapping the handicapped*, 85–86.

35. E. Drame, "Sociocultural context effects on teachers' readiness to refer for learning disabilities," *Exceptional Children* 69, no. 1 (2002): 5–22; Gravois and Rosenfield, "Impact of instructional consultation teams on the disproportionate referral and placement of minority students in special education"; Kovaleski, "Best practices in operating pre-referral intervention teams"; D. Fuchs, L. Fuchs, and M. Bahr, "Mainstream assistance teams: A scientific basis for the art of consultation," *Exceptional Children* 57 (1990): 128–139; W. Hartman and T. Fay, *Cost-effectiveness of instructional support teams in Pennsylvania* (Palo Alto, CA: Center for Special Education Finance, 1996).

36. S. Knotek, "Bias in problem solving and the social process of student study teams: A Qualitative investigation," *Journal of Special Education* 37, no. 1 (2003): 2–14; L. Costas, S. A. Rosenfield, and T. A. Gravois, "Impact of instructional consultation on teacher satisfaction and skill development," Paper delivered American Psychological Association Meeting, Toronto, March 2003.

37. Ibid.

38. Mehan, Hetweck, and Meihls, *Handicapping the Handicapped,* 85–86.

39. "Individuals with Disabilities Education Act of 2004," in *P.L. 108-446* (2004).

40. Skiba et al., "The context of minority disproportionality."

41. Harry and Klingner, *Why are so many minorities in special education?*

CHAPTER 7

1. B. Bekink and M. Bekink, "Children with disabilities and the right to education: A call for action," *Stellenbosch Law Review* 1 (2005): 125–145; Constitution of the Republic of South Africa, 1996.

2. Department of Education, *White paper on education and training in a democratic South Africa* (Pretoria: Government Printer, 1995); Department of Education, *White paper on an integrated disability strategy* (Pretoria: Government Printer, 1997); South African Schools Act 84 (1996).

3. P. Engelbrecht, "The implementation of inclusive education in South Africa after ten years of democracy," *European Journal of Psychology of Education* 21, no. 3 (2006): 253–264; K. C. Moloi, S. J. Gravett, and N. F. Petersen, "Globalization and its impact on education with specific reference to education in South Africa," *Educational Management, Administration & Leadership* 37 no. 2 (2009): 278–297.

4. Department of Education, *Education white paper 6: Special needs education: Building an inclusive education and training system* (Pretoria: Government Printer, 2001).

5. Engelbrecht, "The implementation of inclusive education in South Africa after ten years of democracy."

6. As cited in N. Karvelas, "Exploring the human rights understandings of educators," (PhD diss., University of Pretoria, South Africa, 2007).

7. R. Ng, "Toward an integrative approach to equity in education," in *Pedagogies of difference: Rethinking education for social change*, ed. P. P Trifona (London: Routledge Falmer, 2003), 206–218.

8. J. Beckmann, "Aspects of student equity and higher education in South Africa," *South African Journal of Higher Education* 22, no. 4 (2008): 773–788.

9. L. M. Du Plessis, "Conceptualising 'law' and 'justice' (1): 'Law', 'justice' and 'legal justice' (theoretical reflections)," *Stellenbosch Law Review* 3 (1992): 278–292.

10. Beckmann, "Aspects of student equity and higher education in South Africa."

11. Ng, "Toward an integrative approach to equity in education."

12. Beckmann, "Aspects of student equity and higher education in South Africa."

13. Department of Education, *Education white paper 6: Special needs education.*

14. OECD, *Reviews of national policies for education: South Africa* (Paris: OECD, 2008).

15. B. Van Rooyen, "In/exclusion and (dis)ability: (de)constructions of *Education white paper 6: Special needs education*" (master's thesis, Stellenbosch University, 2002).

16. P. Christie, "Inclusive education in South Africa: Achieving equity and majority rights," in *World yearbook of education*, ed. H. Daniels and P. Garner (London: Kogan Publishers, 1999), 150–168; Human Sciences Research Council, *Monitoring child well-being: A South African rights-based approach* (Pretoria: Human Sciences Research Council, 2007); J. Jansen, "The race for education policy after apartheid," in *Implementing education policies: The South African experience*, ed. Y. Sayed and J. Jansen (Lansdowne, South Africa: UCT Press, 2001), 12–24; OECD, *Reviews of national policies for education: South Africa.*

17. E. Fiske and H. Ladd, "Racial equity in education: How far has South Africa come?" *Perspectives in Education* 24, no. 2 (2006): 95–108.

18. Department of Education, *National education infrastructure management system (NEIMS)* (Pretoria: Government Printer, 2007).

19. De Lannoy, S Pendlebury, and N Rudolph, "Education: Children living far from school," 2009, www.childrencount.ci.org.za/indicator.php?id=6&indicator=46.

20. Department of Education, *National education infrastructure management system* (2007).

21. Human Sciences Research Council, *Changing class: Education and social change in post-apartheid South Africa* (Pretoria: HSRC Press, 2005).

22. Human Sciences Research Council, *Monitoring child well-being: A South African rights-based approach.*

23. OECD, *Reviews of national policies for education: South Africa.*

24. Statistics South Africa, *Prevalence of disability in South Africa* (Pretoria: Statistics South Africa, 2005).

25. Ibid.

26. Department of Education, *Education white paper 6: Special needs education.*

27. OECD, *Reviews of national policies for education: South Africa.*

28. Department of Education, *Education white paper 6: Special needs education.*

29. OECD, *Reviews of national policies for education: South Africa.*

30. Ibid.

31. L. M. Dreyer, "An evaluation of a learning support model in primary schools in the West Coast/Winelands area" (PhD diss., Stellenbosch University, 2008); Engelbrecht, "The implementation of inclusive education in South Africa after ten years of democracy"; N Muthukrishna and S. Sader, "Social capital and the development of inclusive schools and communities," *Perspectives in Education* 22, no. 1 (2004): 17–26; E. Swart and R. Pettipher, "Barriers teachers experience in implementing inclusive education," *International Journal of Special Education* 15, no. 80 (2000): 75–80.

32. Department of Education, *National strategy on screening, identification, assessment and support: School pack* (Pretoria: Department of Education, 2008); Department of Education, *Learner retention in the South African schooling system* (Pretoria: Department of Education, 2008); OECD, *Reviews of national policies for education: South Africa.*

33. E. Berger, "The right to education under the South African Constitution," *Columbia Law Review* 103 no. 3 (2003): 614–661.

34. Fiske and Ladd, "Racial equity in education"; C. Soudien, "'Constituting the class': An analysis of the process of 'integration' in South African schools," in *Changing class: Education and social change in post-apartheid South Africa*, ed. L. Chisholm (Cape Town: HSRC Press, 2004), 89–114.

35. A. Spreen and S. Vally, "Education rights, education policies and inequality in South Africa," *International Journal of Educational Development* 26, no. 4 (2006): 352–362.

36. A. J. Artiles and E. B. Kozleski, "Beyond convictions: Interrogating culture, history, and power in inclusive education," *Journal of Language Arts* 84, no. 4 (2007): 351–358.

37. Dreyer, "An evaluation of a learning support model in primary schools in the West Coast/Winelands area"; Engelbrecht, "The implementation of inclusive education in South Africa after ten years of democracy"; P. Engelbrect, "Using visual

images to make sense of inclusive education in South Africa," presentation at *International Special Education Conference* (Glasgow, Scotland, 2005).

38. Soudien, "'Constituting the class'."

39. L. Green and P. Engelbrecht, "Exploring and understanding challenges: An introduction to inclusive education," in *Responding to the challenges of inclusive education in southern Africa*, ed. P. Engelbrecht and L. Green (Pretoria: Van Schaik, 2007), 2–9.

40. Howell, "Changing public and professional discourse," in *Responding to the challenges of inclusive education in southern Africa*, 89–100.

41. Y. Sayed, "Educational exclusion and inclusion: Key debates and issues," *Perspectives in Education* 21, no. 3 (2003): 1–12.

42. T. Booth and M. Ainscow, *Index for inclusion: Developing learning and participation in schools* (London: Center for Studies on Inclusive Education, 2002); P. Engelbrecht, M. Oswald, and C. Forlin, "Promoting the implementation of inclusive education in primary schools in South Africa," *British Journal of Special Education* 33, no. 3 (2006): 121–129.

43. P. Engelbrecht and M. Oswald, "Trailing the index for inclusion," research report (Stellenbosch, South Africa: Stellenbosch University, 2005).

44. Engelbrecht, Oswald, and Forlin, "Promoting the implementation of inclusive education in primary schools in South Africa."

45. Daniels, "Bringing marginalized people to the centre, the potential of visual methods," research report (Stellenbosch, South Africa: Stellenbosch University, 2003).

46. Ibid; S. B. Merriam, *Qualitative research in practice. Examples for discussion and analysis* (San Francisco: Jossey-Bass, 2002).

47. Sayed, "Educational exclusion and inclusion."

48. J. A. Baker, "Contributions of teacher-child relationships to positive school adjustment during elementary school," *Journal of School Psychology* 44, no. 3 (2006): 211–229.

49. Human Sciences Research Council *Changing class: Education and social change in post-apartheid South Africa.*

50. Department of Basic Education, *Education for all country report 2009: South Africa* (Pretoria: Department of Basic Education, 2009).

51. Soudien, "'Constituting the class'."

52. Ibid.

53. Fiske and Ladd, "Racial equity in education"; Soudien, "'Constituting the class'."

54. Department of Education, *Education white paperEducation white paper 6: Special needs education.*

55. J. Artiles et al., "Beyond distributive equity: A cultural historical critique of the racialization of disability," presented at the research forum "A comparative analysis of equity in inclusive education,"Center for Advanced Study in the Behavioral Sciences, Stanford University, Palo Alto, CA, 2009.

56. M. Ainscow, T. Booth, and A. Dyson, "Understanding and developing inclusive practises in schools: A collaborative action research network," *International Journal of Inclusive Education* 8, no. 2 (2004): 125–139; Dreyer, "An evaluation of a learning support model in primary schools in the West Coast/Winelands area"; Engelbrecht, "Using visual images to make sense of inclusive education in South Africa"; Engelbrecht and Oswald, "Trailing the index for inclusion"; C. Dyer,

"Researching the implementation of educational policy: A backward mapping approach," *Comparative Education* 35, no. 1 (1999): 45–61.

57. Soudien, "'Constituting the class'."
58. Ibid.
59. J. Artiles and A. Dyson, "Inclusive education in the globalization age: The promise of comparative cultural-historical analysis," in *Contextualising inclusive education*, ed. D. Mitchell (London: Routledge, 2005), 24–36; Soudien, "'Constituting the class'."

CHAPTER 8

1. M. S. Khaparde, "Educational research in India: Policy and practice," *Educational Research for Policy and Practice* 1, no. 1 (2002): 23–33.
2. S. Bhattacharya, "Introduction," in *Education and the disprivileged: Nineteenth and twentieth century India*, ed. S. Bhattacharya (Hyderabad, India: Orient Longman, 2002), 1–32.
3. Ministry of Human Resource and Development, *National policy of education, 1986* (New Delhi: GOI, 1986).
4. There is also a system of non-formal education. NFE is an organized educational activity, with significant flexibility in terms of organization, timing, and duration of teaching and learning, age group of learners, content and methodology of instruction, and assessment procedures. It is this characteristic feature of NFE, which has made it a critical mode for reaching out to the hardest-to-reach group of children and youth, both in rural and urban India, in order to achieve the much desired goal of education for all.
5. Ministry of Human Resource Development, *Revised programme of action* (New Delhi: Government of India, 1992); V. Ramachandran, "Introduction," in *Gender and social equity in primary education: Hierarchies of access*,ed. V. Ramachandran (New Delhi: Sage, 2004), 1–31.
6. UNESCO, *EFA Global monitoring report: Statistics* (Paris: UNESCO, 2008).
7. UNESCO, *EEFA Global Monitoring Report* (Paris: UNESCO, 2006).
8. C. Mehta, *Progress towards UEE: Analytical tables*(New Delhi: National University of Educational Policy and Administration, 2008).
9. Ibid.
10. M. Kremer et al., "Teacher absence in India: A snapshot," *Journal of the European Economic Association* 3, no. 2–3 (2005): 658–667.
11. S. Seetharamu, "Status of elementary teachers in India: A review," in *India education report: A profile of basic education*,ed. R. Govinda (New Delhi: Oxford University Press, 2002), 190–201.
12. N. Rao, K-M. Cheng, and K. Narain, "Primary schooling in China and India: Understanding how socio-contextual factors moderate the role of the state," *International Review of Education* 49, no. 1–2 (2003): 153–176.
13. Global Monitoring Review Team, *Reaching and teaching the most marginalized*, GMR 2010 Discussion Document (Paris: UNESCO, 2008), n.p.
14. Ministry of Human Resource and Development, *National Policy of Education—1986*, 9.
15. A. De Haan, "Social policy: Towards inclusive institutions," presentation at the conference "New Frontiers of Social Policy,"Arusha, Tanzania, 2005.

16. "India: Data and Statistics," World Bank, www.worldbank.org.in/WBSITE/ EXTERNAL/COUNTRIES/SOUTHASIAEXT/INDIAEXTN/0,,menuPK:295609~ pagePK:141132~piPK:141109~theSitePK:295584,00.html.

17. A. Banerjee and R. Somanathan, "The political economy of public goods: Some evidence from India," *Journal of Development Economics* 82, no. 2 (2007):, 287–314.

18. S. Bhalotra and B. Zamora, "Social divisions in education in India," in *Handbook of muslims in India*, ed. A. Sharif and R. Basant (New Delhi: Oxford University Press, 2008).

19. Global Monitoring Review Team, *Reaching and teaching the most marginalized.*

20. World Bank, *Attaining the millenium development goals in india: role of public policy and service delivery* (New Delhi: Human Development Unit, South Asia Region, 2004).

21. National Council of Educational Research and Training, *National focus group on work and education*, position paper (New Delhi: National Council of Educational Research and Training, 2007.

22. P. Appasamy et al., "Social exclusion in respect to basic needs in India," in *Social exclusion: Rhetoric, reality, responses,*ed. G. Rodgers, C. Gore, and J. Figueiredo (Geneva: International Institute for Labour Studies, 1995), 40–51.

23. P. O'Keefe, *People with disabilities in India: From commitments to outcomes* (Paris: The World Bank, 2007).

24. S. Majumdar, "Educational programs for the disadvantaged groups," in *Governance of school education in India*, ed. M. Mukhopadhyay and R. S. Tyagi (New Delhi: NIEPA, 2001).

25. R. Jeffery and N. Singal, "Disability estimates in India: A changing landscape of socio-political struggle," *Economic and Political Weekly* 43, no. 12–13 (2008): 22–24; N. Singal, *Forgotten youth: Disability and development in India* (Cambridge: RECOUP, 2008).

26. National Sample Survey Organization, "Disabled persons in India, NSS 58th round " in *National Sample Survey Organization* (Delhi: Ministry of of Statistics and Programme Implementation, 2003).

27. S. Mukhopadhyay and M. N. G. Mani, "Education of children with special needs," in *India education report: A profile of basic education*, ed. R. Govinda (New Delhi: Oxford University Press, 2002); National Council of Educational Research and Training, *The national focus group on education of children with special needs*; Ministry of HumanResourceDevelopment, *AnnualReportfor2004–2005* (New Delhi: Government of India, 2005).

28. N. Singal, "Inclusive education in India: international concept, national interpretation," *International Journal of Disability, Development and Education* 53, no. 3 (2006): 351–369.

29. N. K. Jangira, "Special education," in *Fifth survey of educational research 1988– 1992: Trend reports* (New Delhi: National Council for Educational Research and Training, 1997).

30. Ibid., 496.

31. A. De and T. Endow, *Public expenditure on education in India: Recent trends and outcomes* (Cambridge: RECOUP 2008); J. B. G.Tilak, "Political economy of external aid for education in India," *Journal of Asian Public Policy* 1, no. 1 (2008): 32–51.

32. De and Endow, *Public expenditure on education in India.*"
33. S. Mukhopadhyay, "Management of educational programs for people with visual impairment," in *See with the blind: Trends in education of the visually impaired,* ed. C. Frenandez et al. (Bangalore, India: Christoffel-Blindenmission and Books for Change, 1999).
34. M. Kalyanpur, "Equality, quality and quantity: Challenges in inclusive education policy and service provision in India," *International Journal of Inclusive Education* 12, no. 3 (2007): 243–262
35. Singal, "Inclusive education in India."
36. N. Singal, "Exploring inclusive education in an Indian context" (PhD diss. University of Cambridge, 2004).
37. N. Singal et al., "Exploring the outcomes of schooling for young people with disabilities," presentation in RECOUP mid-term dissemination workshop, New Delhi, 2008.
38. Rehabilitation Council of India, "Draft national policy on special education,"in *Workshop on appropriate models of education for children with special needs* (New Delhi: Rehabilitation Council of India, 2001), 6.
39. Ministry of Human Resource Development, *The integrated education for disabled children scheme* (New Delhi: Government of India, 1992).
40. Ibid.
41. B. Troyna and C. Vincent, "'The ideology of expertism': The framing of special education and racial equality policies in the local state," in *Disability and the dilemmas of education and justice,* ed. C. Christensen and F. Rizvi (Buckingham, UK: Open University Press, 1996), 131–144.
42. Planning Commission, *A handbook for parents of children with disabilities* (New Delhi: Planning Commission, Education Division, 2003), 22.
43. Singal, "Exploring inclusive education in an Indian context."
44. Ministry of Human Resource and Development, *A manual for planning and implementation of inclusive education in SSA* (New Delhi: Government of India, 2003).
45. District Primary Education Programme, *A report on national level workshop: Towards inclusive schools in DPEP* (Noida, India: Ed.CIL, 2001).
46. Central Advisory Board of Education, *Post-war educational development in India*(New Delhi: Ministry of Education, 1944), 109; Education Commission, *Education and national development* (New Delhi: Ministry of Education, 1996).
47. Justice and Company AffairsMinistry of Law, "The Persons with Disabilities (Equal Opportunities, Protection of Rights and Full Participation) Act, 1995," (New Delhi: Government of India, 1996), 109; Ministry of Human Resource and Development, "National Policy of Education, 1986."
48. Rehabilitation Council of India, "Draft national policy on special education."
49. National Sample Survey Organization, *Disabled persons in India, NSS 58th round.*"
50. Ibid.
51. Ministry of Human Resource and Development, *A manual for planning and implementation of inclusive education in SSA,* 23.
52. Ibid.
53. K. Sharma, "Education of children with special needs: Policy perspectives," in *Educational policies in India: Analysis and review of promise and performance,* ed. N. Rao (New Delhi: NIEPA, 2002), 407.

54. W. Wolfensberger, "Social role valorization: A proposed new term for the principle of normalization," *Mental Retardation* 21 (1983): 234–239.

55. M. Young, *Justice and the politics of difference* (Princeton, NJ: Princeton University Press, 1990).

56. S. Swarup, "Teacher preparation policy," in *Workshop on Appropriate Models of Education for children with Special Needs* (New Delhi: Rehabilitation Council of India, 2001).

57. Planning Commission, *A handbook for parents of children with disabilities*, 31.

58. Singal, "Exploring inclusive education in an Indian context."

59. Singal et al., "Exploring the outcomes of schooling for young people with disabilities."

60. Ibid.

61. G. B. Nambissan, "Dealing with deprivation," *Seminar* 493(2000): 50–55; J. Dreze and A. Sen, "Basic education as a political issue," *Journal of Educational Planning and Administration* 11, no. 1 (1995): 1–26.

62. M. Minow, *Making all the difference: Inclusion, exclusion and American law* (Ithaca, NY: Cornell University Press, 1990).

63. S. K. Sharma, *Distributive justice under Indian constitution: With reference to right to equality and property* (New Delhi: Deep and Deep Publications, 1989).

64. Ibid.

65. Planning Commission, *A handbook for parents of children with disabilities*; Ministry of Human Resource Development, *The Integrated Education for Disabled Children Scheme*.

66. J. Rawls, *A theory of justice* (Oxford: Clarendon, 1972).

67. S. Dorn and C. Christensen, "Competing notions of social justice and contradictions in special education reform," *Journal of Special Education* 31 (1997): 181–98.

68. J. Lewis, "Let's remember the 'education' in inclusive education," *British Journal of Special Education* 27, no. 4 (2003): 202.

CHAPTER 9

1. National Law of Education, 2006.

2. UNESCO, *The right to education for people with disabilities* (Paris: UNESCO, 2004).

3. C. Skliar, "Pensar a l'autre sans conditions: Depuis l'héritage, l'hospitalité et l'éducation" *Le Télémaque* 29 (2006): 125–146.

4. S. Schram, *After welfare: The culture of postindustrial social policy* (New York: New York University Press., 2000), 7.

5. Dussel, "Educational restructuring and the reshaping of school governance in Argentina.," in *Education restructuring: International perspectives on travelling policies*, ed. T.S. Popkewitz and S Lindblad (Greenwich, CT: Information Age Publishing, 2004), 3–20.

6. J. Auyero, "Evita como performance: Mediación y resolución de problemas entre los pobres urbanos del Gran Buenos Aires " in *Favores por votos? Estudios sobre el clientelismo político contemporáneo*, ed. J. Auyero (Buenos Aires: Editorial Losada, 1997), 167–233.

7. With the exception of Eduardo de la Vega, *Las trampas de la escuela integradora* [The deceit of integration in schooling] (Buenos Aires: Novudec, 2008); UNESCO,

Education for all: Report to the world conference (Paris: UNESCO, 1990); UNESCO, *The Salamanca statement and framework for action on special needs education* (Paris: UNESCO, 1994).

8. National Law of Education, 2006, article 7.

9. Ibid., article 42.

10. Ibid., article 43.

11. Legislature of the Autonous City of Buenos Aires, Law of Public Policies for Full Educational Inclusion *3.331* (2009), 7.

12. Vacchieri, ed. *La incidencia política de la sociedad civil* (Buenos Aires: Siglo XXI, 2008).

13. S. Dubrovsky, *La integración escolar como problemática profesional* [School integration as a profesional problem] (Buenos Aires: Noveduc, 2005).

14. UNESCO, *The right to education for people with disabilities.*

15. Argentinean Office of Information and Evaluation of Educational Quality, *Relevamiento estadístico anual* (Buenos Aires: National Ministry of Education 2009).

16. M. F. Santarrone and C. Kaufman, "Los discapacitados sociales: La política de educación especial durante la última dictadura Argentina " *Cultura, Lenguaje y Representación* 2 (2005): 75–78.

17. S. Cimolai, "La construcción de los problemas del alumnado en los legajos escolares: Un estudio en dos escuelas públicas EGB de la provincia de Buenos Aires" (PhD diss., University of San Andrés, 2005); A. G. Toscano, "Voces y discursos sobre la educabilidad de los niños en la construcción de los legajos escolares" (PhD diss., University of San Andrés, 2005).

18. UNESCO, *The right to education for people with disabilities.*

19. Ibid., 245.

20. Ibid.

21. Ibid., 247.

22. Ibid., 249.

23. Skliar, *La educación (que es) del otro: Argumentos y desiertos de argumentos en educación* [The education (that is) of the other: Arguments and deserts of arguments in education] (Buenos Aires: Noveduc, 2007); C. Skliar and M. Téllez, *Conmover la educación: Ensayos para una pedagogía de la diferencia* [Moving education: Essays for a pedagogy of difference] (Buenos Aires: Noveduc, 2009).

24. Skliar, P. Gentili, and F. Stubrin, "La inclusión, la responsabilidad y la ética educativa " *Voces de la Alteridad de las Diferencias* 2, no. 6 (2008): 3–27.

25. Skliar, *¿Y si el otro no estuviera ahí? Notas para una pedagogía (improbable) de la diferencia* [If the other were not there? Notes for a pedagogy of difference] (Buenos Aires: Miño y Dávila, 2003).

26. J. Larrosa, "Una lengua para la conversación," in *Entre pedagogía y literatura*, ed. J. Larrosa and C. Skliar (Buenos Aires: Editorial Miño y Dávila, 2006), 25–40; M. Morey, "De la conversación ideal: Decálogo provisional," in *Pequeñas doctrinas de la soledad*, ed. M. Morey (Mexico City: Editorial Sexto Piso, 2007), 413–430.

27. Bárcena, *La esfinge muda: El aprendizaje del dolor después de Auschwitz* [The mute Sphinx: Learning about pain after Auschwitz] (Barcelona: Anthropos, 2001); J. C. Mélich, *La ausencia de testimonio: Ética y pedagogía en los relatos del Holocausto* [The absence of testimony: Ethics and pedagogy in Holocaust narrations] (Barcelona: Anthropos, 2001).

28. J. Derrida, *De la hospitalidad* [Of hospitality] (Buenos Aires: Amorrortu Editores, 2001).

29. J. García Molina, *Imágenes de la distancia* [Images of distance] (Barcelona: Laertes, 2008).

30. M. Blanchot, *La comunidad inconfesable* [The unconfessable community] (Madrid: Arena Libros, 1999), 112.

31. Dussel, "¿Se renueva el orden disciplinario escolar? Una lectura de los reglamentos de convivencia en la Argentina de la post-crisis," *Revista Mexicana de Investigación Educativa* 10, no. 27 (2005): 1109–1121.

32. UNESCO, *Aprender a vivir juntos: ¿Hemos fracasado?* (Paris: UNESCO, 2001).

33. UNESCO, *"Learning: The treasure within,"* (Paris: UNESCO, 1996), 1.

34. UNESCO, *Aprender a vivir juntos*, 28–29.

35. Ibid., 11.

36. J. Nancy, *La comunidad enfrentada* [The confronted community] (Buenos Aires: Ediciones La Cebra, 2001), 51.

37. J. Derrida, *Aprender (por fin) a vivir* [Learning to live, finally] (Buenos Aires: Amorrortu Editores, 2007), 11.

38. N. Pérez de Lara, "De la primera diferencia a las diferencias otras," in *Experiencia y alteridad en educación*, ed. C. Skliar and J. Larrosa (Rosario, Argentina: Homo Sapiens, 2009), 45–78.

39. Skliar, *¿Y si el otro no estuviera ahí?*

CHAPTER 10

1. E. W. Soja, *Thirdspace: Journeys to Los Angeles and other real-and-imagined places* (Oxford: Basil Blackwell, 1996).

2. F. J. Nieuwenhuis, *The development of education system in postcolonial Africa: A study of a selected number of African countries* (Pretoria: Human Sciences Research Council, 1996).

3. Children's Act 8 of 2001; Kenya Persons with Disabilities Act 14 of 2003.

4. Ministry of Education, "The development of education: National report of Kenya," paper delivered at International Conference on Inclusive Education, Geneva, 2008.

5. *BBC*, February 11 2008; Children's Act 8 of 2001; *Lessons from Kenya's introduction of free primary education*, briefing paper (Oxford: University of Oxford, Improving Institutions for Pro-Poor Growth, 2009).

6. G. Steiner-Khamsi, ed., *The global politics of educational borrowing and lending* (New York: Teachers College Press, 2004).

7. K. Mutua, "Postcoloniality and special education in Kenya: Negotiating culture and disability," presented at Holmes Scholars meeting, Pennsylvania State University, State College, PA, 2007.

8. The Constitution of Kenya.

9. B. L. Mallory et al., *Traditional and changing views of disability in developing societies: Causes consequences, cautions* (Washington, DC: The National Institute of Disability and Rehabilitation Research, 1993).

10. N. K. Mutua and D. Dimitrov, "Parents' expectations about future outcomes of children with mental retardation in Kenya: Differential effects of child's gender

and severity of mental retardation,"*Journal of Special Education* 35, no. 3 (2001): 172–180; N. K. Mutua, "Macro- and micro-level factors that predict educational participation among children with disabilities in Kenya" (PhD diss., Kent State University, 1999).

11. Y. W. Bradshaw et al., "Borrowing against the future: Children and third world indebtedness," *Social Forces* 71, no. 3 (1993): 629–656; J. Lauglo, "Banking on education and the uses of research: A critique of World Bank priorities and strategies for education," *International Journal of Educational Development* 16, no. 3 (1996): 221–233.

12. P. Bennell, "The cost of schooling in developing countries: Patterns and prospects," *International Journal of Educational Development* 16, no. 3 (1996): 235–248.

13. Mutua and Dimitrov, "Parents' expectations about future outcomes of children with mental retardation in Kenya"; N. K. Mutua, "Importance of parents' expectations and beliefs in the educational participation of children with mental retardation in Kenya," *Education and Training in Mental Retardation and Developmental Disabilities* 32, no. 2 (2001): 148–159.

14. Mutua, "Macro- and micro-level factors that predict educational participation among children with disabilities in Kenya"; Mutua, "Importance of parents' expectations and beliefs in the educational participation of children with mental retardation in Kenya"; United Nations Children's Fund, "Kenya Statistics," www.unicef.org/infobycountry/kenya_statistics.html.

15. UNESCO, *Education for All: Global Monitoring Report* (Paris: UNESCO, 2010).

16. Ngigi and D. Macharia, *Education sector policy: Overview paper* (Nairobi: IT Power East Africa, 2006).

17. Ibid.

18. Ibid.

19. N. K. Mutua, "Policied identities: Children with disabilities," *Educational Studies* 32, no. 3 (2001): 289–300; Mutua and Dimitrov, "Parents' expectations about future outcomes of children with mental retardation in Kenya."

20. T. W. Schultz, *The economic value of education* (New York: Columbia University Press, 1963).

21. P. A. Baran, *The political economy of growth* (New York: Monthly Review Press, 1957).

22. G. Becker, *A treatise on the family* (Cambridge, MA: Harvard University, 1981); R. F. Curtis, "Household and family in theory on inequality," *American Sociological Review* 51 (1986): 168–183.

23. J. Knight and R. Sabot, *Education, productivity, and inequality: The East African natural experiment* (New York: Oxford University Press, 1990); R Rubinson, "Class formation, political organization, and institutional structure: The case of schooling in the United States," *American Journal of Sociology* 92 (1986): 519–548.

24. Schultz, *The economic value of education.*

25. Rubinson, "Class formation, political organization, and institutional structure."

26. Mutua and Dimitrov, "Parents' expectations about future outcomes of children with mental retardation in Kenya"; N. K. Mutua and B. B. Swadener, "Physical disability and the cultural construction of manhood: Dialectics of capitalism and postcoloniality,"*Linking Research and Education in Special Education: An*

International Perspective 1, no. 1 (2005): 16–29; N.K Mutua and B. B Swadener, "Education for all: Decolonizing metaphors of normalcy and disability,"presented at "Education for All" symposium,Madison, WI, 2009.

27. Mutua and Swadener, "Education for all."

28. See S. Linton, *Claiming disability: Knowledge and identity* (New York: New York Press, 1998); M. Oliver, *The politics of disablement* (New York: St. Martin's Press, 1990); R. G. Thomson, *Extraordinary bodies: Figuring physical disability in American culture and literature* (New York: Columbia University Press, 1998).

29. Frederick Johnson, in *A standard Swahili-English dictionary* (Oxford: Oxford University Press, 1939).

30. N. Erevelles and N. K. Mutua, "I am a woman now! Rewriting cartographies of girlhood from the critical standpoint of disability," in *Geographies of girlhood: Identity in-between*, ed. P. Bettis and N. Adams (London: Lawrence Erlbaum Associates, 2005), 253–270.

31. L. J. Davis, *Enforcing normalcy: Disability, deafness and the body* (London: Verso, 1995); Linton, *Claiming disability*.

32. Thomson, *Extraordinary bodies*, 13.

33. M. Corker and T. Shakespeare, eds., *Disability/postmodernity: Embodying disability theory* (London/New York: Continuum, 2002), 14.

34. Ibid.

35. Thomas and M. Corker, "A journey around the social model," in *Disability/postmodernity: Embodying disability theory*, ed. M. Corker and T. Shakespeare (London/New York: Continuum, 2002), 18–31.

36. Loomba, *Colonialism/postcolonialism* (London/New York: Routledge, 2001).

37. Barnes, "Disability and the myth of the independent researcher," *Disability and Society* 11, no. 1 (1996): 107–110; Oliver, *The politics of disablement*.

38. L. Rogers and B. B Swadener, *Semiotics and dis/ability: Interrogating categories of difference* (Albany: State University of New York Press, 2001).

39. N. Erevelles, "Disability in the new world order," in *Color of violence: The Incite! anthology* (Berkeley, CA: University of California Press, 2006), 22–31.

40. As cited in ibid., 29.

41. Mutua, "Policied identities."

42. Corker and Shakespeare, *Disability/postmodernity: Embodying disability theory*.

43. Talle, "A child is a child: Disability and equality among the Kenya Maasai," in *Disability and culture*, ed. B Ingstad and S. R Whyte (Berkeley, CA: University of California Press, 1995), 56–72.

44. Thomson, *Extraordinary bodies*.

45. See, for example, M. Corker and S. French, eds., *Disability discourse* (Buckingham, UK: Open University Press, 1999).

46. Thomas, "Disability theory: Key ideas, issues and thinkers," in *Disability studies today*, ed. C. Barnes, M. Oliver, and L. Burton (London: Polity Press 2002), 38–57.

47. Mutua and Swadener, "Education for all."

48. J. S. Mbiti, *Introduction to African religion*, 2nd ed. (Nairobi: East African Educational Publishers Ltd., 1988).

49. P. Devlieger, "Why disabled? The cultural understanding of physical disabilities in an African society," in *Disability and culture*, ed. B Ingstad and S. R Whyte (Berkeley, CA: University of California Press, 1995), 94–106.

50. Davis, *Enforcing normalcy: Disability, deafness and the body*.

51. Mbiti, *Introduction to African religion*.

52. M. Emirbayer and A Mische, "What is agency?"*American Journal of Sociology* 103, no. 4 (1998): 962–1023.

CONCLUSION

1. Antonio Gramsci, *Prison notebooks*, vol. 3 (1930–1931; New York: Columbia University Press, 2007), 159.

2. Only fifty years ago, we had little comparative data for planning public education around the world. Gray's account of learning to read in various nations focused mostly on reading processes and writing systems with little on access to school and/or literacy (W. Gray, *The teaching of reading and writing: An international survey* [Paris: UNESCO, 1956]). Downing gathered papers on learning to read in twelve nations, but with little agreement on what data should be included and analyzed. The paper on Japan showed how the writing systems available to children were managed by aphasic adults; schooling was not considered. The paper on Israel analyzed disparities in reading competencies across European and indigenous Jewish children regardless of how they were taught (whether by whole-word or phonics); social factors were considered. The paper on Denmark tied high literacy to an absence of reading tests before puberty (then, but no longer true) to suggest that leaving children to their own developmental schedules might eventually bring them to a common competence. The materials could not yet support a comparative study of literacy. The stakes were higher than the knowledge base. See J. Downing, *Comparative reading: Cross-national studies of behavior and processes in reading and writing* (New York: Macmillan, 1973).

    Starting in 1966, Thorndike administered his own tests to survey literacy in fifteen countries. His findings should have disrupted the modern state story about knowledge, schooling, and progress: "Although one is very hesitant to attach any meaning to some of the relationships that appear, in total it must be admitted that the study provides very little evidence of the impact of the school or of specific school factors on the progress of students in reading." See R. L. Thorndike, *Reading comprehension in fifteen countries* (New York: Halsted Press, 1973).

3. Sanford Schram, *Words of welfare* (Minneapolis: University of Minnesota Press, 1995).

4. As Gregory Bateson once said about the self-fulfilling circles of life in a culture, every category is subject to the "responses of people to the responses of people"; see *Naven* (Stanford: Stanford University Press, 1936), 175.

5. See J. and J. Comaroff, *Ethnicity, Inc.* (Chicago: University of Chicago Press, 2009).

6. R. McDermott, S. Goldman, and H. Varenne, "The cultural work of learning disabilities," *Educational Researcher*, 35, no. 6 (2006): 12–17. For a related account, see L. J. Rogers and B. B. Swadener, *Semiotics and disability: Interrogating categories of difference* (New York: SUNY Press, 2001).

7. See C. Hill and E. Larson, *Children and reading tests* (Mahwah, NJ: Lawrence Erlbaum, 2000); for the same problems made more complex by trying to compare performances across tests in different languages, see C. Hill and K. Parry (eds.), *From testing to assessment* (London: Longman, 1994).

8. For a brief history of names for American children in trouble, see D. Tyack, *Seeking common ground: Public schools in a diverse society* (Cambridge, MA: Harvard University Press, 2003). Almost a century ago, James Joyce had little Stephen Daedalus beaten by his teacher for being a "lazy idle loafer" and a "schemer"; *A portrait of the artist as a young man* (New York: Viking, 1964), 49.

9. J. Scott, *Seeing Like a State* (New Haven, CT: Yale University Press, 1999).

10. L. Dumont, *Homo hierarchicus* (Chicago: University of Chicago Press, 1970).

11. See R. McDermott, J. Raley, and I. Seyer-Ochi, "Race and class in a culture of risk," *Review of Research in Education,* 33, no. 1 (2009): 101–116.

12. The last two are paired because McDermott and Edgar are from New York and can't distinguish *pawn* from *porn* by their pronunciation and because we found one shop in Oakland that catered to both desires: two balls or three, goes the insider joke.

13. The Chinese used national tests for over a millennium. Although completely different in content, format, and standards of interpretation from western examinations, they were nicely tied to the hierarchical organization of markets in traditional China; G. W. Skinner, "The structure of Chinese history," *Journal of Asian Studies* 44, no. 2 (1985): 271–292.

14. Tutoring is an increasingly necessary tool for standardized test-measured school success. The well-to-do fear a regression to the mean. Even in Dallas, horses can't get the job done on the SATs. Just for fun, contrast the role of horses in Dallas and the social degradation of Sissy Jupe, the student from a circus family in Dickens's *Hard Times.* It is not the horse that makes the difference.

15. Smith, *An inquiry into the nature and causes of the wealth of nations* (1776; New York: Modern Library, 1994). E. Rothschild, *Economic sentiments: Adam Smith, condorcet, and the Enlightenment* (Cambridge, MA: Harvard University Press, 2001).

ABOUT THE EDITORS

Alfredo J. Artiles is professor of Culture, Society, and Education in the School of Social Transformation at Arizona State University. His interdisciplinary scholarship examines the ways cultural practices and ideologies of difference mediate school responses to students' needs. His research also focuses on teacher learning for social justice. Artiles has published extensively for research, policy, and practice audiences in education, psychology, and related disciplines. His work has been published or reprinted in English, Spanish, French, Portuguese, and Hungarian. He is editor of the *International Multilingual Research Journal*, and edits the book series Disability, Culture, and Equity (Teachers College Press). Artiles has made over 240 professional presentations in the United States, Latin America, Africa, and Europe. He is vice president of the American Educational Research Association's (AERA) Division on the Social Contexts of Education (2009–2011), an AERA Fellow, a Spencer Foundation/National Academy of Education Postdoctoral Fellow, and a Resident Fellow at the Center for Advanced Study in the Behavioral Sciences (Stanford University). His work has been supported by the U.S. Department of Education, the Spencer Foundation, the University of California's Linguistic Minority Research Institute, Vanderbilt University's Learning Sciences Institute, and the Motorola Foundation, among others.

Elizabeth B. Kozleski holds an EdD from the University of Northern Colorado. She is a professor of Culture, Society, and Education in ASU's School of Social Transformation. She holds the UNESCO Chair in Inclusive International Research and the national 2011 TED-Pearson award for Teacher Education. Her scholarship theorizes and examines systems transformation in schools; how identity, culture, ability, and practices are negotiated in classrooms and schools; and how schools become purposeful sites for professional learning. Her work has been recognized internationally and includes a coedited (with Alfredo Artiles) book series, Disability, Culture, and Equity (Teachers College Press).

Federico R. Waitoller is an assistant professor at the Special Education Department in the College of Education at the University of Illinois at Chicago. He has been awarded the American Educational Research Association Minority Dissertation Fellowship and has presented his work at national and international conferences and research forums. His research agenda focuses on contemporary equity challenges in inclusive and urban education. In particular, he studies the role of institutions and educational reforms in mediating teachers' identity and learning for inclusive education and the overrepresentation of minority students in special education. Waitoller has published his work in national and international peer-reviewed journals and in edited volumes. His most recent publications (with colleagues) include "The Miners Canary: A Review of Overrepresentation Research and Explanations" (*Journal of Special Education*) and "Teacher Learning for Inclusive Education: Understanding Teaching as a Cultural and Political Act," (*International Journal of Inclusive Education*).

ABOUT THE CONTRIBUTORS

Roey Ahram is a senior project associate at the New York State Technical Assistance Center on Disproportionality and a doctoral student at New York University's Steinhardt School of Culture, Education, and Development in the department of Teaching and Learning. A former high school mathematics teacher, he currently works with school districts to help identify and address the root causes related to the overrepresentation of African American and Hispanic students in groups identified as students with disabilities. His research focuses on education policy, equity, and disabilities studies.

Girma Berhanu was born and grew up in Ethiopia. He obtained a BA degree in sociology from the Addis Ababa University. He received a research degree and a master's degree in pedagogy in 1996 from the University of Göteborg; in 2001, he earned a PhD in special education from the same university. He was a research associate at the International Centre for the Enhancement of Learning Potential (ICELP) in Israel from 1999 to 2001. Currently, he is associate professor at the Department of Education and Special Education, University of Gothenburg, Sweden. Berhanu is fervently engaged in discussion of equity issues in the fields of (special) education, multi/intercultural education and communication, and group-based inequalities in scholastic achievement. Currently, he teaches research method courses at postgraduate levels.

Gottfried Biewer has been professor for Special Needs and Inclusive Education at the University of Vienna since 2004. After working as a teacher in the field of special-needs education, he became postdoctoral lecturer at the University of Applied Sciences in Nuremberg and the University of Rostock, assistant professor at the University of Munich, associate professor (Privatdozent) at the University of Koblenz-Landau, and professor at the University of Giessen (all in Germany). His main research interests are inclusive education, comparative research in special-needs education, vocational participation, and life-course research of persons with disabilities. In these areas, he is currently leading several research projects for the Austrian Science Fund (FWF) and the European Science Foundation (ESF).

Inés Dussel is senior researcher at the Latin American School for the Social Sciences (FLACSO/Argentina) and visiting professor at DIE-CINVESTAV-México. She has authored six books, edited two volumes, and contributed extensively to refereed journals and academic books. Her areas of interest lie in the intersections between the history and theory of pedagogy and political philosophy. Dussel is currently doing research on the relationships between new media and schooling.

Alan Dyson is professor of education at The University of Manchester, where he codirects the Centre for Equity in Education and leads work on education in urban contexts. His research interests are in the relationship between social and educational inclusion in urban contexts and, particularly, in the relationship between education and other areas of public policy. Recent work includes evaluations of the national extended (full-service) schools initiatives in England, a review of the research literature on schools and communities, and studies of the role of education in reducing health inequalities in England and in Europe. In 2001, he led the production of the Open File on Inclusive Education for UNESCO, and his recent books (with colleagues) include *Beyond the School Gates: Can Full Service and Extended Schools Overcome Disadvantage?*, *Education and Poverty in Affluent Countries*, and *Improving Schools, Developing Inclusion*—all published by Routledge. Dyson has worked in universities since 1988. Prior to that, he spent thirteen years as a teacher, mainly in urban comprehensive schools.

Brian Edgar is writing a doctoral dissertation at Stanford University after a career as a cook and high school English teacher in New York City.

Petra Engelbrecht, PhD, is at present professor of education for the Faculty of Education at Canterbury Christ Church University, Canterbury, United Kingdom. She was senior director of research at Stellenbosch University, South Africa (2004–2007) and executive dean of Faculty of Education Sciences at North-West University, South Africa (2007–2010). She is an acknowledged and respected researcher in the field of inclusive education and equity and human rights as well as research capacity development in higher education. Engelbrecht has led and is still leading several international research projects funded by various international agencies on the implementation of inclusive education and equity in various countries. She has published widely in peer-reviewed journals and has edited four books on inclusive education in the Southern African context. Recognition for her research and her role in education includes a Medal of Honor granted in 2009 by the South African Academy of the Sciences and the Arts in recognition of her contribution to the development of inclusive education and research in education in Southern Africa.

Edward Fergus is the deputy director of the Metropolitan Center for Urban Education at New York University. A former high school teacher, Fergus now provides technical assistance and analysis on education policy and research to school districts. He is currently the coprincipal investigator of a study of single-sex schools for boys of color (funded by the Gates Foundation), the New York State Technical Assistance Center on Disproportionality, and various other research and programmatic endeavors focused on disproportionality and educational opportunity. He has published various articles on disproportionality in special education, race/ethnicity in schools, and is the author of *Skin Color and Identity Formation: Perceptions of Opportunity and Academic Orientation Among Mexican and Puerto Rican Youth*, published by Routledge.

Roger Jeffery has been professor of sociology of South Asia at the University of Edinburgh since 1997. His work has focused on public health policy, social demography, education, and pharmaceuticals regulation, with fieldwork in rural north India on several occasions since 1982. He was the Edinburgh principal investigator (PI) on the RECOUP project (2005–2010) and is Co-PI on the "Access to Medicines in Africa and South Asia" project (2010–2013), as well as PI on "Biomedical and Health Experimentation in South Asia" (2010–2012). His most recent books are, edited with Anthony Heath, *Change and Diversity: Economics, Politics and Society in Contemporary India*, (OUP, 2010); and (with Craig Jeffrey and Patricia Jeffery), *Degrees Without Freedom*, published in 2008 by Stanford UP.

Lisa Jones is a researcher in the Centre for Equity in Education at The University of Manchester. Her research interests focus on issues of social inequality in education, including social class. Her doctoral research explored novice teachers and their social class identities, and she has done further work on urban teacher education. Recent studies have included the national evaluation of extended services (the equivalent in England of full-service) schools, and a study of the contribution of education to reducing health inequalities in Europe. Her publications (with colleagues) include *Education and Poverty: A Critical Review of Theory, Policy and Practice* and *Education and Poverty in Affluent Countries* (Routledge).

Kirstin Kerr is a researcher in the Centre for Equity in Education at The University of Manchester, and program director of the MSc in Educational Research. Her research is concerned with understanding how educational inequalities come to be ingrained in particular neighborhoods and communities, and how policy can develop more effective approaches to breaking the link between education, disadvantage and place. Kerr has recently led studies exploring: the impacts of schools' community-engagement activities (for the Specialist Schools and Academies Trust); the future for area-based initiatives in education (for the Economic and Social Research Council); the relationship between schools and social inequality (for the British Educational Research Association); and how schools work with other agencies to address local community needs (for The Leverhulme Trust). Her work has been widely disseminated to policy makers and practitioners through the Centre for Equity in Education's annual reports. These chart the state of equity in the English education system and have led to invited audiences with senior political advisors and with Ofsted, the schools inspectorate.

Jessica M. Löser has a doctorate in philosophy in the field of special education and worked as a pre-service teacher for one and a half years at a school for students with language difficulties. She began working as a research assistant at Leibniz University Hannover's department of special education in 2004. In her doctoral thesis, she compared schools in Canada, Sweden, and Germany in terms of linguistic and cultural diversity. Her fieldwork in Canada and Sweden was supported by a scholarship from the German Academic Exchange Service. Löser's research interests focus on issues of equity in inclusive education, multicultural education, and comparative education. She has presented her research results at conferences in Europe and North America and has taught in the field of education at the Universities of Bielefeld, Lüneburg, and Hannover at the undergraduate and graduate levels.

Mikael Luciak is a postdoctoral researcher in the Department of Education at the University of Vienna. His research, teaching, and academic writing focus on intercultural education, the schooling of ethnic minorities (in particular, Roma) in comparative perspective, disproportionality in special education, culture and disability, inclusive education, and equity as well as disability studies. Luciak studied at the University of Vienna (educational sciences), at San Francisco State University (counseling), and at the University of California in Berkeley (social and cultural studies in education). He has held positions as assistant professor at the University of Economics in Vienna and at the University of Vienna, and he held various guest lectureships at universities in Europe and the United States. He has also worked as educational expert for the European Monitoring Centre on Racism and Xenophobia (EUMC). Luciak is board member of the International Association for Intercultural Education (IAIE), serves on the editorial board of the journal Intercultural Education and the SAGE Encyclopedia of Diversity in Education, and is a member of numerous expert networks,including the OECD/CERI Teacher Education for Diversity Project, Network of Experts in Social Sciences of Education (NESSE), Network of Universities from the Capitals of Europe (UNICA—Working Group Equal Opportunities), and International Initiative for Inclusive Education (Equity Alliance at Arizona State University).

Christopher L. Lukinbeal is an assistant professor in the School of Geography and Development at the University of Arizona. He is also the director of the Master's of Science in Geographic Information Systems Technology program. His research specializes in media, landscape, urban studies, and geographic information systems. In more than thirty academic articles and countless professional presentations, Lukinbeal has endeavored to promote the new field of study media geography. He is the coeditor of *Aether: The Journal of Media Geography* (www.aetherjournal.org) and coeditor of the book, *The Geography of Cinema—a Cinematic World*. More recently, Lukinbeal's research has engaged civic and place engagement in Latino neighborhoods in the United States. This ongoing research focuses on issues of segregation, social capital, social justice, and place-identity formation. His research has been funded by the National Science Foundation, National Endowment for the Humanities, NASA, Southwest Consortium for Environmental Research and Policy, the Arizona Humanities Council, and the Arizona Board of Regents.

Ray McDermott is a cultural anthropologist and a professor at the School of Education at Stanford University. He takes a broad interest in the analysis of human communication, the organization of school success and failure, and the history and use of various literacies around the world. His work includes studies of inner-city public schools, after-school classrooms, and the function of information technologies in different cultures. At present, he is working on the intellectual history of ideas like genius, intelligence, race, and capital. His current research includes interaction analysis and social structure, the political economy of learning, writing systems, and educational and psychological anthropology.

Kagendo Mutua is associate professor of Special Education in the College of Education, Department of Special Education and Multiple Abilities at the University of Alabama. Her research interests center around cross-cultural studies of educational access and participation of children and adolescents with significant disabilities. She utilizes postcolonial and disability studies perspectives in her research to understand how dis/ability embodiment impacts access and participation. Her work has been published in several journals, including the *Journal of Special Education*, *International Journal of Disability, Development and Education*, and *Educational Studies*. She teaches graduate and undergraduate courses on characteristics of and methods for teaching students with severe disabilities and secondary/transition programming. Mutua has serves as coeditor of a book series titled Research on Education in Africa, the Caribbean and Middle East, published by InfoAge. She is an associate editor for the Multicultural Learning and Teaching Journal (2009–present), and also serves as a member of the Editorial Board for International Critical Childhood Policy Studies Journal (2009–present) and the *American Educational Research Journal* (Teaching, Learning, and Human Development) (2010–2012). She is coeditor of the award-winning book *Decolonizing Research: Critical Personal Narratives* (with Beth Blue Swadener), published by SUNY Press.

Beth Scarloss is a sociologist of education with a specialty in classroom organization. She is also an assistant professor of education at Frostburg State University, Maryland.

Nidhi Singal is a lecturer in inclusive education in the Faculty of Education at the University of Cambridge. Her research interests are in the area of Education for All. Her work has included the use of both qualitative and quantitative approaches in investigating the impact of changing international discourses on educational systems globally. Her work is particularly focused on challenging the exclusion of marginalized groups. Singhal was the International Team Leader for a five-year project (2005–2010), funded by the Department for International

Development (UK), which investigated the impact of education on people with disabilities living in poverty in Ghana, Kenya, India, and Pakistan. Her work has been widely published in various international journals.

Carlos Skliar is a senior researcher at the Latin American School for the Social Sciences (FLACSO/Argentina) and a researcher at the Argentinean National Council of Technical and Scientific Research (CONICET). He has authored four books, edited six volumes, and has contributed extensively to refereed journals and academic books. His areas of interest lie in the intersections between the history and theory of pedagogy and political philosophy. Skliar is currently doing research on the relationships between schools and the inclusion of students who are considered different.

Beth Blue Swadener is professor of Culture, Society, and Education and of Justice and Social Inquiry at Arizona State University. Her research focuses on internationally comparative social policy, child, and family issues in sub-Saharan Africa, and children's rights and voices in research and program planning. She has published nine books, including *Reconceptualizing the Early Childhood Curriculm; Children and Families "At Promise;" Does the Village Still Raise the Child?; Decolonizing Research in Cross-Cultural Contexts;* and *Power and Voice in Research with Children*, as well as numerous articles and book chapters. Swadener is currently codirecting the statewide external evaluation of First Things First, utilizing a mixed-method longitudinal design and a child care demand and capacity study. She is also a cofounder and president of the board of the Jirani Project, assisting children and youth in Kenya orphaned by AIDS.

Rolf Werning is professor in the Faculty of Humanities, Department for Special Education at Leibniz University Hannover in Germany. After receiving his state examination at the University of Dortmund in 1985, he conducted PhD research in the field of emotional and behavior difficulties and worked in an interdisciplinary therapeutic team for counseling families. He then taught at a special school for children with severe learning difficulties. Beginning in 1994, he worked as a research assistant at the University of Bielefeld for three years before his appointment to the professorship for pedagogy for students with severe learning difficulties at the Leibniz University Hannover. From 2009 to 2011 he was the dean of the Faculty of Humanities. His research focuses on children who are socially disadvantaged and who fail in school. Therefore his special interests are equity in education and inclusive education. He is the spokesman of the research community Preschool Education and Development. His research has been supported by the Federal Ministry of Education and Research and the Ministry of Research and Culture in Lower Saxony.

INDEX